PRAISE FOR
KARMA
&KISMET

"... a skillful writer who bring readers directly into his experiences as a young man searching for a sense of belonging. ... he vividly writes of his first psychedelic trip in 1968: 'The Mescaline journey ... has blasted me into a profound new awareness of inner space, of being, of potential for healing, of psychological and spiritual growth." He's also a meticulous chronicler of the times and places in which he lived, from South Africa under apartheid to an ashram in Canada where he studied yogic teachings. Shandler paints a detailed portrait of his pain due to his father's rejection, his fear and anger when he faced antisemitism, his disappointment with the political wranglings in yogic factions, and finding his path to psychological peace and financial success.

A thoughtful, emotionally forthright, and often engaging retrospective."

—*Kirkus Reviews*

"... Shandler's writing, from the initial dramatic escape from his irate father to the transformative closing tributes, exudes remarkable authenticity and fervor, effortlessly immersing readers in the heart of his personal odyssey. With an authentic and passionate voice, he artfully unravels his tale, rendering it not only enthralling but profoundly resonant ... an emotional roller coaster featuring a cast of multifaceted characters. Readers are compelled to accompany him on his journey and battle for inner serenity and self-acceptance ... a quest across continents, seeking personal growth and ultimately finding serenity and spiritual fulfillment."

—**2024 Nonfiction Finalist American Writing Awards**

"As a young man who came of age in the sixties and seventies (and still working on it in 2024), reading Michael Shandler's moving memoir felt like sitting with an old friend, recounting the ups and downs of a seeker's life. Who of us has not had fraught relationships with our parents, sought love and acceptance from peers, struggled with our cultural and spiritual baggage, seeking to move forward? Shandler's work resonates so much with those of us who managed to go through all of this, broke karmic chains of abuse, and humbly came to a place of acceptance and comfort with our lives. I was moved to tears and laughter many times throughout this beautiful recounting of one man's life. Highly recommended."

—**Dean Cycon**, attorney, activist, social entrepreneur and author of *Javatrekker: Dispatches from the World of Fair Trade Coffee* and *Finding Home (Hungary, 1945)*.

"On a search for meaning that deepens through decades, Michael Shandler takes us from a South African childhood to an Israeli kibbutz to the spiritual-seeking sixties in the United States and on to a successful career consulting leaders and their organizations. He began translating what he'd learned early, when he wrote some of the first books on alternative lifestyles, introducing new ways to be in relationships, navigate marriage and family, and become vegetarian. Now he shows us how openness, curiosity, and compassion guided him through a long life—and led him to write this absorbing and inspiring memoir."

—**Mirabai Bush**, founder, Center for Contemplative Mind in Society and author, with Ram Dass, *Walking Each Other Home: Conversations on Loving and Dying*, mirabaibush.com

"A rare memoir that grabs us by the scruff of the neck from its opening lines and takes us on a man's personal adventure as he embarks on a search for love, acceptance, and a 'forgiveness' both longed for and long overdue. Drama, conflict, pathos, passion, success and failure are the signposts that propel Michael Shandler forward on his unique journey of self-discovery. A journey described with sensitivity, painful honesty, and an astuteness of observation that is the hallmark of a great writer. Perhaps more than anything else, *Karma and Kismet* crackles with humor, often at times in Shandler's life when there was little to laugh about. Absolutely unputdownable!"

—Stewart Ross Carry, freelance scriptwriter and editor, www.ScriptNav.com

"Michael Shandler's descriptions of his remarkable life experiences are moving, vivid, and deeply engaging and touch on many aspects of our shared humanity. Shandler's midlife reconciliation with his abusive father is an inspiring example of healing long-standing conflict."

—Professor Emeritus Ervin Staub, founding director of The Psychology of Peace and Violence Program, University of Massachusetts.

"I enjoyed reading *Karma and Kismet* from beginning to end. What makes this story so compelling is the resolute courage with which Michael Shandler entrusts himself to the truth as the witness and arbiter of life's meaning."

—Joel Agee, author of *In the House of My Fear* and *The Stone World*

"Sometimes wry, sometimes sad, Shandler's excellent memoir illustrates the power of persistence in overcoming childhood adversity in an engaging narrative that readers won't want to put down."

—Laurie Pearlman, PhD, trauma specialist, 2019 Lifetime Achievement recipient, trauma division, American Psychological Association

"In the end, *Karma and Kismet* is a story of challenge, perseverance, resilience, and triumph. As Shandler notes (in his epilogue), 'I am one of the lucky ones—one of those who escapes the confines of his karma and finds healing, love, reconciliation, purpose, and belonging.'"

—**Earl J. Glusac, MD, professor of pathology and dermatology, Yale University School of Medicine**

"An engaging, fascinating journey through realms that most people rarely take the time to consider. But Shandler leads them there in a way that is immensely human, showing not just the seeking but the flaws that come with it, the family dynamics, the politics that pervade even the most spiritually aspirational of places, and, in the end, the juxtaposition of the daily struggles of finding a living with the continuing search for existence, meaning, and place. Shandler bridges the personal with the universal and has created a well-written, accessible account of a life's path through exploration to a measure of contentment. We can all learn from that."

— **Greg Fields, author of *Through the Waters and the Wild* and *Arc of the Comet***

"If ever there was the perfect teaching template for how to introduce the writer's POV with a bang, this is it: 'Bam!' and a few lines later, we're hooked. The dialogue and action, both so authentic in tone, and the easy, fluid style of a natural storyteller do exactly what they're supposed to do. Character is plot, and plot is character—joined at the hip and driving the story forward with such momentum that we're dragged along by the ear like naughty schoolkids."

—*Page Turner Reviews*

"The author's writing is characterized by its directness and a deeply personal touch. This authenticity not only makes for an intriguing narrative but also leaves a profound impact on the reader. Through the author's words, readers are able to connect with the vulnerability and authenticity of Shandler's journey, allowing them to share in the experiences and emotions that shape his story. *Karma and Kismet* is a journey of profound self-reflection, a quest for acceptance and tranquility in a world that at times appears hostile and unwelcoming."

—**2024 Winner Inspirational Nonfiction, Literary Global Book Awards**

"[This book] opens up an awareness of the potential for spiritual and psychological understanding . . . [and shows] an abundance of wit and energy . . . particularly during Shandler's experimentation with altered states of consciousness.

"The abuse Shandler suffers at the hands of his father is expertly handled and deeply affecting. . . . The tense family dynamics in the Shandler household are sharply observed and compelling, especially his volatile relationship with his father, which is rendered in vivid detail. . . .

"A thoughtful, emotional, and engaging narrative that will particularly appeal to those seeking personal growth and self-fulfillment."

—**The BookLife Prize**

Karma and Kismet

by Michael Shandler

© Copyright 2024 Michael Shandler

ISBN 979-8-88824-382-4

All rights reserved. No part of this publication may be reproduced, stored in a retrieval system, or transmitted in any form or by any means—electronic, mechanical, photocopy, recording, or any other—except for brief quotations in printed reviews, without the prior written permission of the author.

Published by

3705 Shore Drive
Virginia Beach, VA 23455
800-435-4811
www.koehlerbooks.com

Karma & Kismet

A Spiritual Quest Across Continents, Cultures, and Consciousness

MICHAEL SHANDLER

VIRGINIA BEACH
CAPE CHARLES

*To my family—
past, present, and future.
And to the kind individuals
who helped me on the way.*

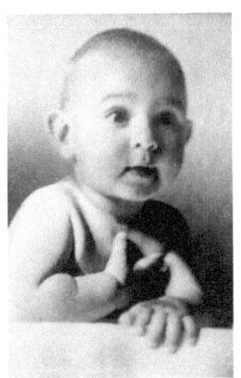

AUTHOR'S NOTE

Karma and Kismet is a story of change, adaptation, and transformation rooted in the mire of a dysfunctional family and a sick society. Wrenched from home at age thirteen and dispatched to a remote area where I couldn't understand or speak the language, gnawing questioning began to surface inside me: *Who am I? Where and with whom do I belong?* At first imposed by my parents and society, then by choice, a series of cross-cultural immersions deepened this existential inquiry. In time, signifying a letting go of the past and the emergence of new beginnings, my prior names fell away and were replaced by new ones.

Several characters in these pages are no longer with us—may they rest in peace—but some are still here. A few living character's real names have been changed.

WINTER, 1970
SOMEWHERE IN THE PRAIRIES, CANADA

The VW van, an already funky relic, its paint faded from orange to a dull yellow, sputters through the endless white wilderness, black smoke spewing from its exhaust. The van's heater, more appropriate to tropical climes, circulates arctic air. Ice fogs the windows. My buddy Jerry and I make accommodations. To save our feet from freezing, we place a brick on the accelerator to keep it flat against the floorboards, pushing the old van to its max on the dead straight road ahead. We sit cross-legged, meditation-style, wrap ourselves in Mexican blankets, and chant *Om* until its vibration transforms the freezing van into a sacred temple. We turn on the cassette recording of our new teacher, Ram Dass. His voice keeps us company. He has just returned from India with an important transmission:

Following a spiritual path will lead to a permanent high without the need for psychedelic drugs.

We are more than ripe for these new teachings.

"Just be here . . . now!"

"Here. Now . . . when *then* becomes *now*, you'll have super consciousness and know exactly what to do."

We have escaped, left Vancouver before our house got busted. We're headed to higher ground. Ram Dass—his journey from stuffy Harvard professor to psychedelic Pied Piper to yogi—resonates with the spiritual yearning awoken in us and many thousands of others.

Little do I know that in a few months, I will be in a very different car—a classic silver Jag, speeding from Toronto to St. Louis, perched on its cushy red leather seats, chanting *Om* with Ram Dass—the real Ram Dass—in the driver's seat.

PART ONE: KARMA

Double, double, toil and trouble
Fire burn, and cauldron bubble!
—*William Shakespeare*

ONE
CAPE TOWN, SOUTH AFRICA, 1955

BAM!

A stunning backhand slams my head into the sharp edge of the hardwood chair.

"You're nine years old and eating like a pig! I told you to stop clinking your spoon on your teeth!"

Ears ringing, head buzzing, blood runs from a cut near my right eye. I spring to my feet, fury and vengeance bursting out.

"You're not my father!"

The words reverberate in the air, an indignance and outrage I've never dared to express. Dad's face morphs in incendiary fury. He charges at me with fire in his eyes, his arms outstretched, reaching to catch me and beat the living shit out of me. I run for my life. He is two or three seconds behind me, my scrawny schoolboy legs pumping as fast as they can. I bolt out of the dining room, down the hallway, past my room, and out the back door. I fly over the back stoop and bound down the slippery lane along the length of the house. Dad gives close chase, his frantic steps telegraphing his intention.

I get to the heavy gate at the end of the lane—solid wood—over three feet high and about as wide. A large black cast-iron latch secures it in place. Frantically, I undo the latch, pull the heavy gate open, slip through, and, lickety-split, slam it closed. A second later, Dad plows full speed into the gate. As if in slow motion, his body flies right over it and makes a hard landing on the other side. Scraped and bleeding, he slowly gets up, shaking off the hurt. Without a glance in my direction, he drags himself back to the house.

I crouch near the gate, as unsure of myself as I had been about escaping moments before.

I rack my brain. *Who can I speak to? Who would understand?* No one. *Where can I go?* Perhaps my fort in the big tree at the Vineyard Hotel around the corner, but they might have floodlights, and they'd spot me. Forget it. *What about the river? Or a cave on the mountain?* No, it's too dark. Besides, there are lots of baboons. They're treacherous, stronger than people, with long fangs and sharp claws. I can't go back into the house and face Dad's wrath. There's no option. The house is quiet. I press my soaked handkerchief against the cut near my eye. The minutes slowly click by. Darkness surrounds me like a heavy velvet blanket. Somewhere, a dog barks. I check my watch. Just after 8 p.m. An hour after dinner. I'm afraid. Alone. Helpless. The scene of me bolting out of the house and Dad flying over the gate runs through my mind again and again. I closed that gate to protect myself, but Dad ran right into it. Jesus.

I wonder what my sister Penny is doing. Just sixteen months younger than me, she and I are best buddies, always playing next to each other or riding our bikes in the street, and sometimes fighting like cat and dog. Maybe she could help me.

Mom and Dad circa 1955

The front door of the house opens, but instead of Penny, Mom comes out. Somehow, Mom knows where I'm hiding. She heads straight for the gate where I'm crouching in the shadows. Beautiful, in the latest European style, a dress she fashioned herself, I inevitably wince when she speaks. Her accent grates—a weird mixture of her Austrian upbringing, her time in Palestine, and the more recent South African influences. She can't help me out of this one. She can't protect me. The two black eyes she hid behind sunglasses for weeks are still vivid. I made a vow then: when I'm big and strong, I'll never let him do that again.

"Look, Gary," Mom says in the tone of voice she uses when she thinks she has a perfect solution. "You be the clever one. Just say you're sorry."

"*Me?* Say *I'm* sorry? Sorry for what? I didn't do *anything!*"

Mom puts the palm of her hand up as if to stop an oncoming train.

"Just be clever," she implores. "It costs nothing to say you're sorry. Be smart! Be a *chacham!*"

"I'll never say I'm sorry," I tell her. "I'm *not* sorry." I'm talking tough, but I know I will pay the price of a phony apology in exchange for my place in the family. I slowly follow her back to the house.

Dad lays on the couch with ice bundled in a handkerchief pressed to his face. His shirt is rumpled, and a sleeve is torn near the shoulder. A little over an hour ago, he had sat at the head of the table, clean-shaven and handsome in his work suit and tie, smoking, staring into space, not saying a word. Sometimes—we never know when—Dad will slip into his private world, and we will all sit as quiet as mice, waiting on tenterhooks for him to come back. Dad is unpredictable and sometimes explosive. I make sure not to stand too close to the couch.

"Tell Dad you're sorry," Mom coaxes.

Almost inaudibly, I mutter, "I'm sorry."

Dad launches into a lecture from his supine position on the couch. "What do you think I work myself to the bone for?" he begins. "It's all for you kids. Do you think money grows on trees?"

I stand silently, watching him. His body slowly transforms into a miniature version of itself. He drones on. His face grows very small. A faraway voice emanates from a puppet head, its pimple mouth moving up and down.

After a long time, magic words rouse me from my spell. "Now give me a hug and go to bed." I shuffle toward him.

"I hope you've learned your lesson," he says as I lean over to hug him.

I say nothing. I have learned a lesson, but not the one Dad intends. I've begun to learn a lesson that will stay with me my whole life. I vow I will always be alert, on my toes, bobbing around like a boxer, weaving, dodging, feinting, moving, constantly vigilant, never allowing myself to become a target, ready in an instant for anything. Run. Hide. Fight. Lie. Pretend. Say the real truth when you need to. Speak what's forbidden. Whatever it takes. But above all, be vigilant.

Sleep with one eye open. Don't get sucker punched again. By anyone.

TWO

A few months after my fake apology, Dad surprises me with a brand-new cricket bat made in Pakistan. The Pakistanis are great cricketers and make excellent cricket bats. I'm over the moon with excitement. Dad knows I'm sports crazy. He understands. Mom doesn't. It's not a compliment when she says, "You're sports *meshuga!*" She means it's an unfortunate affliction.

I lovingly bathe my new bat in linseed oil for a whole week to properly season it. One day, Dad's younger brother, my uncle George, comes over to the house, and I proudly show him my new bat. Uncle George takes the bat in his hands, slowly inspects it, and tells me, "You know, if your father hadn't gone off to fight the Nazis, he would have made the Province team. Your dad was a great spin bowler. But he just wasn't the same when he came back."

I'm impressed. Dad was a great cricketer! If he could have played for Province, he could have played for the whole country!

Occasionally, Dad comes home early from work. If he's in a good mood, I beg him to play cricket with me like an overeager puppy desperate for a walk with his master—"Please Dad! Please!" Nothing thrills me more than playing cricket with my father who would have played for Province.

Dad bowls first and I bat. He takes the ball without saying a word. I love to face his incredible spin. We use the driveway as our pitch.

While we play, I forget everything. I'm not afraid. Only the ball matters, seeing it from the moment it leaves Dad's hand, reading the spin in midair, stroking it away before it hits the wickets. Dad bowls amazing balls that gyrate crazily—offbreaks that swing in from the batsman's right, leg-breaks that spin toward the wickets from the left, even the occasional googly; he bowls out of the back of his hand, fooling me with its unexpected spin before it smashes the wickets. I must be on my toes, ready for Dad's trick balls. Then, when I've batted for a while, he'll take the bat, and I'll bowl for him. I love the challenge of trying to get the ball past him onto the wickets. I crave these cricketing sessions, connecting in this special way, but they are few and far between. Gradually, they will peter out.

I remain alert, sniffing the air like a bloodhound. Where is he really? Might he go off? Will he freak out when he gets home from work? No one in the family knows. We walk on eggshells around him, waiting, watching, pretending nonchalance. I dare not make eye contact with Penny at the dinner table—an escaped giggle could spell disaster. But he's my dad. I love him, and I want him to love me, be happy when he sees me, and be proud of me.

In our small single-story house, the atmosphere is often tense. Mom and Dad argue, mostly about money. I don't know what to do or where to go. I don't understand money. I don't know where it comes from, only that it takes damn hard work and you can't waste a penny. When they fight, I keep one eye on my escape route. Other times, I might slip up, do something wrong or forget to do something. Any miscalculation might awaken Dad's wrath. I constantly track, living in secret fear. I go to bed early every night to avoid him—out of sight, out of mind—but my strategy isn't foolproof. From time to time, I hear Dad's footfalls outside my door.

Suddenly, he opens the door, switches on the light, checks out what I'm doing, switches off the light, and without a word, closes the door. I lie in the darkness, wondering what he is looking for.

Why is he keeping tabs on me?

When Dad leaves on one of his regular business trips every six weeks, I stand in the driveway, waving goodbye like a loving son. As soon as his car is out of sight, I feel relief and guilty for feeling relief. Aren't you just supposed to simply love your father and miss him when he goes away?

Constant watchfulness becomes second nature, a habit of heightened alertness continually reinforced by my situation. With continual practice, my vigilance becomes increasingly acute, providing instant threat assessment. I practice reading people, ready to make a move, a strength that will serve me, that will help me survive, but this strength constantly relied upon becomes a great weakness.

THREE
1956—1960

I've been a pupil at Grove Primary for my first three years of school. Penny and I walk there together every day. She's two grades below me. I like my teachers. They're kind and gentle. I'm not afraid of them, and I like to please them by correctly answering their questions. I'm the smartest boy in class. Only Yvette, the dark-haired girl with the violet eyes, and Norma, the tall fair-haired one, get better marks than me.

One day, out of the blue, Dad announces, "You're ten now, and you've outgrown Grove. Next term, you're starting at SACS—the South African College School. It's the oldest school in the country—boys only—and you'll get the best English South African education there."

This news comes as a complete surprise, but I accept the change. When the term begins, I shyly wear my new uniform—a navy blazer with the SACS badge, navy blue, sky blue, and white striped tie, gray shorts with creases, and school cap with the SACS badge. I take to the prestige of the oldest school in the country.

Located on the eastern slopes of Table Mountain, SACS is a short bus ride from our house. Tall oaks and old pines line the rugby and cricket fields, tennis courts, and swimming pool. There are 650 pupils—all boys.

My new teacher, Ms. Van Dyk, tracks each boy's academic progress by listing the students' names on a large cardboard chart that hangs at the front of the classroom. When you get everything correct on an exam, you are entitled to draw a small star in crayon next to your name. After a few months of numerous spelling and arithmetic tests every day, I notice that some of the boys have a lot of stars, and others fewer. I have among the least. Embarrassed that the other boys will soon discover me as a dummy, I begin adding extra stars next to my name. When I get a legitimate star, I sometimes add an extra one. Or two. After a while, my stars begin to look more or less like the others. Ms. Van Dyk doesn't seem to notice, and I don't think about my deceit for more than a few seconds. I fit in.

One morning, Ms. Van Dyk leads our class down a long corridor toward the carpentry room. I whistle aimlessly. The notes come out high and perfectly pitched, echoing in the corridor. I try a few more high notes just to hear their reverberation.

Ms. Van Dyk spins around and looks directly at me.

"Silence, Gary!" she yells. "Whistling between classes is against school rules. You should know this by now!" Her anger catches me off guard. Trapped and exposed, I lie to her face.

"It wasn't me."

Ms. Van Dyk does not hesitate. "What? Follow me to Principal Hunter's office. Right now!"

I turn on my heel and march behind her to Hunter's office, the much-feared principal and school disciplinarian. Hunter is notorious for giving excruciating "cuts," the South African term for whippings with a bamboo cane. Hunter's fearsome reputation is well-earned. One hot sunny morning, he ordered all 650 boys to the school auditorium. We waited, not knowing why we'd been called to this special assembly. A boy fainted from the heat and stuffiness in the auditorium. A teacher helped him away. Then Hunter appeared, dragging one of my petrified classmates onto the stage. Shouting in outraged spurts, he informed us that this was the elusive thief who had been stealing money and watches. He manhandled the frightened boy and, with all of us looking on in abject horror, bent him over the back of a chair and began caning him. The swish of the cane cut through the air with the most terrifying sound I'd ever heard. By the fourth cut, the poor boy was squirming and squealing for mercy. In the audience, we fruitlessly tried to avoid the devastating spectacle unfolding. Not in the least daunted by the boy's frantic pleas for mercy, Hunter delivered two more cuts—the regulation maximum of six—and then expelled the boy, shouting, "May this be a lesson to all of you!" My poor classmate dragged his broken body and spirit out of the auditorium.

The scene haunts me, and now I'm about to meet Hunter. Ms. Van Dyk's high heels clopping on the concrete corridor announce her determination to deliver me to my fate.

I'm sticking to my story, I tell myself with great trepidation.

Ms. Van Dyk strides past the principal's secretary and raps on Hunter's office door.

Without waiting for a response, she opens the door and disappears inside. I wait, terrified. Hunter's secretary smiles and offers me a seat next to her desk. I sit, coaching myself to keep my story straight. Trying to prevent myself from shaking in fear. Finally, the door opens. There stands Hunter, all six-foot-two of him, blocking the light coming from the doorway.

"Come in here, Gary," his deep voice orders. He sits behind his immense desk, and I stand in front of it.

"Well, what's this I hear about you whistling in the corridor?" Hunter begins. "You've been at SACS long enough to know the rules! You're supposed to be quiet when walking between classrooms. We're not running a circus here."

"No, sir, of course not, sir. But, sir, I also heard the whistling, but it didn't come from me."

"What? If it wasn't you, *who* whistled?"

"I heard it too, but I didn't actually see who whistled, sir."

I can tell that in the face of my denial, Hunter cannot just cane me. He needs some proof. I begin to feel more confident. As Hunter mulls things over, he lights a cigarette, takes a few drags, and eyes me through the smoke. I see the brown-orange tobacco stains on his fingers.

Finally, he says, "Gary, get back to your class. If you're sent here again, sure as I'm sitting here, I'll give you cuts. Now get out."

I've gotten away with it. A tremendous relief. No one can prove that I was the whistler.

When I return to homeroom, Ms. Van Dyk looks perplexed that I'm not in obvious pain.

You're such an old fuddy-duddy, Van Dyk, I mutter to myself. *What's wrong with whistling?*

The next day, at the end of the 11 o'clock break, when the bell rings, we line up according to class. When the bell stops peeling, I'm in line but still horsing around with one of my classmates. Suddenly, Hunter pops up from behind a line of students. He's been hiding there, waiting to pounce on me. He wastes no time.

"Playing the fool after the bell! I've caught you red-handed, Gary! My office. Right now!"

In Hunter's office, a large umbrella stand filled with bamboo canes of various lengths and thicknesses sits to the right of his desk. Each cane is about three to four feet long, ranging in thickness from 3/8 to

5/8 of an inch. Long used for corporal punishment, bamboo canes are favored for their strength and durability but, most importantly, for the pain they inflict. Their job is to keep us in line. They sit silently in their receptacle, broadcasting their dark purpose.

Hunter moves a wooden chair, turns it so its back faces me, and commands, "Bend over and hold onto the chair." Then he turns and rummages around, fiddling with several canes before settling on one. He practices swinging the cane through the air with a few terrifying swooshes. Then he positions my butt to his satisfaction and steps back. An eternity passes before he delivers the first cut. I hear the swish first and then immediately feel a searing pain as the cane cuts through my thin shorts and underpants. Two more cuts follow.

My ass is on fire. I want to dip it in ice water. But true to macho South African culture, I show no signs of my throbbing ass or the humiliation of a thrashing. By the time I'm back in class, I've come up with a strategy for buffering the pain of future canings. I will wear a pair of gym shorts underneath my regular pants, a daily habit I will keep up until I finish high school at age eighteen.

I hate SACS' strictness and its emphasis on academic excellence. I do the minimum requirements for classes and look for other ways to excel. The real action begins outside the classroom on SACS' playing fields. Something about a healthy mind *and* a healthy body. There's cricket, rugby, swimming, tennis, judo, and boxing. New worlds of possibility open. I need no prodding. I jump in, and I'm a natural. I love playing sports of all kinds. By my third year, I'm a member of the top athletic, cricket, and rugby teams, and I've beaten the previous cricket ball record by over nine yards, a feat noted in a one-liner in the sports section of the *Cape Times*. I've found the best way to belong at

SACS. I'm a sports hero, admired by my peers and the younger boys. I don't have to be a brilliant student. I just need to pass. The class brains demonstrate their intelligence daily, but they can't touch me on the playing field.

But, before each match, I have a big hurdle to overcome. Myself. It always starts the night before the game. I barely sleep and wake up weak and sick to my stomach. I cannot eat. I arrive at the playing field a complete wreck, pale, weak, and nauseous. Somehow, I tie the laces to my boots. The whistle blows, signaling us to run onto the field. I cannot feel my legs. I have no strength. I'm trembling. The whistle blows again, and the game begins. Someone passes the ball to me, and I catch it and bring it close to my body. I feel its smooth leather, and the kryptonite weakening me dissolves in an instant. I'm strong, fast, and savvy. And confident. I'm a winner. Everyone knows to feed me the ball. I forget my pregame jitters—until the night before the next game when the kryptonite strangles me again and only lets go when I touch the ball. But no one knows this. I'm a star. I've found a place at SACS where my vigilance and focus are paying off. Hunter occasionally announces my latest sports contributions at morning assembly.

One Saturday morning, our rugby team plays against St. Josephs, the Catholic school, one of our archenemies. I go through my usual sick beginning but then play like I'm possessed. The flyhalf kicks the ball over the heads of the St. Joseph backline. I'm through them in a second. I catch the ball on its first bounce and score. I score again. I'm unstoppable. We trounce them.

Monday afternoon following the game, after school, I head home on the bus's upper deck. A neighborhood kid in a St. Joseph's uniform spies me as soon as I sit down. He's a skinny, freckled, weakling who squints at me in recognition.

"I saw you play on Saturday," he begins. "It was a fluke you scored two tries! You were lucky to win. You're just a bunch of fucking loser Jew boys!"

Without thinking, I punch him right between the eyes. They puff up black and blue. That shuts him up. The punk gets off the bus a sorry mess but then yells up the stairs, "I know who you are and where you live. When my father sees these black eyes, he'll kill you!" Suddenly, I'm filled with a deep apprehension. Fighting in school uniform is the biggest no-no at SACS, right up there with stealing. School colors are a tradition to be upheld with the utmost decorum. The school rules are crystal clear: fighting and ungentlemanly behavior in school uniform will result in severe caning and certain expulsion.

When Dad comes home, I don't even bother checking out where he's at; I immediately tell him what's happened, including the piece where the punk calls our team a bunch of fucking lowlife Jew boys. Dad says nothing. He doesn't seem angry.

My opponent's father has also just arrived home because his car skids to a halt outside a few minutes later. And he storms onto our stoop. Unlike his shrimpy son, he is enormous, and the front door shakes on its hinges as he bangs it. I cower inside. When Dad opens the door a few inches, the big man tries to push his way into the house, but Dad manages to push him out and closes it just in time. The Goliath stands on the stoop and yells, "I'm reporting your little shit to SACS!"

Three agonizing days go by. I don't sleep. Dad tells me Hunter has called him in to discuss my behavior. He seems thoughtful but says nothing further. Another day drags by, and then Hunter calls me to his office. I'm quaking in my boots, sick to my stomach. The canes in their receptacle near Hunter's desk are an ever-present reminder of the regulations and the consequences of breaking them.

"Gary, you know this as well as anyone. You are one of our best athletes, but fighting in school uniform is absolutely forbidden! This boy's father is insisting the matter be properly addressed."

"Yes, sir."

"Do you not realize I have no choice but to give you six of the best and expel you? There are no exceptions. Do you have anything to say?"

"Yes, sir, I know the rules, but sir, that Catholic kid swore at my religion." Hunter takes this in for a few seconds.

"Swore at your religion? Speak, boy. What exactly did he say?"

I hesitate, swallow, and blurt out the truth. "Sir, he called our SACS team a bunch of fucking loser Jew boys. I refuse to take that from anyone."

Hunter sits silently, smoking while I stand there. I've let it all hang out. Swear words and all. I've told the truth. I've taken a stand. I'm filled with the courage of the righteous.

I can't articulate my feelings about my Jewishness, but it goes very deep—an ancient identity seared into my flesh when I was eight days old. When I take a leak, I hold my Jewish commitment in my hand while stealing furtive glances at the uncircumcised strangeness of my classmates. Three afternoons a week for seven years, I sat through boring Hebrew classes. I sang my Bar Mitzvah in front of the whole community. And Mom often reminded us that the Nazis expelled her family from Austria because they were Jews. "Just imagine, not a single country in the entire world would give our family a visa. Not even the Americans. Only the Zionists in Palestine risked their lives to save us. Never forget Israel!"

Hunter smokes half a cigarette. He says nothing. His face disappears in clouds of smoke. All I can see are the yellow-brown nicotine stains on his fingers. A tense silence permeates the smoky room. I've taken a massive risk. Staked my destiny to my Jewishness.

Then, with a frustrated wave of his hand, Hunter says, "Get out!"

That's it! No cuts. No expulsion. No warning. Nothing. I'm free! I can't believe my last-minute reprieve. I've told the truth. I've escaped humiliation, disgrace, and painful punishment. An unspoken justice has been served—a higher justice than school rules. Sometimes, telling the truth will protect me. Standing up for my Jewishness is worth the risk.

After Christmas, I begin my first term at SACS High. Here, matriculating eighteen-year-olds—prefects—inspect you upon arrival at the school gates. Black shoes polished and shining, our uniform impeccable—gray socks, gray trousers with knife-edge creases, buttoned-up white shirt, navy blue, light blue, and white striped SACS tie, navy blue barathea blazer with the SACS badge on the breast pocket, and a gray felt hat with the school colors prominently visible around the brim. The prefects' job is to make sure we know and obey the rules, and the school uniform is where it all begins. The message: *Take this seriously, or your life will be hell.*

The term begins in the summer heat, and Mr. Irvine's sweltering Latin classroom is more suited to sleeping than learning. He stands in front of the class, mumbling barely audible Latin. Latin sounds like nonsensical gibberish to my ears, and I tune out, snoozing my way through class. I achieve 19 percent on the multiple-choice exam, which goes to show you will learn *something* even if you don't pay attention. I'm convinced that I will never learn Latin. I feel no connection to the language. What use is a dead language? Slowly, I come to realize that I've just failed the subject that most symbolizes British heritage in South Africa. After all, I am a student at the vaunted South African College School, preparing for my future as one of South Africa's English elite. I've never failed a subject before, but there's no doubt I will fail this year. What a disgrace! A failure in my very first term at SACS High. What a dummy! By the time I finish high school, I'll be a stooped and sad old man with a scraggly beard squeezed into a desk next to students so young they will not yet have experienced their first erection. What can I do? I depend on my parents—no, mostly Dad—for decisions about my education and future. Dad tells me what to do, and I do it as best I can.

Mercifully, the term ends, and we're on holiday for a few weeks. I immerse myself in my well-learned expertise—playing at Muizenberg Beach, surfing the waves, and checking out the girls at the Snake Pit. I meet Joyce, a pretty blue-eyed Joburg girl staying in a Muizenberg hotel with her parents for the holidays. In Joyce's arms, I quickly forget my Latin dilemma.

The fall term and a repeat of Latin looms when Dad calls home from one of his business trips. He's in a town called Oudtshoorn—pronounced "Oat-sorn"—about 300 miles from Cape Town. The small Afrikaner country town is known for one thing—it's the world's ostrich capital.

Mom holds the receiver, so I can hear what Dad is saying. "I've found the right school for Gary! Oudtshoorn Boys High!" Dad's voice sounds excited, leaving no room for debate or discussion. "I've already spoken to the principal. Very understanding. Everything's set. He'll live in the boarding house a mile from the school. After the holidays, we'll take a trip to Oudtshoorn and drop him off. The boys are Afrikaners from farms in the district. It will be good for him to learn Afrikaans. It is our second language, after all. Tell him he won't have to study Latin in Oudtshoorn."

He has me there. I know I'm a failure. Still, I storm around the house yelling, "I'm not going to school with Afrikaners and ostriches!"

For a while, Mom says nothing, but then she admits, "I don't understand why he's sending you to live with *dummkopf* peasants. The Afrikaners were Nazis during the war!"

It begins to dawn on me that I am being sent away—far away. To an unknown place.

Cast out. A failure. A reject with no say. I just go along.

FOUR
1960

A barren and stony wilderness stretches before us. No water. No trees. Flat, dusty brown desert. Thorn bushes. Small rocks. An occasional aloe. I didn't know the earth could look this desolate. I thought the whole world was like Cape Town—iconic Table Mountain, its cloudy tablecloth swirling in ever-changing formations, the peninsula's turquoise and royal blue Indian and Atlantic oceans, the rocky bays and white-sand beaches, the leafy green oak canopies framing the streets. The baboons on the mountain slopes.

I hear bits of Dad and Mom's conversation in the front seat.

"I can't understand why you're sending him to live with Afrikaners. They're Nazis!" Mom hisses the word with more than her usual disdain. The Nazis destroyed her home in Austria and made her family refugees. She's lucky to be alive. She hates the Nazis. They hate Jews. If Afrikaners are in cahoots with the Nazis, they must hate Jews too.

"Not all Afrikaners are Nazis nowadays," Dad retorts. "I grant you, some Afrikaners were with the Nazis in the war because of their bitter history with the British in this country. But we've come a long way in the last fifteen years. Now, we're pulling together—English, Afrikaners, and Jews."

Ostriches pop up behind fences. As we get closer to our destination, hundreds of the giant bird creatures roam in herds. They are mammoth, much taller than a man, their heads perched on long sinewy necks emanating from broad bodies, covered in long black and white and gray feathers, and carried by muscular legs capable of running at thirty-five miles an hour and sprinting up to forty-five miles an hour, each foot tipped with razor-sharp claws like spears. These are my new neighbors. I've arrived in the world's ostrich farming capital.

I sit in the back seat, wondering why Dad has sent me to this godforsaken ostrich empire.

It doesn't look like much to me.

"Believe me, fortunes were made here," Dad tells us. "By Afrikaners and Jewish immigrants from Lithuania. My people." This piques my interest for a moment. Dad's father—*Zeide*—came from Lithuania. But what do I care about fortunes made a long time ago in a dusty, boring place or about Jewish and Afrikaner business?

Dad ignores my eye-rolling and goes on with his lecture. He thinks it's important.

"Of all things under the sun, a worldwide ostrich feather craze—boas and hats—dominated international women's fashion for forty years before the First World War. Demand was enormous. Ostrich feathers were South Africa's fourth largest export, worth more than gold by weight! The desert around Oudtshoorn was ideal for large-scale ostrich farming, and it became the world's preeminent producer of ostrich feathers. The lure of feather fortunes attracted Jewish immigrants seeking success in a new country. Most of them were Lithuanian Jews escaping pogroms and conscription into the czar's army. They were hardworking, and some became prosperous. Oudtshoorn became known as *Africa's Jerusalem*. Although the Jews and Afrikaners coexisted, competing and collaborating, the tension between them periodically flared into violence—Jewish holdings were burned to the ground. The Afrikaners had long resented the Jews, whom they accused of collaborating with the British to keep them in poverty after the Anglo-Boer War at the turn of the century. But Oudtshoorn's heyday was a long time ago. Nowadays, ostrich feathers make good dusters. Only a small community of Jews have remained here."

A small sign with the Afrikaans word *koshuis*—boarding house—points to a nondescript entrance, and Dad's Peugeot turns onto the dusty grounds. I get out of the car and take my suitcase without a word. Mom says, "Drop your things off and come with us to the Cango Caves. It's just nineteen miles away. A real wonder of the world! Huge chambers of stalagmites and stalactites!"

This is a last-minute gesture of kindness, but at that moment, I don't care about the wonders of the world or being with my parents. I have more important things on my mind. Now that I've landed at my new home, I want to face the reality. Dad understands and suggests that they go on to the hotel in town. They will see me tomorrow. They climb back into the Peugeot and drive off.

A blue-eyed guy with thick blond hair notices me walking toward the boarding house with my suitcase. He's about my age.

"Hullo! You must be the new English boy from Cape Town. I am *Kuiken*." I'm surprised that his English is quite good.

"Kuiken?" I'm curious about the meaning of this strange name. Kuiken quickly lifts his T-shirt, takes a deep breath, and puffs out his chest. An unusual indentation near his breastbone catches my eye. I'm a little shocked that he's exposing his deformity so soon after we've met.

"See? Baby chicken chest! Chick! Kuiken! Come, I will show you everything."

"Your English is very good," I tell him.

"Thank you. Hey, my English friend, he teaches me to speak right. But only one or two boys speak English here, you know."

I'm apprehensive. How will we communicate if I can't speak Afrikaans and they can't speak English? With gestures and pantomimes? I'm at the threshold of a new domain of unknowns. I'm cool. No one will know that I'm sick to my stomach.

He leads me to the front of the building. An open cement stoop runs the entire length of the ground floor, with wooden benches facing outward toward the street. Boys sit on the benches, watching cars roll by. Kuiken introduces me to an older teenager nicknamed Caltex, one of South Africa's popular petrol brands. I have no idea how he came to this nickname, but I don't dare ask. Caltex is sitting on the stoop with a shortwave radio tuned to LM radio, a station out of Lourenco Marques in Mozambique, a country on South Africa's northeastern border. Bill Haley and the Comets belt out "Rock Around the Clock," and Caltex turns up the volume. LM radio plays rock 'n' roll for hours every day, and it will become a lifeline to the outside world. I smile that here in Oudtshoorn, over a thousand miles from Lourenco Marques, we can still get the latest rock music, scarce on the straightlaced South African radio stations. From their astonishment, it appears that several of the boys on the stoop have not heard rock music before. Some laughingly call it, *"Die Duivel se musiek"*—the devil's music. Afrikaners belong to the Dutch Reformed Church, a staunchly conservative branch of Christianity. They are moralistic, whatever that means.

A low wall and a fence enclose the boarding house. The grounds are parched. A few scrub pines peek out of dusty orange gravel. Quince trees laden with hard yellow fruit line the perimeter.

Kuiken, in his role of self-appointed welcoming committee, pulls me away from the music and into the dim concrete interior of the boarding house. There are twenty-five dorm rooms on two floors. The walls, a dirty gray color, look like they haven't been painted in forever. Three windows on one wall of each room overlook the backyard. Out of a window, I see furling clouds of smoke emanating from an oasis of green bamboo. Kuiken notices me looking and says, "We can smoke, but only in the bamboo down there!" I look at him with incredulity. Smoking was such a big no-no in the prefect-monitored halls of my old school, the vaunted South African College School, but here, apparently, farm boys smoke early in life. I remember stealing one of Mom's cigarettes, cavalierly tearing off the filter, lighting it, and inhaling deeply. Three seconds later, I collapsed, lightheaded and sick. I will not be joining those boys in the bamboo bushes.

Large communal bathrooms are located on each floor. Hot water is available once a week. Kuiken warns me to take a shower before the hot water runs out. The study halls are located on either side of the building. I will be expected to study for two hours every afternoon and another two in the evening, except on Sundays, which is the Afrikaner Sabbath. I'm shocked.

I've never spent that much time on schoolwork.

We head to the second floor, walk to the end of a cement corridor, and enter room 18.

"Your room," Kuiken informs me.

Six rickety wooden beds are positioned barrack-style in two rows opposite one another. Each bed is covered in an identical, faded yellow bedspread. Six narrow floor-to-ceiling cupboards take up the entire wall to the right of the door, each cupboard guarded by a prominent lock. Kuiken points to one of the lockers and says it's mine. I put my suitcase down. He shows me my bed, and I'm introduced to my roommates.

Diagonally sits a boy with a narrow waist and shoulders. He has a pimply face with a scraggly beard, a pipe clamped between his teeth, and another weird nickname—*Katderm*—cat gut—like they use for stringing tennis rackets. He is a senior but extremely self-conscious about his English, blushing with embarrassment at his attempt to speak a few sentences. The others laugh at his effort.

Directly opposite me, another lanky boy with white skin, translucent blue eyes, and hair the same color as his face stands by his bed. His nickname, Spook, means ghost, and it provides an apt physical description. Right away, Spook grabs my attention. With a huge mischievous grin, he hops onto his bed, sticks his ass in the air, and lets out a very loud fart that lasts several seconds. I'm embarrassed. "Ach, that's nothing!" Spook informs me. "Once, I farted forty-seven times in a row! That's my record!" Later, I will see for myself that this claim isn't an exaggeration.

Next to Spook's bed sits a boy with wrinkled skin resembling an old man's. The tip of his nose turns up prominently, as though twisted into that position at birth. His buzz cut accentuates the prominent shape of his skull. His small rheumy eyes complete the picture. His nickname—*Renoster*—rhino—fits. He is also a senior and tries to speak English, waving around an unlit pipe.

My fourth Afrikaner roommate has a massive purple birthmark covering half his face. I'm afraid to look at him, concerned I'll be accused of staring. His nickname brands him: *Moerbei*—mulberry. I find it hard to call him this cruel nickname, but I need not worry. Moerbei is a cheerful soul and accepts his nickname without embarrassment or resentment.

I'm pleased to learn that the only other English-speaking boy in the boarding house has a bed in the corner next to mine. Mike claims he's seventeen, but he looks at least twenty-two, with thick bottle glasses and a grizzled and pimply face.

"Howzit *poephol*!" he yells in greeting, calling me an asshole with a skew grin. "Got any wine? I wanna get pissed . . . can't believe I'm back here in this bladdy place again. Hey, got a girlfriend back home?" He laughs raucously as he sticks his thumb between his first and second fingers in the lewd South African gesture for sexual intercourse. "Ach, shame. Hey, how old are you, boy? You just a baby, a little snothead. They chased you out of Cape Town, hey, you little *Kaapenaar*! What did you do? Steal cars? Are you a fuckup?"

I don't quite know how I'm supposed to take this, but I find it funny and laugh, which seems to go over well. I'm grateful I have someone to speak English with, though I'm not sure about this guy.

"Do you speak Afrikaans?" he asks.

"I just know a few words."

"Well, you came to the right place, hey. You can't help learning Afrikaans around here, mind you. They're supposed to teach in

Afrikaans and English—but don't you believe it. It's all Afrikaans!"

I may be only thirteen, and I've only met a few Afrikaners in my life, but I've experienced the tension between the English and the Afrikaners. I've never missed a big game at the Newlands rugby stadium, and I remember when the University of Cape Town's English *Ikeys*—Jew boys—played Stellenbosch University's Afrikaner *Maties*—mates. It was never a normal rugby match between two good teams. This was something more—a war, a do-or-die competition; every second played in a fever pitch of messianic purpose, egged on by vitriol, boos, catcalls, and jeers, in English and Afrikaans, the historical bad blood that went back more than a hundred years. During the Anglo-Boer War, over 27,000 Afrikaner women, children, and elders died in British concentration camps. The embittered Afrikaners had never forgotten their loss to the British or forgiven them for the deaths and suffering of their loved ones.

Then, Mike steps forward a few feet and, leaning into me, tells me quietly, "Look, There's some *bliksems*—real bastards—in this bladdy place. You have to tell them to *voetsek*!—to fuck off! You have to watch out, hey! There's no place for *moffies* or fairies or softies here!" He lies back on his bed. He's told me a lot, and I feel he will be an ally, if not a close friend. I'm in a new world, one I could not have imagined and would not have chosen for myself. But it is my new world, and the first thing I will have to do is learn Afrikaans.

The boarding house runs on a rigid schedule, punctuated by a loud bell rung at precise intervals. I'm used to a certain amount of discipline, but this is in a whole other league. The first bell clangs us awake at 5:40 a.m., and we have twenty minutes to tumble out of bed, get dressed, rush to the crowded bathroom, wait for an empty cubicle to relieve ourselves, wash up, and get back to our rooms before the next bell signals Bible study. Then, each boy sits stiffly on the wooden chair next to his bed, reading his Bible. This is followed by prayer time, and each boy kneels next to his bed, clasps his hands together, closes his eyes, and prays. As if his life depends on it. I mean fervently. I wonder if I will be expected to pray like them. Exactly five minutes later, the bell summons us to breakfast in the dining hall.

After breakfast—a bowl of porridge, a slice of bread smeared with a thin layer of butter and jam, and a cup of weak tea—we walk a mile down the hill to the school for classes. The school building is a classic Victorian built in 1906 from sandstone and decorated with gables and a red roof. It was a handsome building in its day, but now, more than a half-century later, it's rather shabby and neglected. As Mike warned me, all the classes are predominantly in Afrikaans. Situated a block away, the girls' high school may as well be in the next county. It's strictly off-limits.

At 1:15 p.m., school is over for the day, and we walk back to the boarding house under the blazing sun. At the boarding house, a similarly rigid schedule continues. The final bell tolls a 9:45 p.m. lights out. Then, the head prefect, *Muggie*—the bug—storms around the building, yelling loudly at any poor sod stupid enough to be caught outside his room after lights out. When Muggie's in a bad mood, he canes anyone he catches, the outrage in his voice and the caning amplified by the building's cement corridors.

It's taking time for me to get used to my new life. My school uniform, a black blazer with thin maroon and white stripes, feels strange and unfamiliar. I don't feel school pride. The colors are ugly compared to SACS' elegant colors.

My Afrikaans comes along in small spurts. I'm behind in my classes, trying my hardest to understand the Afrikaans instructions and keep my head above water. But most of my life is in the boarding house with strange boys who don't understand me and tease me when

I make elementary mistakes in their language. I have a long way to go before I'll be able to understand and communicate.

I head down to the rugby fields, expecting to be one of the fastest players, a top scorer, to find my home in the under 15A team, but in Oudtshoorn, the rugby is organized by weight—one group over 116 pounds and another group under 116. I weigh 124. I join the group of bigger boys. I'm the smallest, a *lightie* playing with the heavies. My SACS sports stardom means nothing here. I'm relegated to a third-rate team of lumbering giants, and we play against equally huge monster boys. They catch me easily. I'm a pipsqueak. A mouse playing with hungry cats.

I'm disappointed. Perhaps I can play cricket in the summer. There are no weight issues in cricket. It's all about having a good eye and good hands.

Everything in Oudtshoorn is so different. The flat ostrich desert around us ensures no escape or place to run. I can't compare my life in magnificent Cape Town to this dusty world. I'm out of place. A stranger. I miss the simple sense of belonging. My place. But I'm a reject. An outcast. Banished to a reformatory in a godforsaken desert surrounded by huge silent birds who stare at me and seem to be saying, "We are also prisoners."

Bullies begin calling me "*Joodjie*," which they pronounce "Yooikie," a nickname meaning *little Jew*. They say it with the same disdain they use when they talk about *kaffirs*, the most derogatory name for tribal Black people.

After school one day, I sit in the quadrangle closest to my room, sobbing uncontrollably. I really can't explain it, except that everything has caught up to me, and the dam has finally burst. Some older boys shrug as they walk by. "Ag, man, it's homesickness! He misses his mama."

Others simply smirk, smelling my vulnerability. I feel ashamed and embarrassed by reacting like such a baby, but I just can't help crying. The emotions I've held in demand release. I'm imprisoned in this foreign place. I'm nothing more than *Joodjie*—a rejected little Jew in a sea of Afrikaner Christians, abandoned and alone. I want to escape, but running away is impossible. I'd die of thirst in the desert. Besides, where would I go?

As for being homesick, I don't miss Dad's black moods and scary temper that made me tiptoe around in fear. I don't miss the cracks that came when you least expected, the putdowns, being afraid to go back into the house, or apologizing for crimes when I wasn't guilty of a damn thing.

I do miss Mom's Austrian cooking, her Vienna schnitzel, her butter-sautéed *steinpilzen*—from the porcini mushrooms she foraged—and her delicious apple strudel, but I don't miss her sticking her nails in my arms, her feeble attempts to control me, her tattling to Dad, giving him more reason to give me a crack.

But I miss Penny. We are so close in age, and she's my longtime ally, a partner in crime, and a faithful companion. I remember a group of *skollies*—juvenile delinquents—sauntering up Buchan Road looking for trouble. They seized on me, but Penny grabbed a half-brick, ran toward the *skollies*, and threw it directly at them. The brick landed in their midst, and they scattered like ninepins, yelling, "The little bitch is *mal!* She's crazy. Let's get the fuck out of here!" That day, Penny taught me a lesson: strike first before the bullies know what hit them.

Gary and Penny, Cape Town, circa 1951

Eventually, the sobbing subsides. I walk back to my room, ashamed. Everyone knows I'm a homesick crybaby. I pass my roommates, Katderm and Renoster, in the corridor. Maybe I'll get some privacy in the room for a moment.

Seven or eight of the boarding house bullies have gathered in my room. They range in age from fifteen to eighteen. The ring leader's name is Dolos, a reference to his rugged strength. A *dolos* is a large, heavy, reinforced concrete form used to protect harbors and coastlines from ocean erosion. Dolos and his cronies encircle me and taunt me. They push me into the center of the human ring they form around me.

I don't understand what they are saying, but their body language and taunts telegraph their plan. Opposite me in the circle stands a boy

I've seen from a safe distance. He slouches casually. His name is Fanie. Looking at him, I realize that Fanie is Dolos's younger brother. Like his brother, he is huge, a good three or four inches taller than me, with at least a twenty-five-pound advantage. Thick and solid, he looks bored and menacing at the same time. It's no contest. That's the point.

I cannot run away. I'm a trapped animal, a beast. Penny's lesson is about to be tested. I spin and land a massive punch with a resounding thwack right on Fanie's chin. His legs wobble. He goes down like a sack of potatoes. A couple of the toughs help Fanie to his feet, his mouth bleeding, his lip split. They avert their eyes and hustle him out. If Fanie had done his job, life would simply go on with this little *Joodjie* knowing who's boss and what's what.

I'm afraid to go outside the dorm room. Everyone has melted away. I don't know where they've taken Fanie. After several minutes, I dare to step through the door into the concrete corridor. I gingerly make my way back toward the red-tiled quadrangle, where only a short time before, I'd been bawling my heart out.

A powerful hand grabs me from behind by my collar, lifts me off my feet, moves my body through the air to the center of the quadrangle, and dumps me on the hard, red tile. A heavy rubber hose slams into my body.

"You punched one of us! *Jou fokken Jood!* You fucking little Jew boy! I'll teach you!"

Loftus, a tall eighteen-year-old feared by everyone, unleashes his hate, whipping me with full force. Large welts spring up on my skin. Swollen red abrasions cover my legs. Loftus, more and more frenzied, rains blows indiscriminately over my body, my stomach, my back, my head, and my face. I'm helpless to defend myself. I curl into a ball, trying to protect my head and face. Fighting back is useless. I go inside, deep inside, away from the world. Eventually, Loftus's breath becomes ragged, and he stops. He turns away, muttering obscenities, and leaves me lying on the hard red tiles.

Other boys are not going to help me. They're afraid of Loftus, Dolos, and their cronies. The boarding house has suddenly turned into a hostile place. I've violated the most basic of the unspoken rules. I'm supposed to be the fall guy, not Fanie. I'm so alone.

My spirit somehow remains intact. I want to do something. There must be something I can do, someone I can speak to. Someone more powerful who will help me, who will protect me. I know the boarding house father, Meneer Van Rensburg, nicknamed "*Wan*," lives in a small house nearby. Maybe Wan can help. After all, he's supposed to be the housefather. Though I've never been the kind of kid who appeals to his parents or teachers for protection, I drag myself to Wan's house and ring the doorbell.

Wan answers the door, and without a word, I drop my pants and show him my swollen and bruised legs. I don't care anymore. I lift my shirt and display the welts on my back and stomach. He looks at my face and sees my unsuccessful self-protection.

"Who did this to you?" he asks. The whole story pours out. Wan listens intently, his face turning a deep crimson with anger.

"Come with me!" he says as he strides rapidly toward the boarding house. I can tell he is really pissed off, and it's not with me. I follow him. He instructs a few boys to gather everyone in the south study hall. Boys stream into the study hall. Soon, it's overflowing. Wan tells those lingering outside the door to come into the room and sit on the floor. I find a seat at one of the study tables. Once everyone is settled, Wan stands between the tables and launches into a tirade that goes on for over half an hour. He yells at the top of his lungs, leaving no doubt that these boys are being reprimanded. Later, Zirk, a sympathetic Afrikaner, explains that Wan has outlined a vision of inclusion and tolerance, that as Whites in South Africa, we need to stick together, and that traditional *Boer* or Afrikaner culture welcomes guests, including the

English. Even Jews.

Wan makes a few other interventions. The first is that Fanie and I will share the same dining table, taking turns as table leaders from that day forward. This doesn't sound like a big deal, but practically, it carries weight because the table leader portions the meat ration out to the boys who sit around the table like a pack of hungry wolves. Fanie and I take our assignment seriously. Over time, I understand that Fanie is a gentle giant, set up by his brother, Dolos, and the other bullies. A quiet respect grows between us, and I never fear retribution from him.

Wan's second intervention isolates Loftus and restricts his movement. Except for attending classes, Loftus is confined to a small room where he lives alone. A strict restraining order forbids him from having any contact with me. Even so, I live in fear that Loftus, who seems unhinged, will attack me. When we occasionally pass each other in the corridor, he stares at me with intense hatred, mouthing curses and threats.

A few boys go out of their way to let me know that they have friendly intentions—a smile, a wink, even the occasional "Good morning!" in English. I feel friendly toward one of these Afrikaners right away. He's about my age but taller than me, with an amused smile permanently plastered on his face. A thick curl hangs stubbornly above one eyebrow. Between my beginner's Afrikaans, his rough English, and gestures, we communicate essentials. His nickname, *Boompie*, means sapling, and if you look, you can see why the boys have given him this nickname. He looks like a young tree shooting up. Boompie seems as curious about me as I am about him. We both like hanging out on the stoop and listening to LM radio with Caltex and some other guys. He's not like the dour Afrikaners who believe listening to rock 'n' roll is evil.

The biggest thing Boompie and I have in common is that we

are both adventurers. One day, we agree to meet after lights out in the corridor near the rear exit. Boompie tells me to wear *takkies*—sneakers—so we can prowl around without being heard.

A half-hour after lights out, we meet in the dark, near the rear exit of the building. Muggie, the prefect, is nowhere to be seen. It's quiet. With a nod to each other, we open the back door and step outside into the moonlight. We make our way down the road adjacent to the boarding house. After a few minutes, we come to a house shrouded in darkness, but in the moonlight, tall vines laden with huge bunches of ripe grapes provide a feast for hungry eyes.

We open the gate and, like two shadows, skirt the front lawn, furtively making our way to the side of the house. In a few seconds, we stand under the vines. What a treasure trove!

We cut off numerous heavy bunches and gently place them into a pillowcase we've brought along. Of course, we taste many grapes just to make sure they are of appropriate quality. In a few minutes, we've collected enough to make us both quite ill, especially if we scarf them down in a single sugar-rush orgy. We head back, carrying our bounty up the road.

We arrive at the rear of the boarding house and check out the situation to make sure the coast is clear. All seems fine, so we head for the back door. Suddenly, a large figure steps out from behind a tree, shining a blinding flashlight directly at us.

"What are you two *mamparas* up to?"

Oh, my God, it's Wan! Even I know that a *mampara* is a dolt, a stupid incompetent. A fool. A weak-willed klutzy thief.

Caught red-handed, we stand there sheepishly. Strangely enough, Wan doesn't seem angry. Actually, he seems a bit amused.

"Ach, yah, man, that lady down the road. She phoned me and told me two little *mamparas* were stealing her grapes. Tomorrow after school, you will go back to her house and apologize. And come and see me after lunch. Now get yourselves to bed!"

Wan says nothing about the grapes, so we carry our stolen loot inside.

That night, I barely sleep. I keep thinking that Wan will punish us for stealing. Will he give us cuts? Probably. We'll each get at least four or maybe six cuts. Not stealing is one of the Ten Commandments. Afrikaners take the holy book seriously. I've never heard of anyone getting five cuts. For some reason, if you get cuts, you get three, four, or six, never five.

School the next morning drags. After the last period, we walk back to the boarding house for lunch under the blazing sun. I can barely eat. One of the other boys scrapes my food onto his plate and wolfs it down without blinking.

After lunch, Boompie and I head to Wan's house. He meets us at the door. He's already changed out of his teacher's suit and tie and greets us in his shorts, his legs like tree trunks. He can see that we're shitting ourselves.

"Okay, you two *mamparas*. You see that Volkswagen?" He points to his blue VW bug, a 1957 model. "Clean my car inside and out. Take it around back and use the hose there. Here's the keys!" He tosses them to Boompie, turns on his heel, and heads back toward his house.

"And don't forget to say you're sorry to that lady!" he says over his shoulder.

Boompie and I look at each other and grin. *What a relief!* Clean Wan's car and say we're sorry to some old lady? Wow! My mood shifts from fear to elation.

Like many country boys, Boompie has been driving cars since he was ten or eleven. He quickly jumps into the VW, turns the key, and brings the engine to life.

"Hop in! I'll teach you to drive!"

I don't need a second invitation. Boompie drives the bug like an old hand, parking it on the sunbaked gravel road around the back of the building. We clean the car like we're purging ourselves of a great sin. We know we are damn lucky.

When we're satisfied that the car sparkles inside and out, Boompie turns to me and says, "Look, man, the secret to driving a stick shift is working the clutch and the petrol right. This is the clutch," he says, motioning to his left hand. "And this is the petrol," he says, moving his right hand. "Now, watch, clutch in, left foot down. Then, put it in first, give petrol only a little, and gently let the clutch out. You try!" I jump in the driver's seat, push the clutch to the floor, and start the car.

"Now give a little petrol and let the clutch out slowly!" I push the accelerator gently until I hear the engine revving, and then gingerly let out the clutch. The car begins to move!

Boompie yells, "*Yislike*, man, you are driving good! Now stop—brake a little, clutch in!"

I do as I'm told, and the car comes to a halt.

"That's it! Now you just have to practice!"

I spend the next hour practicing starting and stopping, and when I can do it smoothly, Boompie says, "Okay, good, man. Now you drive it back to Wan's house!" And I do. My first time driving. This Afrikaner world has its perks. Wan is pleased with our handiwork.

Our punishment not yet complete, Boompie and I creep back to the scene of our crime. We knock on the door. After a brief delay, the door opens, and an old, wrinkled lady stands before us. She squints like a frightened owl in the bright sunlight.

"Oh, you the boys who was here last night. The grape thieves. The *mamparas*!" I can tell from her accent that English is not her native tongue.

"Yes, we are very sorry for taking your grapes," I blurt while Boompie earnestly nods in agreement.

"*Ons is baie jammer, Mevrou*. We are very sorry, Mevrou," Boompie adds in Afrikaans.

"But why did you boys steal the grapes?" the old lady asks with a suspicious look. Before we answer, she continues, "Are you hungry? Do they not feed you enough in that boarding house?"

"No, they feed us. We are not hungry. We just like grapes very much."

"Well, ask next time, you hear?"

"Yes, Mevrou!"

With that, we head back to Boompie's room. We pull out the pillowcase, dump the huge bunches of grapes onto his bed, and scarf ourselves sick. I'm happy. We've gotten away with it. I love grapes, and I've learned to drive. And not all Afrikaners are Nazis, no matter what Mom says, including the German boy from South West Africa, nicknamed *Stuka*, after the WWII German dive-bomber.

We have a ten-day holiday at term break, long enough to head home. I take a taxi to the Oudtshoorn train station. My train will traverse three or four mountains before arriving at the Cape twenty-four hours later. As I clamber out of the taxi at the station, I freeze in fear. Loftus and one of his cronies, Cecil, are buying tickets. Since there is only one train a day, it's obvious they will be on the same train as me. They spy me right away.

"Just wait till we get on the train, Joodjie. You're fucking dead. Wan can't help you now!"

When the train comes into the station, I quickly climb aboard, find my compartment, and stow my suitcase. Then I find a toilet and lock myself in it. For a while, all is quiet, but then I hear Loftus and Cecil yelling, "Where the fuck is that little Jew? Joodjie, where the fuck are you?"

Closer and closer they come. Finally, they arrive outside the toilet where I'm hiding. They bang on the door.

"Joodjie! Come out! You're fucking dead." I don't say a word. I barely breathe. I hear them getting frustrated outside the door, and finally, one of them says, "Let's go get pissed. We can deal with this little shit later."

I wait several minutes, open the door, and find my way into another carriage. Desperately, I look for an empty compartment. I find one quickly, climb to the top bunk, cover myself in some bedding, and hide. It's not long before I hear Loftus and Cecil. By now, they're drunk. I hear them yelling. Their words are slurred and menacing; I stay hidden—quiet as a mouse.

After a while, they arrive at the compartment. They noisily slide the door open and look inside. The alcohol odor is overpowering, wafting into my hiding place beneath the blankets on the top bunk.

"He's not here!" Cecil announces. And then they leave, cursing me. I just lie still, covered, waiting. The train arrives in a coastal town called Mossel Bay. I dare a peek out the window. I see Loftus and Cecil weaving their way unsteadily down the platform. Yes! They get off here. The train begins moving again, and I come out. Free!

Back in Cape Town, I'm out of place. An outsider. I head to the Snake Pit at Muizenberg Beach. I recognize many characters from my pre-Oudtshoorn days, but I'm no longer a part of them. I'm different. The only Jewish kid sent away to live with Afrikaners and ostriches.

At least Dad hasn't hit me since I've been home.

I go fishing in St. James. It's easy to find fresh bait on the rocks. I cast my line into the rough surf. My forefinger sits gently on the line, attuned to the telltale nibbling of a hungry fish. I forget my loneliness. Then, *thud! Thud!* Something big is nosing around my bait! I strike and know I've hooked a fish! It's heavy and strong. A fighter. I let it go and then reel in. Let it go, and reel in. Again and again. It tires and lays heavy in the foaming sea. I reel it in. It's a *galjoen*—South Africa's national fish—the most delicious fish found only at the Cape. I'm ecstatic! I turn to make my way back to the beach, and suddenly, Dad's there. He's standing on the rocks above me, clapping and smiling with delight. He's seen everything! "I knew you'd be here," he says. "It's exactly where I would fish too. Well done!"

The Barmitzvah boy in his blue suit, circa November, 1959

FIVE

Sundays in the boarding house are a big deal. The Afrikaners dress in suits and ties and go off to church. They're gone for hours. I'm alone in the big building, which is now strangely quiet. At first, I'm unsure of what to do. I feel my otherness, my difference, my Jewishness. I don't want to draw any unnecessary attention to myself. Eventually, I dress like the others, like it's my Sabbath. I wear my dark blue Bar Mitzvah suit. I blend in.

At lunch, we sit at our assigned tables, salivating like civilized wolves, everyone's hair slicked down, on their best behavior. A teacher drones on in earnest Afrikaans for ten long minutes. I understand little, though his frequent entreaties to *Yesus* are rather obvious. As a reward, Sabbath lunch makes up for the rest of the week. There's more food than other meals and more variety. More meat and gravy. White meat—pork. Not kosher. Although our family isn't religious, we adhere to basic kosher rules. I've never eaten pork before. But I learn that I will have to eat it or go hungry.

As I settle in, I begin to understand how Afrikaner piety can work in my favor. Since the Sabbath is so important to the Afrikaners, the Jewish Sabbath surely will be honored without question. My attendance at Sabbath services on Friday evenings and Saturdays will be expected and respected. But after I leave the boarding house, no one checks my whereabouts. I go anywhere, and no one is any the wiser. If I play my cards right, I'm unsupervised for large parts of every weekend. The question is, where to go? I walk on High Street and check out the Afrikaner *meisies*; some are pretty, but how do I talk to them? I sit in the big café or go to the bioscope. I walk back up the hill to the boarding house. No one asks me where I've been.

One long weekend, parents arrive outside the boarding house in their dusty *bakkies*—pickup trucks. Every boy jumps on board, looking forward to a three-day vacation with family, but my family is far away. I hide in my dorm room alone.

Suddenly, I hear a voice yelling. "Joodjie! Joodjie! You come to my farm!" It's Renoster, one of my roommates. He and I have a strange kind of relationship. He seems fascinated with me and calls me *Joodjie* but without the malice of the bullies. I feel like an exotic pet. He likes showing me off to his friends.

So, I head out with Renoster and his father in the back of their *bakkie*. We drive for about an hour until we came to a valley surrounded by mountains. In the middle of the valley sits an old Cape Dutch farmhouse with a large white gable over the front stoop. We are welcomed by Renoster's mother, whom people respectfully call *Mevrou*. She is a big woman and wears a *doekkie*—a scarf—on her head, which gives the impression of modesty. Renoster's extended family gathers in Mevrou's kitchen. She pours sweet tea into big mugs and feeds us dried rusks. We sit around the table, dunking the rusks into the tea and chatting. I'm pretty sure that I'm the first English-speaking person who has spent any time with this family and certain I'm the first Jew any of them has encountered. I'm basically ignored. I understand a smattering of words. From time to time, I sense they are talking about me. They sneak furtive glances. I'm an alien—a little Jew captured by Afrikaner Christians.

More than one Christian has called me "fucking Jew boy!" and I've given more than one Jew-hater a black eye. I don't trust Christians. I'm afraid of them. Christian Austrian Nazis turned on my grandparents, uncles, and Mom. Neighbors ransacked their house. My grandfather had to bribe his way out of a concentration camp. They escaped to Palestine before it was called Israel.

Left: Mom's family in Austria before Kristallnacht, 1938.
Right: Zeide and Granny at my Bar Mitzvah, Cape Town, 1959

Alone in the safety of the family car, Dad's father, Zeide, dared to mock Christians with a cruelty of his own. On Sunday drives to Hout Bay, a fishing village on Cape Town's Atlantic Seaboard, we drove through a park, where a large crucifix towered over the landscape. As we approached the statue, Zeide began his refrain: "Look! Look! The *kvetch*! The *kvetch*!"

We all laughed in great mirth. We had heard the joke numerous times. But Zeide's timing was impeccable, and his thick Lithuanian accent somehow added to the joke. I never understood exactly what *kvetch* meant. It was at the expense of the *goyim*. Zeide embodied the part of us that sought revenge from our oppressors.

Renoster's mother leads me to an old and lumpy mattress. I'm uncomfortable in this bed. I sleep fitfully. One eye open. Who are these strange people? What will they do to me? Before dawn, Renoster shakes me awake. Men gather. We eat a hearty breakfast with copious cups of strong *koffie* simmered on the stove for hours. Soon, they make a plan for the day. *Mevrou* packs food. The men file outside into the dawn. I trail behind, the last in a line of ten men, each carrying a Lee Enfield rifle of First World War vintage. I wonder what we are going to hunt, and Renoster lifts one arm, sticks his face into his armpit, and makes monkey sounds.

"*Bobbejaan*! Baboons!"

After trekking through the mountainous territory for hours, we stop for *koffie*, dried rusks, and *biltong*—strips of antelope the farmers themselves have hunted and air-dried with salt and special spices to preserve the meat without refrigeration. It's delicious. I piece together that the farmers are hunting the baboons because they've infiltrated their farmlands and caused havoc. The baboons are nothing more than pests. "*Hulle is dood!* They're dead!" one of the farmers mutters, drawing his finger across his throat.

I know from my days in Cape Town that baboons are smart. They understand humans. One time, while hiking near Cape Point, a baboon hid behind a rock and snatched my lunch out of my hand as I passed by. Before I realized I'd been robbed, the baboon jumped onto the branch of a nearby tree, where he inspected my lunch. He devoured my sandwiches in seconds and tossed the rest. I stood sputtering.

I contemplate the prospect of coming upon a troop of baboons and shooting them. I can't help thinking that this would be something like shooting people. But still, I continue trudging behind the hunters. It's not like they're asking my opinion.

We walk all day, up and down steep ravines, covering a lot of ground. Finally, late in the afternoon, we return to the farm empty-handed. The men are disappointed. There've been no sightings of the baboons at all. They've disappeared as if they knew we were coming for them. Like I said, baboons are aware of human ways.

Back at the farm, Renoster and his brother load one of the old Lee Enfields and aim at a large rock in a field a few hundred yards away. Though I've shot a pellet gun many times, I've never shot with a real rifle. This rifle is serious—A.303. It's loud and demands attention and respect. Renoster offers the gun to me. It's heavy and smooth with handling over many years. I love shooting. There's something so satisfying about the power, precision, and control. Of course, I'm shooting a rock, not a baboon.

The next day, Sunday, everyone cleans up for the Sabbath, the men slicking their hair down and wearing ill-fitting suits. They go off to church. I stay around the farm. By midday, they return, and *Mevrou* unfolds a feast of pork, *mielies*—maize, roasted potatoes, gravy, and *koeksisters*, a honey-filled donut-like desert. The meal is washed down with sweet *koffie*. The fact that I'm eating pork doesn't faze me. By now, I've learned that if I refuse pork, I will simply go hungry. Mevrou's helpings are big, and I tuck in. To a hungry boy, food speaks a universal language.

I return to the boarding house. This is the first time I've been with Afrikaners in a family setting. It's strange not understanding what people are saying, but I can tell that they are kind. I've been shown a different slice of life. Renoster's family has been generous and accepted me in their own way. I'm grateful to have been invited to their farm, but a few weeks later, things change between Renoster and me.

After living in Oudtshoorn for several months, to fit in, I've tried on some of the customs of the other boys. One custom is the ritual prayer. Boys get on their knees next to their beds, close their eyes, clasp their hands together, and move their lips without a sound. You can tell they are earnest. The way they pray is alien to me. I've grown up with Jewish prayer—reading long sections of unintelligible Hebrew, with people chanting in unison, humming or singing boisterously, all while *davening*, swaying back and forth, uttering their prayers aloud. A few times when I've been in danger, I've asked God for help. Once when my cousin Raymond and I paddled a rowboat around Gordon's Bay, a sudden surge of wind pulled us out to sea. Then, I prayed. Raymond's quick thinking and bravery saved our lives, but as soon as I got back to solid ground, I forgot about God. One hot Sunday afternoon in my dorm room, during the two-hour "rest and reflection" period, I try out the Afrikaner way of praying to God. I take my turn kneeling and silently praying.

I'm on my knees, concentrating, when I feel a wet, sticky sensation in my hair. It smells like oranges. Orange peels! Someone is fucking with me. I'm exposed—a fake, wannabe Christian. Humiliated, I lash out, punching backward toward the source of the orange peels. My fist finds a target in someone's crotch, and as I turn around, I see Renoster go down like a felled tree. I've hit him in the balls. He lays on the floor, writhing in agony. One of the boys runs to find a teacher. A doctor is called.

From that point on, every few days, Renoster collapses not ten feet from where I sleep.

The boys gather around him, murmuring in sympathy, waiting

for the latest excruciating episode to subside. I'm not sure if the pain Renoster feels is real or whether this is an elaborate face-saving way of getting back at me. I'm probably in denial.

One day, a letter arrives for me. It's handwritten and signed by Renoster's father. It's all in Afrikaans, so I ask Boompie to translate it. He just shakes his head. I look at him expectantly. He hesitates for a few long seconds, then tells me, "Renoster's father wants you dead. You will not escape his anger, and he will take pleasure in seeing you, *verdomde Jood*—damn Jew, croak like a dying frog."

Somehow, I ignore or pretend to ignore this threat, like it's just the rantings of a madman. Inside, I'm anything but nonchalant. A week later, I'm summoned to the room of one of the teachers, a man nicknamed *Koos Krap*—Koos the Crab. He's so named because, although powerfully built, he's severely bowlegged. When he walks, he gives the impression that he's moving sideways, like a crab. Krap gets right down to business.

"Why did you hit Renoster in the balls?" he demands.

I tell him that Renoster rubbed orange peels in my hair while I was praying. I protected myself. Koos Krap takes this in, but his mind is made. I'm guilty.

"*Nou kom. Buk*—bend over for cuts," he demands. Pointing to a chair, he wields a large cane.

In my halting Afrikaans, I stand my ground. "*Ek sal nie buk nie!*—I won't bend over!"

Krap repeats himself, this time with more authority. "*Kom hier nou! Buk!*" He brandishes the cane in his huge hand, convinced that thrashing me is the just course of action and that I should submit to my punishment.

But, full of the righteousness of my cause, I once more refuse.

"Excuse me, Meneer, but I told you before—Renoster rubbed orange peels in my hair while I was praying."

Krap doesn't know what to do. He looks confused and defeated. He's finally heard my side of things. Fucking with someone while they pray isn't okay. He gives up and dismisses me, his frustration evident. I leave his room. I hear no more on the matter—not from Koos Krap or anyone else.

As final exams loom, Renoster's attacks diminish. The end of the year arrives. Renoster graduates. Gone. I'm free of guilt and justification. His graduation coincides with the graduation of most of the bullies, promising a new phase in my life. I've gained a reputation from knocking out Fanie and hitting Renoster in the balls. Wan has made it clear I'm not to be bullied. No one dares pick on Joodjie.

SIX

During my second year, I'm invited to the Safari Ostrich Farm—one of the oldest and largest ostrich ranches in South Africa—for Passover. The Lipschitz family's prominence dates back to the bygone feather frenzy era.

The Seder is held in a magnificent sandstone "feather palace," an opulent home built during the heyday. There's a warmth to the scene. The candles burn brightly on the table, and the ceremonial Seder plate is familiar and sacred, reminding me of Seders at Uncle Nathan and Auntie Milly's. Each year, Uncle Nathan tells the same joke—the one with the punchline in some indecipherable Slavic language. Everyone erupts in stitches. My family—the whole *mishpocha*—is no doubt over at Uncle Nathan's right now.

At this more lavish Seder, a bottle of sweet wine has found its way to the table populated by kids, the young, invited minions of Oudtshoorn. Several of us join the ritual, dutifully downing large gulps of the wine at the appointed times. Soon, we are giggling, followed by tittering and waves of riotous laughter. The leader of the service waits. Mrs. Lipschitz shakes her head in consternation.

It's time for the *Manishtana*—the Four Questions at the heart of the Seder. Per tradition, the youngest boy, a bright eleven-year-old, asks the first question. He stands at the kids' table, wobbling and waving around a goblet of wine that overflows with his erratic movements. He looks around at the gathered congregation, squinting like a biblical scholar.

"*Ma nishtana halaila hazeh?*—Why is this night different from all other nights?" His voice is high-pitched. He sounds like a girl.

Pregnant seconds pass. Then the eleven-year-old doubles up in laughter. He manages a feeble "Isn't it obvious? Isn't it obvious?" and explodes into another fit, collapsing with hysterical laughter on the floor.

The adults don't find his drunken answer satisfactory, but his hysterics are contagious. In seconds, we're all rolling on the floor. We are *shikker*. The adults have lost control. As mysteriously as the wine appeared at our table, it now disappears. It's a night to remember.

While all the adults look away in disgust, one comes over, surveys the scene, and smiles.

"Hi, I'm Lily Kushner." She speaks directly to me. "You're Gary, the boy from Cape Town." Embarrassed, I acknowledge this fact.

"You must come over to our house. It's just a short walk from the boarding house. Come for *Shabbat* dinner on Friday. You can swim in our pool whenever you want!"

Wow! What an invitation!

Friday evening. I'm sitting at the Kushner's dinner table. Lilly has two sons. Mervyn is about twenty, and Derek is sixteen, a few years ahead of me at school. I've never experienced a family meal like this. It's friendly and relaxed. Lilly says something about needing to feed hungry boys. The maid, Meeta, delivers plates piled with chicken and brisket from the kitchen. I haven't seen this much food in a long time. I follow Mervyn and Derek's example. I tuck in, eating as much as I can. When the meal is finally over, I'm truly stuffed. I can't eat another mouthful.

Then, Mervyn yells to Meeta in the kitchen, "Meeta, bring the turkey!"

Meeta trots out of the kitchen empty-handed, laughing her head off.

"You so silly, Master Mervyn!"

In no time, I become a fixture at the Kushner house, at ease in their home as my own. Actually, more at ease. I lounge around their pool, jumping in and splashing around with Mervyn, Derek, and other neighborhood kids. It's an oasis of fun and hospitality.

One afternoon, I head into the town of Oudtshoorn, dressed for the occasion in my favorite bright orange, tight-fitting shirt, a gift from Uncle George. As I walk down the hill toward town, I feel a pair of eyes boring into me. One of my teachers, nicknamed *Sleiper*—literally *prowler*—is riding his bike, very slowly, a few yards behind me. I turn and see the judgment on his face.

"You look like a *tzotzi*!" he says with a sniff of disdain at my bright orange shirt, a reference to the flashy dress of Black city gangsters. "You're not in Cape Town now, boy. Have more respect, *Kaapenaar*!" I get the message. I go back to the boarding house and change my shirt, and I won't wear it again. I'm learning to fit in.

The only café in town is a popular meeting place for high school and college students.

Two chain-smoking, heavily mustached Greek brothers, who speak to me in English with thick Greek accents, run the place. Girls meet there in giggling groups. I sit ogling them, trying to figure out how I can land a girlfriend. I'm too shy. I can't even speak their language.

There's also a single bioscope movie theater in town, with matinees on Wednesdays and Saturdays. These three places—the Kushner's, the Greek café, and the bioscope—become my frequent hangouts.

I'm adept at concocting bogus errands or fake doctor's appointments to get out of the boarding house. In town, I take in cowboys and crooks flicks. At least it's cool inside the bioscope.

One Wednesday matinee, just before the main film, they show a short. On the screen, a beautiful long-haired blond drives a baby-blue MG sports car around the Cape Peninsula. Here in bright technicolor is the magnificent peninsula that I know like the back of my hand. I feel a pang of homesickness; then I realize something else. I actually know the blond bombshell on the screen. She's Mom's old friend's daughter, Eve, the gawky teenager I've known at a distance since I was little.

Boy, has she grown up? Now, she's a genuine stunner.

After the movie, I head for the Greek café and join a bunch of other truant guys. I recognize Mike, Moerbei, and Spook, my roommates. They've all been at the bioscope.

I blurt out, "You know what, guys? I know the star of that short! The gorgeous blond!"

Spook says, "What blond?"

"The one in the baby-blue sports car. You know, in the short? At the beginning. Driving around the Cape."

Mike blows out a cloud of smoke and says, "Is that so, hey? Well, I know the queen of England!"

"No, really! She's even come to our house in Cape Town. I've been to her house too! Her mother's my mother's best friend!"

"Yes. And the queen's my mother's best friend, and she lives in Buckingham Palace! If you know her so well, what's her name? What's her mother's name?"

"Her mother's name is Traute, and her name's Eve," I exclaim.

"Well, Joodjie, you're a real bullshit artist!" The group thinks this is the greatest joke and laughs their heads off. I'm pissed. I can't prove it to these hicks, but it's true.

That Sunday morning, when the others are at church, Mom calls the public phone downstairs. I've been eagerly awaiting her call.

"What's new?" she says.

I blurt out my news. "Well, I went to the bioscope. I saw Eve in a short film. Wow! What a star!"

"Oh, yes!" Mom says. "The one with her driving around in the fancy sports car. Eve has me to thank for her good looks! I told Traute, 'I know how to make her beautiful.' And look at her now. She's a model." I flashback to the endless parade of women with their dresses on hangers, their high heels clopping down the driveway to Mom's workroom to bask in her European beauty and fashion advice.

I meet a few friends at the bioscope. Among them is one girl, Vivienne. She's a few years older than me. She's not the prettiest girl, but she's very friendly, and I like girls. She takes me under her wing. In the last row of the balcony, she introduces me to French kissing.

"You simply must learn," she explains. I acquiesce to age and experience.

"Open your mouth wide!" she instructs, demonstrating with a yawn.

"Keep your lips soft like a dog taking a treat. Here, let me show how!"

She's on me in a second, with her lips on mine, her mouth wide open. I do my best, keep my mouth relaxed, and meet her full-on. Her tongue slides in my mouth, going all around my teeth—like she's inspecting to see if they're all there. She wiggles her tongue around and puts it right on mine! It's hard not to gag. Finally, after an eternity, she's satisfied. "That's how you do it!" she says. "But you've got to put more feeling into it!"

Vivienne hints with a broad smile that Marie, a pretty Afrikaans girl, has expressed interest in me. I'm excited at the prospect. Marie might appreciate my skill at French kissing.

So ends my second year in Oudtshoorn.

After an uneventful summer in Cape Town, working part of the time in Dad's factory, I return to Oudtshoorn for my third year. I've adjusted to the school, boarding house, and Afrikaners. The overt anti-Semitic comments have more or less petered out. My grades have improved. I speak Afrikaans fluently. Meneer Visser, our Afrikaans teacher, is as pleased as punch. Smiling broadly, he compliments me in front of the class. "No one would guess you're an English *Kaapenaar*. Now, you're a real *Boerejood*!"

SEVEN
JANUARY 1965.

I'm eighteen. Ten days ago, I graduated from high school.

I'm standing in the Castle's quad—not a palace sort of castle: the Castle—a massive stone edifice on the Grand Parade in downtown Cape Town, a pentagonal fortress, sometimes prison, now army base, a monument to the subjugation of South Africa's native peoples. The tradition continues. I've been drafted into the all-White South African army. I'm trapped.

An officer, stiff, his chest laden with medals, barks, "*Manne*, men, you are the hope of our nation! You are the chosen ones—the ones who will preserve the freedom of our great Republic." I look around at my conscripted brethren.

Moments after we arrive at the Castle, a team of military barbers descends on us—no ifs, ands, or buts—and shaves the lot of us. We look like plucked chickens. If we're the hope of South Africa, this country has a serious problem. I want to know where they're going to send us.

Finally, the officer says, "You men are blessed, hey. You're going to *Potch*. We got a lot of history in Potchefstroom. The *Voortrekkers* founded it." He wanes nostalgic about South Africa's storied White history, the treaties, and clauses, which I've spent years learning by heart.

I don't feel blessed. It's back to Afrikaner territory for me.

The last two years have been marked by my return to Cape Town. After my third year in Oudtshoorn, Dad announced my homecoming and enrolled me in a new school for my final two years—Wynberg Boy's High. It was a shock. I'd gotten used to Oudtshoorn. I'd become a *Boerejood*. Our house on Buchan Road had been sold. The family was living in a cramped suite of rooms in a residential hotel in Rondebosch, eating breakfast and dinner in a large formal dining room with stuffy guests and obsequies waiters. For the first six months, I slept in a closet-like room. Then we moved into a fancy new house on the slopes of Table Mountain in Newlands. Wynberg Boys was a throwback to my days at SACS. I played rugby and cricket and made a few friends. Fortunately, there was no Latin requirement. Most of my time was taken up preparing for the dreaded matric exams. That sucked big time. But it's all behind me. Now, I'm in the army!

Jesus.

The officer delivering the induction speech finishes with a warning: "We have a serious problem in this country. *Die swartgevaar*. The black danger. Make no mistake, hey. We must be prepared to defend ourselves." It's early 1965, and they need White men. We're a small minority in a sea of Blacks. I've been snared by the government's dark tentacles, and there's no way out.

As the train chugs northward, I'm sick to my stomach. I don't want to be here. Try as they have, the indoctrination has failed. I'm not a proud South African. The country's history is alien to me. I love the land and the sea, but I'm a Jew. An outsider. Bullied by Afrikaners and English alike.

The Potchefstroom training camp is in a sprawling military base, about a hundred miles from Johannesburg. We're in the hinterland. Far from the Cape. Each barrack, large bungalow style buildings, holds about forty or fifty steel cots. The floors, the toilets, the showers shine. The trainers call new recruits "*roofies*." Basic training aims to toughen us up through psychological intimidation, emotional abuse, sleep deprivation, and physical exhaustion.

A few weeks into basic training, I'm woken by loud yells and a deafening cacophony.

Clang! Clang! Clang!

It's 3 a.m.

The Permanent Force sergeant, the one with a single eye looking straight ahead and the other wandering in every direction, clandestinely called *One Eye*, bangs large steel trash can lids together. He screams, "*Word wakker, jong! Word wakker!* Wakey, wakey, assholes!" He clangs the lids a few more times to make sure all the *roofies* get the message.

One Eye is a freak, a drunk with obvious complexes. His only pleasure is to take out his life frustrations on his underlings, his purpose to be as menacing and threatening as possible. God forbid he takes note of you for any reason. When he stands really close, you unflinchingly inhale his putrid breath and the alcohol fumes from last night's binge. Sometimes, he leans into you with a wandering eye, his ponging sweaty body so close it's almost sexual, a twisted, evil grin on his face.

"Today will be the worst day of your shitty little lives!" he announces. I numbly tumble out of bed and dive into fatigues and boots. Every *roofie* does the same. All of us are forced into subservience. We're becoming united through shared oppression.

We march for hours until the sun is high on the Transvaal veld.

This is followed by long sessions in the obstacle course with One Eye and his assistants screaming and swearing at us as we frantically climb large wooden ladders, rappel with ropes from high platforms, or slide on our bellies through narrow tunnels. For weeks, we run and march through the heat of the day. We grow tired. We make mistakes. One Eye has a multitude of punishments he employs. He'll make us run the field with our rifles held overhead till our arms collapse. He seethes. "You motherless scum. You fucking soft *moffies*. You pussy queers! Now clean the shitters and use a toothbrush, you dumb fucks!" After hours of meticulous toilet scrubbing, he says, "Are you fuckers blind? This place is still filthy. You're fucking with me, hey!"

When we aren't marching, we're running, and when we aren't running, we're disassembling and reassembling our rifles till we can practically do it in our sleep. We clean and iron already-spotless clothes. There's the constant threat of inspection. We sleep. One Eye wakes us after a few hours and threatens us with a forced twenty-five-mile march with a sixty-pound pack. Then mysteriously allows us to sleep for a few more precious hours. The army food is bad—worse than at boarding school—but we're hungry and wolf it down.

One day, we're taken by truck to the shooting range. One Eye delivers a sermon on the intricacies of the new FN rifle. "You're lucky fucks!" he tells us with a sneer. "The first group of *roofies* to get the new rifles from Belgium, mind you. Now we got the best rifles in the world, hey! Those fucking *kaffirs* better be quiet!"

We learn how to load the magazine, to aim, to squeeze the trigger, all the basics. One of my fellow *roofies* casually refers to his FN as a gun. This sets One Eye off on a tirade.

"You dumb fucks!" Spit flies in every direction. "You better learn the difference between a gun and a rifle!" He grabs his crotch with one hand and holds up his weapon in the air with the other. He launches into a ridiculous falsetto, mocking us with each syllable.

"This is my rifle.
This is my gun.
This is for shooting.
This is for fun!"

We all laugh as One Eye gazes at us with thinly veiled contempt.

I'm confident that I've done quite well in target shooting, but for some reason, there's a delay in retrieving my shooting score. One Eye addresses me directly. His voice drips with sarcasm. "You completely missed the fucking target. Jesus Christ! Are you a fucking malingerer? Are you blind, man? It's like you shot a bunch of blanks!" I'm puzzled. One Eye hesitates, then hands me another five bullets. "Okay, man. Let me see how you shoot!"

I load the FN and lie on my belly as we've been trained. About 250 yards away, the target pops up. I aim and squeeze the trigger. I shoot the five bullets. One Eye trudges down the range while I wait to hear my score. Minutes later, he returns, shaking his head.

"You are fucking blind, man. You almost hit the next target. Fucking useless! God help us if we have to rely on you!"

I can't understand it. I'm sure I saw the target pretty clearly.

We return to our bungalows. My feet have been bothering me for a few hours. I'm happy to finally take off my boots and socks. I have a problem with my right foot's big toe. It looks swollen, and the nail oozes. I will not be able to put my boot back on.

A sergeant drives me to the military hospital a few miles from the training base. After two hours, a doctor takes one look at my toe and declares, "Ag, man, the nail will have to come out."

He reaches for a large needle and injects it directly into the infected area. Then, looking at his watch for twenty seconds, he cuts my toenail into four strips and yanks each of them out.

Then he says, "Well, that's that. You're out of commission until your nail heals."

For three long weeks, I bide my time in the military hospital. Recuperation feels something like watching paint dry. It's the same day after day: talk to a few guys, play cards, read crappy books, walk around, sun myself, and sleep. I'm surprised that there are so many guys here. Most are "Permanent Force"—"PF's"—the real South African army. The rest are various *roofies* like me—recovering from some injury sustained in basic training. I think that the army has forgotten about me.

One morning, a corporal takes me back to the training camp. I'm now a stranger. My Capetonian bunkmates have all been reallocated. I'm assigned to a bungalow of Afrikaners. Most are from the Orange Free State and the Transvaal. At least I can speak Afrikaans. I try to catch up to the guys, but it soon becomes obvious that in the three weeks I've spent laying around in the hospital, they've been hardening up. I'm like an injured antelope, easy prey for predators.

A few weeks later, a snap inspection is called for the following morning. We prepare all night. The inspection covers all our clothes, gear, toilets, bungalow, and most importantly, a meticulously cleaned and oiled rifle.

At about 4 a.m., as I'm putting the final touches on a ceremonial white belt, one of the Free State boys comes up behind me, reaches over, and purposefully knocks the liquid white polish out of my hand. The bottle arcs through the air, finally coming to rest in a white mess on my bed, and, horror of horrors, the thick white oozes down the barrel of my rifle. I look at this asshole in total anguish and disbelief. He laughs in my face and spits out, *"Fokken Jood!"*

I lose it and sock him with a tremendous punch that knocks him off his feet. He lands heavily and bangs his head against a steed bed frame. He gets up slowly. "You fucking Jew boy!" he sneers. "Maybe I can't take you, but Swanepoel will fuck you up!"

There's no time to clean up. The white shoe polish has splattered over everything, covering my blankets, shirts, and rifle. Minutes later, the commandant and his officers march into the bungalow for the inspection. There's no escape. Slowly, the entourage moves from one *roofie* to the next. They inspect every detail. When they arrive at my bed, I'm standing at attention. The commandant sees the white splatter.

"What the hell happened here?" I mumble some feeble excuse. He looks at me with a raised eyebrow. "Group weekend pass denied," he announces and continues with his entourage.

The entire bungalow has been denied the much-awaited weekend pass.

Outside, early morning sunlight glares. The guys mill around, complaining. I understand their rapid Afrikaans.

Some blame the Free State guy who instigated things.

"You should've left him alone!" they tell him. "We could've taken care of this little Jew without getting the entire unit into shit. Too late now, but Swanepoel will teach him." I'm apprehensive. A sudden quiet descends as Swanepoel arrives.

He's big and tough and leaves no room for misimpression. It's like Loftus in Oudtshoorn, only Swanepoel is much bigger. He's gunning for me and gets right to the point. "You punched Van Niekerk, you *hardegat Jood*. I'm gonna fuck you up!" *Hardegat Jood*—a stubborn Jew who needs to be put in his place.

I know I must make the first punch count. I land a left jab to Swanepoel's nose. His eyes water, but it's not a solid hit. It glances off his nose, and he shakes it off like a lion shaking off a flea. Then he grabs me, and in seconds, we're a fury of tangled limbs, wrestling on the ground.

I try to get back on my feet, but Swanepoel easily overpowers me and begins kicking me with his heavy combat boots. I protect my head with my arms, but it's futile. Over and over, Swanepoel's heavy boots land near my left shoulder. I'm overwhelmed with pain. I scream in agony. My shoulder has dislocated.

Swanepoel melts away. An English-speaking cohort helps me up. A sergeant appears. It's obvious that I'm injured. He wastes no time getting a jeep and driving me back to the military hospital. Usually, this sergeant is belligerent, but this time, he's silent. At the hospital, a doctor sees me immediately. After a quick examination, he wraps a large bandage around my shoulder and orders me to rest. Again, I hang around the military hospital, sleeping, playing cards, and rereading the same trashy paperbacks from my last visit not long ago. Weeks later, I'm called in to see the doctor again.

"I'm sending you back to basic camp for the commandant to decide your status." Back at the main camp, I'm brought before the commandant. He sits behind a large desk with five or six officers standing at attention behind him. I come to attention and salute. He returns my salute with a wave of his hand.

"What happened here, man?"

"May I speak freely, sir?"

"Yes, yes. Of course. Tell me what happened."

"Well, sir, they did this to me because I'm Jewish."

The whole story tumbles out and hangs in the air.

The officers standing in a straight line behind the commandant stare mutely ahead. The commandant examines my file. I've been in a military hospital twice during basic training, missing over six weeks. I'm still injured. My shooting scores are abysmal. I'm a problem—a fighter. I'm a Jew.

He looks up and takes off his glasses.

"As commanding officer, I am dismissing you from the South African Defense Forces. You're permanently medically unfit. An honorable discharge." He points out his office window to a wall about fifty yards away and says, "If a *kaffir* comes over that wall, I can't rely on you to pick up a rifle and protect me or anyone else."

He hands me an official-looking document signed and stamped

with the date. Faking disappointment, I protest, but only for a few seconds. I'm elated. I'm done with the army! Two days later, dressed in civvies, I'm on the train back to Cape Town.

EIGHT

I'm afraid of facing Dad. He has strong ideas about how his son should be groomed. First, he sent me to SACS, relying on South Africa's oldest school to educate me in the British colonial mode. I failed Latin and flunked out. Next, he sent me to an Afrikaner boarding school, hoping it would mold me into an upstanding bilingual South African. I became too boorish, perhaps losing too much of my English veneer. And no doubt, he had expected the army to discipline me and make a man of me. But I'm a disappointment again.

As the train chugs over the veld toward Cape Town, I move gingerly, afraid to make any moves that might dislocate my shoulder.

At the train station in Cape Town, I call Dad from a public phone booth.

"Howzit, Dad. . . . I'm back from the army. I've been discharged."

Long silence.

Then Dad's voice crackles. "How can this be? Are you AWOL?"

"No, Dad, the army kicked me out. It's a long story, but they say I'm medically unfit. Don't worry. They say it's an honorable discharge!"

Long silence.

"I'll pick you up at the station."

An hour and a half later, Dad arrives at the station in his new car, a white Plymouth Barracuda with an enormous back window. On the way home, I tell him the whole story. He takes it in. Smokes his cigarette. Says little.

Within days, he hires a lawyer to sue the army for negligence. The lawyer claims the army was responsible for my safety. It seems farfetched to me. Then Dad makes arrangements for me to apprentice as an electrician. He explains it's a great way for me to get the technical background necessary to contribute to his electrical switchboard and wholesale electrical component business. We've never discussed my becoming an electrician, but his explanation makes sense, and having a direction after my unexpected release from the army comes as a relief. With my precarious shoulder, manual work might pose a problem, but I'll manage it. The idea grows on me. I want a practical leg up to follow in Dad's business footsteps. I begin apprenticing at a small electrician's—Faraday's Electric. Apprenticing by day isn't difficult. I compensate for my weak shoulder. Night school, however, proves problematic. Because of my precipitous army dismissal, I'm more than a half year behind my fellow apprentices. I've missed the electrical basics. I'm at sea. I'm back failing Latin again. Except this is the real world.

My shoulder begins dislocating after a few months of working with heavy equipment. The dislocations are excruciating. Now I know how to relocate my arm into the shoulder socket. Apprenticing becomes increasingly difficult. Finally, I see an orthopedic surgeon. "This injury is serious. We'll need to pin your shoulder and relocate the nerve that controls your arm and hand movement." I listen in stunned silence.

"You'll need months of rehab.... You should understand that you'll have a limited range of motion. Your left arm will gradually atrophy."

After the operation, I'm weak and unable to lift anything. My days as an apprentice electrician are over. The surgeon encourages me to brush my teeth with my left hand. He says the circular movement is good for my rehab. It takes months to heal. Dad arranges work for me at his company. He sets me up with a front-of-house job in his business supplying components to electricians throughout the Cape Province.

In the front office, Ms. Rose, Dad's prim secretary with the large blue tortoiseshell glasses, types up invoices and statements. Underneath the blue glasses, she's actually pretty, only about three years older than me, but she's very formal. She works for Dad. He's the boss. I make no attempt to find out her first name. She's just Ms. Rose.

I enjoy working with Charlie, the Cape Colored storekeeper in charge of the warehouse. He speaks a mixture of English and Afrikaans, often in the same sentence. I have to pay attention, or I'll miss the punchline of his outrageous jokes. When the bosses are in their offices, Charlie loves nothing more than putting on a show. He mocks the Afrikaner government's narrow-mindedness and their laws forbidding sexual congregation across the color line, the so-called Immorality Act.

"I'm telling you the real truth, hey! These stupid Afrikaners—the *Boere*—have penis envy! *Hulle is bang vir die swart piel en poes!* Plain and simple, they're afraid of Black cocks and pussies!"

Charlie's ability to be serious around the bosses, especially Dad, starkly contrasts his outrageous antics when the authority is absent. He smokes enormous *zols*, joints rolled in newspaper filled with green *dagga*—cannabis—called Durban Poison. The skunky odor fills the warehouse, his domain. Charlie's eyes are yellow with years of dagga smoking, but he knows the location of every screw and component in the facility. It's easy to learn from Charlie. His irreverent humor—his *chutzpah*—is an unanticipated benefit of working in the warehouse.

One day, the air hangs heavy with Charlie's Durban Poison; no one's around, so he begins performing for me. He takes out his false teeth and pulls his lower lips over his nose, and half of his face disappears! Then he relaxes, and his face returns to normal. He goes about his business, returning minutes later to quickly repeat his face-disappearing act. I laugh in delight.

Neither he nor I see Dad emerging from his office. Dad sees Charlie and I yucking it up. We're both doubled over in laughter. Dad takes me aside and demands, "Why are you hanging around with Charlie? Do you want to become like him?" I say nothing, pretending to heed Dad's warning, but my real answer is *I'd rather have fun with Charlie than be uptight like you!*

Besides, Charlie is showing me the ropes.

One evening, Mom and Dad attend the opening of *The Sound of Music*. It's a musical that takes place in Austria in the late 1930s in the looming shadow of Naziism and WWII. Mom hasn't seen images of her country of origin since she escaped the Nazis herself at fifteen.

About 10 p.m., I hear Dad's car pull into the driveway. They enter the house through the kitchen, near my room. Dad says something, but his voice is muffled. I can't make it out.

Then I hear Mom's voice. Loud. She's yelling at Dad, "You have no soul! You don't really know what happened to my family. You know nothing about the Nazis!"

Dad responds, indignant, defensive, angry, "What are you talking about? I fought the Nazis for damn near five years!"

Mom screams, "You know nothing! You pretend you're pious, but you just go to shul to flirt with the women!"

Her voice trails off as they move down the corridor. The door to their suite closes. My stomach is a knot. I'm nauseous. I don't know what to do. I'd rather be anywhere but here. I hate when they argue.

Suddenly, Dad yells. Mom cries out in fear and pain.

I'm instantly transported back to when I was eight. Penny and I were playing in Mom and Dad's bedroom. Unexpectedly, Mom entered the room, sat in front of her mirror, and began applying her foundation. I thought it odd that she was wearing sunglasses.

Then I saw that she was hiding two ugly black shiners. I knew Dad had done it.

It won't happen again.

I jump out of bed, run down the passage, fling open the door to their suite, and rush in.

Mom is whimpering in anguish, a bloody towel pressed to her face.

"Get out of here!" Dad commands.

I stand firm in front of him.

"I'm not leaving until you control yourself!"

Without another word, he kicks me hard in my midriff. I absorb the force of the kick and fall to the carpet. I spring to my feet and land a solid right on Dad's chin. He stops in his tracks. The skin on his chin is split. As if in a daze, he touches his face and looks at me with bewilderment. His fingers are covered with blood.

"You're my son! You hit me!" he says in stunned disbelief. "That's it." He turns, pulls out a suitcase, and throws clothes into it.

Mom pleads with him, but Dad continues packing. Without another word, he takes his suitcase and walks out. His car starts and drives away.

Mom stands there with her swollen face and screams, "He would never have left if you hadn't lost your temper! You're just like him. Violent. Why did you interfere? He's abandoned us, and it's your fault!"

I'm shocked and confused. I was protecting her. How can she be angry with me? But am I stupid? Have I forgotten? I've never been able to trust her. Not really. She speaks with a forked tongue. She's unreliable. More than once, she lulled me into relaxing my guard, then suddenly dug her nails into my arms to show me she was in charge. Once, she scratched my face, leaving two furrows down my cheeks. I told my teachers I ran into barbed wire.

Did I lose my temper? Did I have the right to raise my hand to my father? What do you do when your father beats your mother? What should I have done if it was wrong to stand up to him? Nothing? Just stayed in my room, pretending to mind my own business? Allow him to beat her up again? If I had let it be, how far would it go the next time or the time after that?

But my dilemma is immediate. I've been working for Dad for months. It's been going well. I've learned a lot. I don't want to lose my job. After a sleepless night, I decide to go to work. Life goes on. Best to get back to normal as soon as possible. I shower, get dressed in my work clothes, and come to the kitchen. Mom asks a relevant question. "Are you *meshuga*?"

I ignore her challenge to my sanity and hitchhike the six miles to Dad's business. I head inside like it's just another day. Dad's office door is shut, the blinds drawn. I hear the low rumbling of his voice speaking on the phone. He stays in his office for a long time, but when he comes out, he seems somehow diminished. A square white bandage covers his chin. He avoids eye contact. I can feel his loathing. I try to go about my work. Soon, he returns to his office, where he remains secluded.

Around noon, my phone rings. A prominent customer places an order for a substantial length of expensive multi-cored underground cable. I write down the order, pass it on to Charlie, and continue working. The cable is duly measured and cut by three men working together. They load it onto a truck, and after a few minutes, it departs.

At around 4 p.m., Dad's office door suddenly flies open. He storms out, heading directly to the counter where I serve customers. His face is contorted in rage.

"What size cable did you tell them to cut?"

"What the customer specked," I sputter. "I wrote it down!" Dad ignores me and continues railing. "You fucked up the size of that cable! The customer is really pissed! He's standing around with a bunch of men and the wrong-size cable. Who's going to pay for their lost time or the cost of that cable?"

I'm flabbergasted.

"But Dad . . . " I stammer.

"Jesus Christ!" Dad yells, becoming more enraged by the second.

"I wrote down exactly what the customer asked!" I insist.

Dad looks around, his eyes settling on the heavy steel bar used to secure the business' front door. He grabs it and hurls it like a spear toward me in one swift motion. I move my head to the left before it smashes into the wall behind me. I look at him in utter disbelief.

"What are you doing? Are you mad? You could have killed me!"

I walk out the door as fast as I can. Tears blind me. I get down to De Vaal Drive and stick out my thumb. In a few minutes, someone stops and gives me a ride toward Newlands.

Mom takes one look at me and gloats. "I told you not to go."

At home, the tension between Mom and Penny becomes more palpable than ever. They've been fighting for years, intermittent outbursts of blame and recrimination. A few days later, I walk past Penny's room. Her door is open. Penny is standing while Mom, on her hands and knees, measures her for a new dress. Penny asks Mom for money, a ritual we both detest.

"Mom, please, I need five rand for the school trip."

"Ask your father!" Mom replies, her voice bitter. Penny and I have heard this refrain umpteen times, but this time, it's different.

"Ouch, Mom! You're sticking pins into me!" Penny yells.

Mom slaps Penny across the face and yells, "I'm sick and tired of being taken for granted by everyone in this family!"

Penny rips off the dress, runs out of the house, and disappears. The next afternoon, she arrives home with a driver from Dad's business. Without a word, she packs up her clothes and leaves with the driver. Via the grapevine, I hear she is staying at Uncle George's, happy to be out of the house and away from Mom.

Mom falls into a deep depression. She wanders from room to room, wondering aloud about her future in South Africa.

"I have no family here," she says with great sadness. "Dad's family has never accepted me." She finds Dad at his hotel and begs him to come back. He refuses, telling her an honest truth: "If I come back, I'll end up killing you or myself."

By standing up to my father, my world has turned upside down. My family is disintegrating. Dad and I are at serious odds. He punched Mom, kicked me, and I punched him.

Then he tried to kill me with that iron bar. What now? I have no job or prospects. I'm a loser.

Aimless and depressed, I begin drinking and hanging out at Muizenberg Beach.

Mom focuses obsessively on the impending divorce. She constantly berates Dad and bemoans Penny's betrayal. I miss Penny, but she and Benny, my closest buddy at Wynberg, have gotten together. I don't see much of them. The beautiful new house feels oddly large and empty. It's a safer but sad and lonely place.

After a few months of aimless debauchery, I land a job as a traveling salesman for a small electrical component wholesaler in the city that sells some of the same lines as Dad's firm. It's small, too small to be competitive with Dad's business. My new employer is happy to have me on board as I'm familiar with their lines and hit the ground running. Still, my new boss wonders why I no longer work for my father. I tell him that we have a personality clash. He clucks understandingly, with a shake of his head and a "*Ja-nee*," the Afrikaans that means "yes-no," but which also sums up the inevitability of father-son conflict.

I find the job of visiting customers in the suburbs of Cape Town easy enough, though a few of them refuse to do business with me because of their allegiance to Dad. I'm pleased to have a job.

NINE

A few months later, I receive a phone call from Ms. Rose, Dad's secretary.

"Your father would like to meet you tomorrow. Can you be here at eight?" After not seeing Dad for months, I'm apprehensive. Why the sudden urgency? I show up at eight the next morning. Dad sits behind his desk, a Mills cigarette clenched between his lips as he compulsively cleans the desk's glass surface with a soft cloth. He's nervous. I am too.

"Look," he says. "I've put out feelers for you. I've located a special training program sponsored by the Dorman Group, an affiliate of ours in Joburg. They're connected to Federal Electric, a big firm in Canada. This opportunity will set you up for the future. The program begins in a week. I have to tell them right away."

I take in Dad's proposal with a mixture of hope and insecurity. The last time I saw him, he seemed unhappy with my work performance. But this Joburg thing sounds like a big deal. Maybe it's the break I need. But what if it's a setup? Just a way to get me out of Cape Town. I'm apprehensive about going to a strange city, Joburg. I've heard nothing good about the place. Dad presses me. I want the war between us to be over. Joburg has a different vibe than Cape Town. For one thing, it teems with Black people, a phenomenon I've not previously experienced. Cape Town's industry and trades are overwhelmingly serviced by Cape Coloreds, who make up half of the city's population. But here, tribal Blacks from the *Bantustans*—the ten government-designated homelands—provide the labor. Where the Cape felt relatively relaxed, here, palpable anger seethes just below the surface, threatening to boil over. Joburg's reputation as a scary place seems well-deserved.

The Dorman Group manufactures electrical switchboards and plumbing components. The training program requires me to spend time in a series of parallel factories, each focused on various manufacturing processes, from sheet metal fabrication to welding and wiring. The offices of the executives are located in a separate wing protected from the noise and activities of the factory floors.

I'm placed initially in steel fabrication. Here, I learn welding and measuring and bending sheet metal into precise shapes. After three months, I'm transferred to switchboard wiring. Day after day, I attach identical wires to color-coded terminals. At night, I dream of copper wire entangling me. Then, with no warning, I'm transferred again—to the plumbing valve factory. On these factory floors, I learn which wires are supposed to go where or how to turn brass valve components to fine tolerances, but so far, I haven't learned much about how the different parts work together or why. I'm bobbing around in a sea of machines and micrometers with little direction, trying to look intelligent.

On the plumbing valve shop floor, simply because I'm White, I'm in charge of nine Black lathe operators, all far more experienced than me. They call me "*Basie*"—Afrikaans for "young boss"—but I'm under no illusion about who is really in charge. The men in my group all come from one of the tribal homelands. These so-called *Bantustans* are supposed to be semi-autonomous regions, separate but equal, according to the government. From what I can tell, the homelands' main source of income derives from their "export" of millions of workers who provide labor for the country's industrial and mining heartland.

Most of the men don't speak English and only a smattering of Afrikaans. Their leaders pantomime to explain things to me. I'm embarrassed by my stupidity and my privilege. One day, I'm handed a cryptic note from Mr. Tangney instructing me to take my men to the carport where the bosses park their cars. Using the existing structure, we're to install corrugated iron siding to create a six-car enclosed garage.

When my measurements for the garage construction leave a conspicuous gap in one of the walls, the men rectify the situation. I'm relieved.

After the walls have been reattached, the men invite me to eat with them. We head to an open lot out of sight of the factory, where they build a small fire. They place a piece of rectangular scrap metal over the flames and barbecue scraggly pieces of lean meat on the hot metal. Soon, the meat is thoroughly cooked, and they offer me a good-sized chunk. When each man has received his share, we sit on our haunches in a circle, eating around the fire. The men joke boisterously, and though I can't understand much, it doesn't matter. I understand the vibes. They've accepted me. They understand the racial situation and don't seem to hold it against me. Their kindness accentuates my loneliness and confusion about what I'm doing in Joburg. After a year at the plant, I'm thoroughly miserable. No one seems to know where this so-called training program should take me. Unlike Dad's sunny description, there's actually no real program. Whatever training I receive is purely a function of the kindness of my current babysitter or the goodwill of the men I'm supposed to be leading.

On Christmas Eve, there's a party for the White management team. I'm included. The Black workers have their own party on the floor of one of the factories. Alcohol flows freely. Everyone is soon inebriated and having a fine time. Although the White and Black parties start off separately, soon, lubricated by plenty of drink, they mix freely, and racial distinctions dissolve in the Christmas spirit.

Mr. Tangney comes by and invites me up to his office for a drink. Already quite plastered, I follow him up the stairs to the executive suite. Tangney casually heads for one of the two visitor's chairs in front of his desk, gesturing for me to sit next to him. Instead, I head for Tangney's comfy chair behind his desk. Here, in the big boss's chair, I sit up straight, put on a serious face, and address Tangney as though he's me, and I'm Tangney himself. "Well, boy, you've been here for quite a while now, and I must say you've done a great job!" I slur.

Tangney seems amused and raises his eyebrows. I plow ahead.

"You've done such a great job that we are going to give you a new position up here in the executive suite. And we're going to double your salary to 150 rands a month!"

This is completely outrageous, and for a moment, even in my drunken state, I know I've gone too far. But Tangney thoughtfully smokes his cigarette and says nothing. He keeps that amused look long after I have nothing left to say. After an awkward silence, I skulk away. As I sober up, I am convinced I'll be fired for my chutzpah—my drunken off-the-wall play-acting.

During the holiday, I meet up with Howie, an ex-Capetonian now living in Joburg.

"I heard your dad got remarried!"

What?

I know the divorce has gone through, but I've heard nothing from

Dad since I arrived in Joburg. The news is jarring, but there's more. Much more. Dad has married Eve, Traute's daughter. Traute was in and out of our house my entire childhood—pinching my cheek and suffocating me in her perfumed bosom. I remember seeing Eve on the screen at the bioscope in Oudtshoorn, driving a sports car around the Cape Peninsula. She's only ten years older than me.

The news of my father's new marriage, that he has said nothing about it to me, highlights the insurmountable gulf between us. Briefly, I consider calling him, but what would I say? *Mazel tov, Dad?* I think of Mom and how it must feel to hear that Dad has married her best friend's daughter. But both Dad and Mom feel a million miles away.

After the holiday, I go back to work. For the first few hours, things proceed normally.

I relax, sure my drunken proposition has been forgotten, but then, I get a message from Mr. Tangney's secretary to stop by. I knew it. This is it. I'll be on the street in a few minutes. I head to Tangney's office to face the music.

"Come in, boy! Come in!" Tangney greets me with a friendly smile. "Did you have a good holiday?" Like I hadn't made a complete fool of myself. I sheepishly head for the chair in front of Tangney's desk, which I drunkenly avoided on my last visit.

"I've been thinking about what you said Christmas Eve," Tangney says matter-of-factly. "We've got a job upstairs here in the plumbing valve division. You would be in charge of customer service for the entire Witwatersrand and the rest of the Transvaal. That's quite a lot of responsibility. And we'll double your salary to 150 rands a month!"

Is he putting me on? No, he's serious. I can't believe that my drunken Christmas party antics have worked out in my favor like this. I'm twenty years old, less experienced than really all the men working here. But the color of my skin and my chutzpah are pushing me on.

"Thank you, sir!" I stammer out my gratitude. Tangney tells me to start the next day.

"Good afternoon. Dorman Plumbing!" I mark down the fifteenth call on my worksheet.

"Hullo, yah, hey, is this the plumbing company?" The man's voice on the other end of the line sounds frustrated, ready to explode.

"Yes, sir, can I help you?"

"I hope so! My house is flooding! All because of your bladdy valve! This piece of rubbish doesn't hold water! What the hell are you going to do about it, man?"

I pause to gather my energy before I deliver my well-rehearsed script.

"Sir, thank you for your call. Per our warranty, defective valves that are under one year from the manufacturing date will be replaced. Can I have the date of manufacture of your valve? It's printed in the brass section at the bottom. Do you happen to have the valve handy?"

"Be serious, man. The valve's installed in my basement, and the basement's flooded. The plumber just spent two days trying to figure out what's happening. I'm a pensioner! I can't afford this! What kind of product are you making, hey?"

"I'm very sorry, sir, but without that date, I cannot proceed to replace the valve."

"Jesus Christ, what a fly-by-night company! I don't need a new valve; I need a new house. Bladdy hell!" With that, he slams down the phone.

Just one of a hundred similar calls I've been taking for months now.

Two years after beginning the "training program," purposelessness gnaws at my hopes. I hear endless irate callers echoing into the future. My job sucks. I'm tired. I have no power to help. I've come to believe the valves are crap—poorly designed and poorly manufactured. I hope that none of these faulty valves are ones I made when I worked on the factory floor. I certainly had a tough time measuring those fine tolerances with the micrometer. Perhaps that's why I got this promotion.

I'm sad and lonely. I can't go back to the Cape. What will I do there? I don't know how to change my situation or myself. I'm paralyzed, stuck in a dark tunnel, a wreck, barely holding on.

TEN

It's early 1967, and the Arab-Israeli conflict begins making the daily newspapers. I'm obsessed with the news. The Arab nations threaten to "push the Jews into the sea." I'm Jewish and connected to Israel. My family has a long history with the place, even when it was still called Palestine. Before he settled in the greener pastures of South Africa, Zeide lived in Palestine. For him, Palestine was a way station from Jew hatred and pogroms in Eastern Europe. In 1939, Zionists saved Mom's family from Hitler's final solution. They risked their lives to bring Jews safely to Palestine. Dad, a South African soldier attached to the British Eighth Army, was stationed in British Mandate Palestine for part of the war. He met Mom at a dance for Jewish soldiers. They were married in Tel Aviv in 1945. I was born the next year in Cape Town.

I practically imbibed Israel in my mother's milk. I can still hear

Mom saying, "Wherever you go, don't forget Israel!" At eleven, I joined Habonim—Zionist scouts—and was chosen *Rosh Machaneh*—leader of the camp. This recognition filled me with pride. It's one of the few times outside of sports that I felt seen.

I cling to BBC radio, waiting for updates.

As the months go by, the conflict becomes more distressing, the rhetoric terrifying. Five Arab armies threaten to wipe the Jews from the face of the earth.

Syria relentlessly shells the *kibbutzim*—the collective farms—in the valley below the Golan Heights. I wait. There's no resolution. Only a slow walk to the annihilation of the only safe place for Jews.

Then, in early April, the Israelis retaliate, shooting down six Syrian MIGS. I celebrate. I plummet when Syria shells Israel fourteen times in the first fifteen days of May.

At night, I return to the rooming house I share with four complaining old ladies. They trap me in the kitchen, wondering why I don't eat dinner with them. There's no diplomatic way of explaining they're not the most attractive and uplifting dinner companions. I think I need to find another place to live.

Then, Egypt joins the fight, moving its army into the Sinai. UN peacekeepers withdraw.

Two Egyptian MIG-21s fly over Israel's nuclear reactor. On May 22, Egypt closes the Straits of Tiran, shutting down shipping to Eilat, Israel's Red Sea port, an act of war. Within two weeks, six Arab countries amass 230,000 troops on Israel's borders. Jordan and Egypt sign a mutual defense pact, declaring, *our goal is clear—to push the Jews into the sea.*

I take a portable shortwave radio to work. I don't want to miss a shred of news. Irate valve customers call and complain incessantly. I listen to them with half an ear, going through the motions. I couldn't care less. Problems with these stupid valves are so mundane. I want to know what's going on in the Middle East. Why is the news so sparse?

After work, I grab a quick bite and head over to the flat of some new friends, the Goldin brothers and their girlfriends. Everyone's Jewish and as concerned as I am about the situation.

We sit around their shortwave radio, waiting for the latest bulletin. We're all in the same boat. On June 5, Israel launches a preemptive strike against her Arab neighbors. We're stunned. We wait. The news is sparse. We're demoralized. We imagine the worst. The Arab armies will annihilate the Jews.

We get a new report: the Israeli Air Force has destroyed nearly 400 military aircraft. Israel claims complete air supremacy. The Goldin brothers scream in jubilation, but within moments, we're back to biting our nails, waiting to hear what will unfold. At work, I can barely concentrate. I couldn't care less about plumbing valves. My job sucks.

On June 7, Israeli troops storm Jerusalem. The Wailing Wall—the most holy of Jewish sites—is in Israeli hands. We hug and cry in relief and hope.

In the next few days, Israel and Syria engage in heavy tank battles in the Golan Heights.

We're glued to the radio. Nothing matters except the news. On June 9, Israeli tanks defeat the Syrians. Israel traps the Egyptian army in the Sinai. Hundreds of tanks and armored vehicles are destroyed. Suddenly, it's over. Israel has beaten the invading Arab armies. The Six-Day War—the miracle war—ends.

It's a moment of great relief. We toast Israel's great victory. David has slain Goliath. We are proud to be Jews.

The Jewish Agency appeals to young South African Jews to volunteer to help in Israel. They offer free airline tickets, board and lodging, and pocket money in exchange for six months on one of Israel's 230 kibbutzim. By working on a collective farm, volunteers will contribute directly to Israel's well-being in the aftermath of the war. I'm stunned by this offer. The only thing that's kept me engaged for months is the situation in Israel. I rush to volunteer. I'm told to be ready to leave for Israel in a week. For the first time in my life, I've chosen my path forward for myself. I'm filled with excitement and purpose.

I can't wait to get out of Joburg. I give notice to a sympathetic Mr. Tangney, pack my belongings, pile them into my car, and head for Cape Town. I drive the thousand miles through the night, arriving at Dad's office just as he's unlocking the door. He's shocked to see me. "What a surprise," he says. "What are you doing here?"

Standing on the sidewalk outside the business, I blurt out, "I've volunteered to go to Israel, Dad."

Dad takes this in and exclaims, "I'm proud of you!" I'm glad he feels that way.

Then he says, "But what will you do when you get back?"

I say nothing. I don't know, and I don't care. I'm psyched about going to Israel. I'm almost twenty-one. I'm heady with excitement. My life has taken an unexpected turn. A life preserver has been thrown into the water. I'm seizing it.

PART TWO: SEEKING

We travel, some of us forever, to seek other states, other lives, other souls.
　　　—*Anais Nin*

What you seek is seeking you.
　　　—*Rumi*

ELEVEN

"Welcome to the Holy Land! Welcome to Israel! We will be landing in Tel Aviv shortly." The pilot's voice stirs me from a restless sleep. I look out the window. Israel's Mediterranean coastline stretches northward and southward. Lebanon to the north, Gaza and Egypt to the south. The sunlight is strong, contrasting the blue ocean and the white breakers with the yellow-brown of the land.

Twenty minutes later, I walk down the passenger stairs, breathe in the baking Middle Eastern heat, and sob. I can't help myself. It's the beginning of the biggest adventure of my life. I've made it to Israel—the third generation in my family to fulfill a connection to the Holy Land. I've arrived in the place that offered a haven to generations of my family, the Promised Land. I'm a part of something bigger than myself. I've dropped my crummy life to join thousands of Jewish volunteers from South Africa, Italy, Britain, Germany, Sweden, Argentina, Australia, New Zealand, Canada, the USA, and other countries that have flocked to Israel. Each person is here to ease the economic stress created by the war. Being a part of an international volunteer effort buoys my spirit.

I'm assigned to a small contingent of Joburg volunteers. I don't know any of them. We're placed in the back of a truck and driven to Moshav Habonim, a collective farm situated between Tel Aviv and Haifa, in an area along the Mediterranean coast, known as Caesarea. We're put up in a simple house. We're unexpected guests. There aren't enough beds. I sleep on the floor in my sleeping bag. Edith, the only young woman in our group, pressured by our hosts, reluctantly prepares meals for five hungry guys and herself.

On our first morning, the men in our group are dispatched into the potato fields. At 7 a.m., it's already hot and promises to be a real scorcher. A tractor driven by a young Israeli upturns rows of potatoes that stretch as far as the eye can see. Showing off his driving skills, he whizzes by us, loudly revving the tractor's engine and grinning at us from his shaded seat while we slave under the boiling sun. I don't like this young punk's attitude. He's arrogant, laughing at us. What an asshole! The stereotype of a surly *Sabra*. The Hebrew word refers to Israelis who were born after Independence in 1948. They're like the native Israeli cactus fruit, prickly on the outside but soft, sweet, and juicy on the inside. Supposedly.

We pile upturned potatoes into stacks of wooden boxes. The sun is unrelenting, much hotter than I'm accustomed to. By evening, I'm so exhausted that I can barely eat. I climb into my sleeping bag and sleep like a dead man. The next day is a repeat of the first day and the day after that. In two weeks, I question whether I've made the right decision to come to Israel. I'm working my ass off, but these Israelis don't seem grateful at all. Just the opposite. I get a distinct feeling that volunteers represent an extra expense and that our hosts resent us. It's like we've been imposed on them. Disillusioned and beaten down by the relentless Cesarean sun, I wonder how long I'll be able to keep up.

To make matters worse, I haven't bonded with the Joburg co-volunteers in my group. One of them, an intense dark prince, flirts at every opportunity with Edith. He gets into his head that I'm also after her, that I'm his competition. Whenever we're around Edith, he puts me down, relishing in my discomfort and my inability to one-up him.

After a month on Moshav Habonim, I'm quite fed up. I decide to visit a few Cape Town acquaintances stationed on a kibbutz south of Tel Aviv called Givat Brenner.

I arrive during lunch. My friends take me directly to the dining hall. I sit down to a meal fit for a king—at least three different types of yogurt, various cheeses, boiled eggs, freshly baked bread, *tachina*—a delicious sesame seed paste—fried chicken, and mounds of Israeli salad made from cucumbers, tomatoes, salt, pepper, and olive oil. It's by far the best meal I've eaten since Mom's Sunday lunch Vienna schnitzel with *steinpilzen* mushrooms and apple strudel for dessert.

Surrounding the central residential areas of the kibbutz and the dining hall are orange orchards and banana plantations, each with a satellite kitchen to feed workers in the field. There's also a commercial dairy, a furniture factory, a canning and juice factory, schools, basketball courts, and a large communal swimming pool. Well-kept gardens and neat paths lead from one area to another. Tractors and small trucks crisscross the kibbutz. People go about their business. Givat Brenner is an established and thriving community.

About thirteen hundred kibbutzniks live communally, sharing their labor and expertise, and receiving security, food, housing, education, childcare, and friendship. All members live in small houses, each with mini kitchens for preparing tea and snacks. Everyone is equal, and each person's contribution is valued. Kibbutz children don't live with their parents. They live together in dormitories with their peer groups, independent of adults, and visit their parents for tea and discussion each afternoon. I've heard that kibbutzniks make fine army officers because their unique upbringing brings out natural leadership tendencies.

Compared to the small and pinched moshav where I've baked in the fields for a month filling boxes of potatoes alongside my unfriendly co-volunteers, Givat Brenner looks inviting. My friends are quick to vouch for me, and after a brief interview and a few phone calls, I'm welcomed as a volunteer resident of Givat Brenner.

The volunteers' house sits in a separate area from the other residences. It has a long wooden porch, with rooms along its entire length. Next door to my simple room lives an Italian couple. They burn incense and have decorated their room with Arab blankets and mosquito netting. It has the vibe of a sacred temple. The guy has long kinky hair and a scraggly beard. He wears an Arab scarf around his head for protection from the sun. The woman has dark hair and blue eyes, and she walks around wearing gauzy Indian clothes that show off her curves. These are the first hippies I've come across. I want to be friends, but their rapid Italian is impossible to understand, and they keep to themselves. Another volunteer from Sweden named Pia is an attractive blond woman in her early thirties. She came to live on the kibbutz months before the war. From time to time, she invites my friends and me to tea. These are spirited events, filled with interesting conversations about the war and Zionism.

The volunteer administration assigns a young kibbutznik by the name of Yehuda as my mentor. Yehuda's a kind and gentle guy, and we get along well. He speaks excellent English and shows me the ropes—where to go, what to do, where to eat in the field. We begin work early in the morning—by 6 a.m.—barely after sunrise before it gets too hot to work outside. If we're working far from the central dining room, we stop for breakfast in one of the field kitchens. Most days,

Yehuda and I work side by side on the massive plantation, where we fertilize row after row of banana trees. Sometimes we work in the residential area maintaining the substantial grounds. Every few hours, we stop for a drink, and after our morning shift, we eat lunch in the central dining room. Then, in the heat of the day, we take a siesta. Our second shift begins in the late afternoon when it's beginning to cool. While we work, Yehuda tells me about his job in the army. I'm curious and pepper him with questions. He's a modest guy who doesn't enjoy speaking about war.

Yehuda slowly introduces me to his kibbutznik friends. They're all officers in the army; Lazer, a commando frogman, regales me with tales of clandestine underwater missions into enemy harbors, and Pietzie, an intelligence officer, isn't talkative but appears permanently amused. They've all grown up together on the kibbutz, away from their parents. They're tight. I can't help feeling envious of their bond.

Spending time on the kibbutz begins to open my eyes to the world in a new way. I feel the sense of purpose and togetherness that everyone around me seems to share. My bleak life in South Africa casts a dark shadow, but with each day that passes, it recedes. My companions are people with different backgrounds and countries of origin. I drink it up. It's heady and exciting. Tending banana trees or the kibbutz's gardens with Yehuda's patient guidance introduces a certain dignity to simple work and how our small part contributes to the collective whole.

Kibbutzniks praise "good workers" to high heaven. I'm a good worker. But there is something in the kibbutz culture that also prizes intellect and knowledge. Kibbutzniks are surprisingly well-read and well-informed. They're not just country hicks on a big farm. Givat Brenner has a library with all kinds of books and magazines, many in English. I like the quiet in the library. I peruse the books and magazines. *Time* and *Life*. Photography books of the Negev desert, the Dead Sea, and Masada.

A book by Eric Berne, a Canadian psychiatrist, attracts my attention. It's called *Games People Play*. Much of the book is rather analytical, but I pick up a few ideas that awaken my curiosity. According to Berne, "Everyone carries his parents inside of him," his "adult," and his "little boy or girl." Parent, adult, child. I meditate on the implications. How am I carrying my parents around? The good and the not-so-good? What are the implications? What is an adult? How does an adult behave? How does the wounded child I'm carrying around impact my thoughts and feelings? What does this mean about my fraught relationship with my parents, especially Dad? I'm drawn to this kind of psychological introspection. It's not the same as being forced to study. I'm pulled inside to the threshold of self-discovery. Being on the kibbutz has begun to open my eyes to new possibilities.

A couple named Amir and Nira have been designated as my kibbutz "parents." They're about ten years older than me and have young children. Nira, a vivacious woman with a mischievous smile, makes me feel at home right away.

"You're very welcome here! Now you are one of our children!" she jokes with a mischievous laugh.

"You must visit us every day for tea and discussion. We want to know about you and your life and your plans!"

If only I had plans, I would gladly share them with Nira. The excitement of my everyday learnings and discoveries fills my consciousness, but I don't have a clue about my future. It's a subject best left alone for the time being.

Amir, a balding guy with twinkling blue eyes, exudes intelligence. He carries himself with easy confidence.

"Your kibbutz father, Amir, is a colonel in the tank corps. A big shot!" Yehuda informs me.

"Maybe he can take you to the Golan Heights, where his guys defeated the Syrians. Let me speak to him."

Two weeks later, I'm sitting in the passenger seat of Amir's jeep. We're driving toward northern Israel and the Golan Heights. The barren, hilly region extends for miles above Israeli farmlands, forming a natural border with Lebanon in the Northwest and Syria to the Northeast. The army that holds the high ground here has the obvious advantage of being able to see what's happening in the valley below. Amir wears battle fatigues and informally salutes soldiers we come across. We follow one of the roads taken by hundreds of tanks during the war toward the summit of the Golan Heights. Amir knows the territory. The terrain meanders steeply upward, and the wreckage of war—burned-out tanks, badly damaged armored cars, and blown-up canons—dot the roadsides.

"From these pillboxes," Amir informs me, pointing to destroyed gun emplacements on the summit, "the Syrians shot Israeli farmers in the valley below. They were sitting ducks."

It's a lot to take in. Here are the remains of war—twisted and charred metal, strewn around by powerful forces bringing death and destruction. In each of these destroyed vehicles, young men like me have died terrible deaths or been maimed for the rest of their lives. The ghosts of their screams still haunt the battlefield. It's a scene from hell and one from which I cannot look away. These soldiers have made the ultimate sacrifice for their country.

Amir drives the jeep onto a narrow plain. Dozens of Israeli tanks are parked, row upon row, facing the battlefield of destroyed Israeli and Syrian tanks.

"We fought tough battles against the Syrians. Many lives were lost on both sides. We will never give back this area and make ourselves vulnerable again." He pauses and then adds an afterthought. "But Israel's most dangerous enemy is Iran."

The mention of Iran catches me off guard. I don't understand. It seems so far away. How can it be Israel's most dangerous enemy? Amir infers that he knows things but can't go into details. It's clear that even after Israel's tremendous victory, enemies—near and far—surround and are invested in Israel's demise. It's only a matter of time before there's more war—more death.

My trip to the Golan Heights impresses upon me some basic realities about Israel. It's a country with a tiny footprint, vulnerable to attack, particularly at its waist, where it's only nine miles wide. The entire country is only 263 miles from north to south. My excursion to the Golan Heights has been exciting, but it has also sobered me, showing me the realities of the war. Plain and simple, war equals death and destruction. I've seen it for myself. Now I'm confronted with a basic issue: If I stay in Israel, I will be conscripted. I will put my life on the line. Am I ready for that level of commitment?

A former American professional basketball player by the name of Norm coaches the kibbutz's high school kids. A tall, lanky guy with long, unkempt brown hair, Norm comes from Brooklyn. He speaks English with a broad accent, which, at first, I have trouble understanding. He played for a team I've never heard of, but that's not surprising, since there's no professional basketball in South Africa. He tells me that he was injured and can no longer play professionally. He came to Givat Brenner to coach the kibbutz kids. One afternoon, after work, Norm invites me to his house, a simple studio with a bed, a small table, a few chairs, and a bathroom. On the table near his bed, there's a glass bowl, half-filled with a dark brown substance. Norm scoops up a handful of it, expertly rolls a cigarette, lights up, and takes a long drag. Then he offers it to me.

"Thank you, but I don't smoke," I say automatically.

"That's cool, man, but this is different," he says. "Have you ever heard of hashish? It's compressed grass, and this is the finest quality hash, smuggled in from Lebanon. Hash has been made in the Middle East for centuries."

He hands the smoldering cigarette to me.

"This is called a joint," he informs me. I hesitatingly take a small puff, inhale it, and hold my breath for a few seconds, as Norm has demonstrated. He takes another puff and passes the joint back to me. I cough from the slight tickle in my throat. This back-and-forth ritual continues for a few minutes. I think of Charlie and his Durban Poison stinking up Dad's warehouse.

Then Norm says, "Hey, man, let's go outside. Things might look a little different out there."

He opens the door, and we step into the bright sunlight. I notice a kibbutznik walking with great purpose in our direction. On his head sits a blue kibbutznik cap. It looks ridiculous. He looks ridiculous. He's on a mission, an earnest mission, taking himself oh so seriously! It's hilarious! I collapse to the ground, shaking with laughter. I look at Norm and burst into fresh guffaws. In a few seconds, he scoops me up and ushers me back into his house.

"Jesus! You gotta be cool, man! You can't let these kibbutzniks know you're stoned. They'll throw us off the kibbutz!"

He looks at me, mumbles something about me being a newbie, and then says, "Wanna come with me to Jerusalem? I know where we can score some great Lebanese hash!" This sounds like a great adventure. Who am I to blow against the wind?

On our next day off, we take a bus to Jerusalem. Norm knows his way around, so I gladly follow. After some late afternoon sightseeing, the sun sets, and we walk through a poorly lit area with high sandstone walls and barbed wire that has been cut and pulled to one side. Norm explains that before the war, this area was the Jordanian border of divided Jerusalem.

Soon, we're in the Arab quarter of the Old City and, in seconds, lost in a maze of winding cobblestone alleys and shops. I'm mesmerized by this mysterious place and its ancient and exotic culture. Multicolored spices with unfamiliar aromas emanate from large burlap sacks. Sesame seed confections in glass containers make my mouth water. Men wearing *kaffiyehs* go about their business. Some sit in open-air cafés smoking from large hookahs. Brightly embroidered pillows, shirts, and scarves hang in small shops. The Muezzin's voice calling people to prayer echoes through the alleyways. Israeli soldiers walk around, rifles slung over their shoulders. The Palestinians seem to accept their presence. Though Norm and I are on an illegal and clandestine mission, somehow, it makes me feel safer knowing there are soldiers around. We move on. We enter a shop from the rear exit of another, and here, Norm greets the owner with an elaborate bow and a friendly *As-salamu alaykum.* We're invited to take tea and offered seats on a pile of colorful rugs with large cushions strewn around. We sit and drink tea as though we have all night. Norm jabbers away, cracking jokes the shopkeeper cannot possibly understand, laughing uproariously at his own punchlines.

After what seems like a very long time, the shopkeeper excuses himself. He disappears out the back exit of the store. In a few minutes, he returns with a brown-paper parcel, wrapped with string. He cuts the string with a curved knife and reveals the contents—a large chunk of brown hashish. Norm makes appreciative noises, whips out his wallet, peels off $20, and gives it to the shopkeeper.

"You want any, man? This is the best shit!"

Mindful of my tight budget, I blurt out, "Well, can I get just a little?"

Norm turns to the shopkeeper again and speaks rapidly in a mixture of Hebrew, Arabic, and English. Once again, the shopkeeper disappears and returns with a smaller package. He cuts it with his curved knife and reveals a chunk of brown hash about five inches long by four inches wide and an inch thick. It's too much. Way too much for me. He holds up the fingers of both hands. "Ten US dollars," he says in English. Ten dollars is a small fortune, but I hand it over. The shopkeeper hands me the hash and pantomimes that I should hide it in my underpants to avoid suspicion. I tuck it in my underpants, where it gives the impression that I'm rather well-hung.

The months that follow on Givat Brenner are highlighted by hash sessions filled with new and exciting sounds, visions, dynamic patterns, and creative ideas. I've discovered new worlds. I've fallen in love with music; it's truly a gift from the gods to humanity. I'm relaxed and happy.

After five months, most of the other volunteers have returned to their home countries, rationalizing that their services are no longer needed. They've fulfilled their duty and are headed back to their own lives, to their own countries. A rumor spreads that the whole international volunteer effort is a Zionist propaganda exercise designed to snare unsuspecting young Jews to make Aliya, to settle in Israel. I don't know what to do or what to think about my own future. I just get up in the morning and meet Yehuda. These days, he often assigns me to work alone.

One beautiful, blue-skied morning, I'm working in the gardens of the kibbutz rest house—a resort where city dwellers come to relax. A young woman, arm in arm with an older woman, walks toward me. She's stunning. I can't take my eyes off her.

To my utter amazement, the young woman stops to talk to me. She speaks in rapid Hebrew, which I can't follow. I explain that my Hebrew is limited, and she switches to English without missing a beat. I love that about the Israelis—they almost always speak English.

"Hi! My name's Yudiet. This is my *ima*!" She uses the Hebrew word for mother. She looks into my eyes and holds my gaze. I'm smitten.

"Are you a *kibbutznik*?" I ask her, stumbling around for something interesting to say.

"We are from Tel Aviv. We are here for a week to rest from the city."

I muster the nerve to invite Yudiet to meet me that evening. Like in a dream, we quickly fall into an intimate relationship. For the next week, we spend every free moment together. Yudiet is unlike any Jewish girl I've met. She seems to genuinely like me and doesn't act like the spoilt Jewish girls I've known before. She's not a *kugel*—an entitled dumpling who expects me to buy her chocolates. After a head-over-heels romance, she and her mother have to return to Ted Aviv.

"Get off the kibbutz! It's a trap! Come to Tel Aviv. Make some money! We can live together!" Yudiet implores me.

"I'll come to Tel Aviv and look around," I reply. I make arrangements to be gone from the kibbutz for a week. The kibbutz administration encourages volunteers to see the country, and since I'm considered a good worker, my request doesn't raise any eyebrows. Yudiet shows me around Tel Aviv. We bake in the sun at the beach, swim in the refreshing Mediterranean, eat felafel in the street, and stroll along Dizengoff with hundreds of other couples. I get a feel for Israel's vibrant social life. It's invigorating. Yudiet's mother is happy to see me again. A little too happy. Eventually, Yudiet shows me an old garage for rent in a seedy part of town. It wouldn't be too difficult to build a rough living space, but that brings up much bigger issues. I like Yudiet, but I'm not ready for the kind of commitment it will take to be with her. The learning curve on so many fronts is too steep. Way too steep. How can I make a living? For starters, I'll have to learn Hebrew. How long did it take me to learn Afrikaans? I have about sixty US dollars to my name and a return ticket to Joburg. I don't know anyone here. And what about getting conscripted into the Israeli army? I care more about Israel than South Africa, but not that much. Not after what I've seen on the Golan Heights.

I tell Yudiet. She cries. Bummed that my adventure with Yudiet has ended, I leave and take the bus back to Givat Brenner. I'm fortunate to have a safe place, and I fall back into my routine. Time is running out. I keep to myself, contemplating my next move. A pretty kibbutznik comes to my room one night. I've noticed her, but we've not met. I'm surprised. I'm not used to women being so direct. She gazes at me for a long time without saying a word. Then she says, "The kibbutz is a small place. You and I would make a good couple." Oh, jeez! If I was a normal man, I'd bed her right now, but I'm not in the mood for another relationship. I freeze. She leaves.

In the afternoons, I visit Amir and Nira for tea. I appreciate their warmth and hospitality. They are the perfect model of family life on the kibbutz—secure, settled, leaders in their community. They have love, belonging, and purpose. I've proved myself as a good worker. I could stay on the kibbutz and create a life like theirs. I'd have a home, food, friends, work, a girlfriend, community, security. But it's not enough. Something in me will not allow me to settle. My co-volunteers have whetted my appetite to experience more of the world.

For years, Mom has talked about her family's desperate escape from the Nazis. How they were rescued by Zionists and brought to a rough and poverty-stricken prewar Palestine. Ernst and Walter, her younger brothers, grew up in Palestine and in the postwar fledgling new state of Israel. Now, nearly thirty years later, they live in Vancouver, on the west coast of Canada. Ernst, the older brother, speaks several languages and left Palestine after the war to become a translator for displaced people in Europe. Then, he joined the merchant marines and landed in Vancouver around 1950. Walter, the younger brother, remained in Palestine until the death of his parents in 1960, when he followed his big brother to Vancouver.

"They did well in Canada," Mom told me. "They learned to work in Israel and became millionaires in the lumber business." Ernst and Walter are mythical family characters, made a bit more real when they sent me a gold watch with a fancy leather band for my Bar Mitzvah. Canada seems like a cold, snowy place, but perhaps I can visit my uncles and check out another country. I can figure things out one step at a time. I write them an honest letter telling them that I don't want to stay in Israel and don't want to go back to South Africa either.

Mom often writes Ernst and Walter detailed letters about her life in Cape Town. They must know some of the gruesome details about our family breakup. In my letter, I admit I have a "personality clash" with my father.

A month goes by. I hear nothing from Ernst and Walter. The winter rains have begun. One afternoon, after work, despondent, I take a flimsy wooden chair out into the muddy road adjacent to the volunteer house. I sit there. No one pays attention to me. Norm, Pia, the Italians, and the other volunteers have already left; only the ghosts of their laughter remain. I'm alone in the world. My options have run out. Going back to South Africa feels like returning to a prison sentence where I will stamp number plates into eternity and live off the favors of others. To return to South Africa is defeat. I don't cry easily, but this day, tears run down my cheeks.

A few days later, a letter arrives from Canada. With eager anticipation, I open it and find a $100 bill pinned to a piece of torn paper. There's one line scrawled on the paper. It's barely legible, but I make it out. "We hope this will help. Maybe we'll see you one day. Ernst and Walter."

I hatch a plan to continue traveling with Vancouver as my main destination. I exchange my ticket to South Africa for a ticket to London, Toronto, and from there to Vancouver. With the $100 Ernst and Walter have sent, if I'm frugal, I'll have just enough for the journey.

TWELVE

I'm on my way to Canada. I'm wearing my suit, with a neat tie and a snazzy fur-lined coat I picked up secondhand in London for a few quid. On my feet, polished brown boots glisten. I look respectable. Very respectable. The remaining chunk of hash from Norm and my clandestine Jerusalem mission is tucked in my underpants.

At Canada Immigration, an officer demands my entry visa. He holds my South African passport by a tiny corner, like it's radioactive. It's January 1968, and the apartheid regime is arguably the most unpopular on the planet. He wants to know exactly how much money I'm carrying. The $61 I have in my pocket doesn't impress him. I tell him, "I'm just on a brief visit to see my uncles in Vancouver." With great reluctance, he stamps my passport with a three-month visa. Whew!

A co-volunteer, Dora, had scribbled her phone number on a slip of paper and invited me to stay with her family when I got to Toronto. I call Dora from a phone booth at the airport. She tells me her father will pick me up. In about an hour, a friendly, clean-cut guy with glasses and a brown fedora shows up. After a brief introduction, he says, "I'm proud of our Jewish youth. I'm pleased Dora served on Givat Brenner. It's expanded her horizons." He shakes my hand again.

It's like a small hero's welcome.

It's snowing lightly, and the ground is covered in a beautiful white carpet. It's cold. Colder than I've ever experienced. It's interesting to breathe freezing air. I like it. It's invigorating.

We arrive in what appears to be an upper-middle-class suburb. Dora and her mother welcome me with big smiles and hugs. It's Friday evening, and they do the whole Shabbat dinner thing. They're really into it—a white table cloth, two white candles, prayers, and chicken dinner. It's familiar and warm. Good to be with friendly people at the beginning of my Canadian adventure.

Dora takes me around Toronto and shows me the city's diverse ethnic areas. It's a much bigger city than I realized. As we visit various neighborhoods, it becomes obvious Dora's interest in me is more than simple friendship. I'm just not attracted to her. She's very nice but too homey, not my type. She places her hand on my arm just a little too long, gazes adoringly into my eyes, and brushes her hand accidentally against mine too many times. I don't want to hurt her feelings. She's been kind to me, but each day with her family makes me more claustrophobic.

They're so nice, their warmth and acceptance seductive, but I'm beginning to smell a rat.

Four days after my arrival, Dora's father invites me to take a walk around the neighborhood. It's quite cold outside, but the fresh air wakes me up. After we've walked a number of blocks, he stops and peers at me. His glasses are misted, and his brown fedora is pulled over his ears.

"May I be frank?" I'm listening but make no response.

"I've been watching you for the past few days. You have a lot of promise. You need a job, and you need to settle down. I run a carpet-manufacturing business here in Toronto, and I need a good man. If you and Dora settle down, I have a good job for you. You'll have a future, and you won't have to worry about money again."

Now I understand that Dora's family thinks I would make a good husband for their daughter. She's an only child, and they're desperate for her to marry. I mumble platitudes about the family's hospitality, that my uncles are expecting me in Vancouver. The disappointment on Dora's father's face is obvious. Soon, Dora begins acting more distant. I'm glad my flight to Vancouver leaves early tomorrow morning.

I arrive at Vancouver airport and step outside to get some fresh air. Dark gray clouds hang overhead like a low-hanging roof, the scene obscured by a damp fog.

A man with dark hair and a neatly trimmed beard strides toward me.

"Goddamn, Gary, you look just like your mother! Those brown eyes! Unmistakable! Let's go! Walter's waiting."

This is Ernst, the older of my two uncles.

Ernst is flamboyant, speaking nonstop in a kind of hybrid accent that betrays his Austrian, Israeli, European, and more recent Canadian histories, jumping from one subject to another. Too much coffee. We get into his car, an old Volvo. A mess. Cigarette butts overflow the ashtray. Ernst chain-smokes, chatting gaily away.

Arrival in Vancouver, January, 1968
Me on the left, Walter (center), Toby, Ernst (right)

We arrive at Walter's apartment, a three-story stucco building on Montcalm Street in the southern part of Vancouver. I'm surprised at the modesty of the area and the apartment building. After Mom's description of her brothers' millionaire status, I'm disappointed. Our house in Cape Town was much more upscale than this, and we weren't millionaires. Not by a long shot. Walter leans out a window on the second floor and waves. Friendly enough. In a minute, we're out of the elevator and walk into the apartment. Walter is as different from Ernst as one can imagine. Short and portly, he gives the impression of a little Napoleon. Where Ernst's flamboyance and eccentricity stand out, Walter's more rational—controlled. I realize what Mom had neglected to tell me about her brothers: Ernst is a schmoozer, Walter a stickler. Jean, Walter's wife, comes from Yorkshire and speaks with a pleasant English accent. In her thirties, she has long blond hair and a quick smile. She wears a simple green dress and hardly any makeup, giving off a very natural air. Quite different from my two chain-smoking uncles.

She seems pleased that I've arrived and fusses around in the kitchen, bringing snacks to the dining table. Walter has married outside the faith.

"I came to Canada ten years ago and met Walter here in Vancouver," Jean tells me. "I'm glad you're here. I've heard so much about you over the years. Your mother writes us regularly." I can't imagine what Mom has said about me.

Walter and Ernst suddenly start yelling at each other across the dining room table.

"Walter!" Ernst yells. He pronounces it *Vulter*.

"I told you not to pay those *ganefs*! They're goddam thieves! Crooks!"

"You never said a word to me!" Walter yells back, contradicting his brother.

Jean looks at me with a quick smile and winks. I like Jean right away—her warmth and sense of humor. She can be with Walter and Ernst and not take them as seriously as they take themselves. I wonder what it's like for Jean to be married to Walter and have Ernst around as a spare wheel. And now me.

Toby, my two-year-old cousin, clings to Jean. He seems intimidated by the intensity of Ernst and Walter's brief exchange. Toby has a pixie nose and long white hair that Jean trims to shoulder length. Walter mutters, "Jeanie, I tell you, Toby looks like a girl. Can't you give him a boy's haircut—short back and sides?"

As I sit around my uncles' dining room table, I remember a story about Mom's family.

A few days after the Nazis marched into Austria in 1938, they arrested my grandfather, Samuel, and dispatched him to Dachau, the infamous concentration camp. The Nazis had not yet developed their so-called "final solution," and after three months, Samuel managed to bribe his way out.

Mom would repeat the story over and over about what happened after Samuel's return. "When he came back from Dachau, I met Papa at the Graz train station," she told me with tears in her eyes. "He was all dressed up like he had gone away on a business trip to Vienna. I hugged him, but I was hugging a skeleton. His hair had turned white. He was such a dignified man, so learned, a scholar of Esperanto, but he was broken.

"Days after his return, men arrived. They made Papa sign some papers and then, room by room, confiscated everything of value: our furniture, Persian rugs, antiques, paintings. Everything. A commissioner took over Papa's clothing business, and he was forced to stay home. The message was unmistakable: Jews were not welcome in the Third Reich. More and more of our neighbors were being arrested. Papa frantically searched for a country willing to provide a visa to our family, but not one would have us. I was fifteen, and the Jewish Agency sponsored me for summer camp on a kibbutz in Palestine. Ten-year-old Ernst and six-year-old Walter were placed in a Jewish orphanage in Vienna. Rumors had it that the orphanage children would be sent to Sweden. I went with Papa to say goodbye to my brothers before I left for Palestine. At lunchtime, bigger boys stole my little brothers' food. Samuel flew into a rage. He said, 'I'm taking you boys out of this place right now. Either we'll live together, or we'll die together, but we will be together.' This was *bashert*—because the Nazis killed all the children in the orphanage."

Now, sitting at their dining table in Vancouver, thirty years after the orphanage, it's difficult to see how any boys could have ever bullied either Ernst or Walter.

After dinner, Ernst heads directly for a wooden rocking chair in the living room. He rocks back and forth for a minute or so. Then he begins loudly snoring.

Walter yells, "Ernst, go home! Take Gary with you."

We get into Ernst's Volvo, and he drives two blocks to another squat apartment building. We enter the building from the rear and head down some dark stairs into the basement. Heating units hum in the dark. Ernst fumbles for a light switch, but even with the light on, the hallway is dingy and smells musty. He inserts a key into a door. We enter a room in which two double beds dominate the cramped space. High up one wall, a single rectangular window lets in a sliver of light. The air is stale with cigarette smoke. A dirty light brown rug covers the floor. The place hasn't been cleaned or swept in a long time. A few graying posters and pictures take up most of the wall space. When I ask about a toilet, Ernst points vaguely down the corridor. I find the toilet. It stinks of urine, and the shower is coated in brown scum.

I'm just coming out of the bathroom when a loud voice pierces my thoughts. "Who the hell are you?"

An old and disheveled man shuffles into view down the passage. He looks at least ninety and reeks of alcohol. A cigarette hangs from his wrinkled lips. He looks me up and down.

"Good evening, sir. I'm just staying with Ernst for a little while."

"Just staying for a little while, eh, laddie?" the old codger mocks. "I've told that Ernst a thousand times, he's got to talk to me first before he brings anyone here!"

Ernst arrives and explains that the old guy is his next-door neighbor. When we're alone, Ernst tells me to ignore him. "He's senile and drunk half the time."

He points to one of the beds. "You take that one." He gets undressed and climbs into the other bed in his long underwear. He lights up. He's found a second wind. He sits in his bed, smoking cigarette after cigarette, asking me questions but not waiting for my answers. He talks and talks. At first, it's kind of interesting, but after a while, I can't follow any longer. I'm jetlagged and badly need to sleep. Ernst's monologue goes on and on—about Israel, the Jews, the Holocaust, South Africa, my mother. He tells me he met my father in Palestine during the war. "Handsome guy! You don't get along with him, eh?"

No doubt Mom has detailed our terrible fight in one of her aerograms. I'm desperate to sleep. Ernst continues like there's no tomorrow. Around 2 a.m., he mercifully falls asleep, again snoring loudly. I sleep fitfully until the alarm jangles us awake. It's pitch-dark outside.

We tumble out of bed, taking quick turns in the bathroom, then get dressed. Ernst curses in Russian and Arabic. We stumble outside and head over to Walter and Jean's apartment. Jean has coffee ready. We eat a hearty breakfast. Ernst sits at the table, dozing. As if by some invisible signal, Walter and Ernst both light up cigarettes, stand up, and head out the door. I assume I should follow.

Ernst and Walter's lumber mill is located on a big sawdust lot in an industrial area near Vancouver called New Westminster. British Columbia is famous for its wooded forests. Large, local mills provide for the province's lumber needs. The lumber-manufacturing process generates a byproduct of scrap lumber. Ernst and Walter's business concept: purchase the big mills' scrap cheaply, sort it according to size, and remanufacture the scrap into popular shorter lengths. The mill also produces cedar shingles and pickets for fencing, all made from the same scrap cedar end-cuts. They sell the new products at a handsome profit.

Ernst and Walter run the lumber mill Israeli style. Nothing wasted. Everyone works. Hard. No exceptions. No executives in corner offices giving off superior airs. They charge around the mill in heavy forklifts, moving loads of scrap lumber into position for sorting. They're loud and aggressive. They remind me of the nasty young Sabra gloating from his shaded tractor seat while we volunteers slaved in the heat on Moshav Habonim.

After a brief introduction to the mill's operation, Walter leads me to what appears to be a mountain of wood. Upon closer inspection, I see that the enormous pile is made up of thousands of bundles, each eighteen inches wide, four inches thick, and four feet in length, held together by twine. Nearby, a machine whirs. Walter inserts the end of a bundle into the machine, pulls upward, and a rounded half-point magically appears at the end of the bundle. Then he turns the bundle around, again inserts it into the machine, pulls up, and a rounded point appears on the end of the entire bundle. Oh, I get it. Picket fencing. Walter gestures to the mountain of bundled lumber.

"Okay, this is how we point pickets! Now you know what to do. You should have enough work to keep you busy for months! So long!" He laughs, jumps on his forklift, and careens off. Thus, my new occupation begins. Sisyphus should have used this pile of pickets instead of a stone to make his point. My back aches from bending and lifting the pickets all day. I'm sick of the sound of the blades cutting the picket points every few seconds. I'm going to die of boredom. Are Ernst and Walter testing me? Seeing what I'm made out of?

Now and then, Ernst stops by. He checks out what I'm doing, makes some inane comments, and then leaves. One day, he sidles by and stuffs a $20 bill into my hand.

"You poor slob! Take this. Buy something for yourself!"

I haven't made money in a year, so I'm happy to have a few bucks in my pocket. The whole money thing is kind of weird with Ernst and Walter. They sure don't live like the millionaires Mom said they were. On the other hand, the mill is busy, saws going constantly. Nothing has been said about wages, and I haven't asked. They're putting me up and feeding me. I don't want to be crass and ask them directly what pointing twenty million cedar pickets is worth.

Each day for lunch, we meet in the office, a small stand-alone building centrally located on the sawdust road that traverses the mill. We eat ham on white bread with butter. Not kosher. Ernst takes advantage of a brief lull and launches into one of his almost constant musings.

"Sometime in '38, a family friend arrived from another city. His head was bandaged. He told us he had been injured in a pogrom against Jews. We were scared, but Papa insisted, 'I fought for the Germans in the Great War. I was awarded medals for bravery! They won't harm us.' Then on November 9, 1938, Kristallnacht happened. I remember a woman screaming, 'They're burning down the synagogue!' I saw the flames. The Graz synagogue was a beautiful temple. We were shaking. Mama was petrified. She took to bed. Papa kept saying, 'Don't worry. I've been loyal. I'll show them my medals. They'll leave us alone.' Papa and his stupid medals. He thought they would magically save us. He was wrong. The Nazis came for him and took him away with all the other Jewish men. You can't imagine. When our neighbor resisted, they shot him in the street."

"Ernst! Enough already with the past!" Walter interrupts with a disgusted look.

Ernst holds up his hands, as though in surrender. "I know. I know."

Walter's building some steam. "We were saved from Hitler. But six million others didn't make it. Don't you forget that!"

"And you," Ernst retorts. "You, of all people, shouldn't forget you grew up in Israel. You paid your dues for being a Jew. Fought for Israel against those bloody Egyptians in Sinai. That's why you're such a prickly bastard—an Israeli Sabra through and through!"

Walter stands up and shouts, "Jesus, Ernst, we're supposed to be making a living! I'm not listening to any more of your bullshit *bobbe meises*—grandmother tales. We've got work to do!"

With that, we file out of the office, and I head back to my picket mountain. It still looks about as high as when I started weeks ago. I so badly wanted to discover unimagined worlds. I thought Canada would show me new things, but picket-hell is not exactly what I had in mind.

THIRTEEN

Months of hard work at the mill drag by under charcoal skies and relentless rain. Ernst has moved into his girlfriend's place. I'm blessedly alone in the dismal basement room. I've become a landed immigrant. Ernst made all the arrangements. I'm legal. Walter gives me checks every two weeks. I buy a cheap car, a light blue Simca Aronde in surprisingly good shape, a French car with massive wheels on the back, a mini-monster car.

I'm learning my way around Vancouver, exploring the city. Spring comes; the city explodes into a riot of cherry blossoms and flowers. The surrounding mountains, a majestic snow-peaked backdrop, become visible. The temperature is pleasant.

People venture out, glad for the sunshine. A new breed of people appear on the streets. They remind me of the Italians on the kibbutz.

They have their style—beads, faded jeans with colorful bell-bottom inserts. The women wear long dresses. Some place flowers in their hair. Flower children. West Coast hippies.

The more time I spend wandering around, the more I appreciate the Northwest Pacific beauty. I walk around Stanley Park, looking back toward the city's downtown skyline. I watch magnificent sunsets from Look Park, which faces west toward Vancouver Island. The monotonous gray colors that seemed ubiquitous have transformed into greens and blues. I spend hours at UBC's Museum of Anthropology, checking out the indigenous British Columbian people's artifacts. I love learning about the spirit of the Northwest.

In Chinatown, in an alley, I discover a hole-in-the-wall restaurant called the Green Door. The food is delicious. Then I discover the Red Door and the Orange Door. They're all really good, and the price is the same—one dollar.

I'm drawn repeatedly to one area of the city near the beach on the west side, known as Kitsilano. People call it Kits for short, a busy thoroughfare teeming with hippies and small shops. It's the place to see and be seen.

One day, attracted by the Rolling Stones blasting from the stereo inside, I wander into a store off West Fourth that sells hippie clothes, beads, and posters. A huge blown-up black-and-white poster of a smiling, oily-looking man looks down from a wall. The photographer caught the subject in a moment of apparent embarrassment. I don't know who he is or why his likeness is on the wall, but I immediately know my answer to the caption at the bottom of the poster: *Would you buy a used car from this man?*

Hell no. He looks like a shifty crook, the worst stereotype of a used car salesman. Someone sees me studying the poster. I ask, "Who's that?" The person looks at me like I've just arrived from outer space.

"That's Tricky Dick Nixon! He's going to be the next president of the US of A." I'm curious about the hippies. They're unhurried but have a sense of purpose. It's easy to distinguish between them and the more conventional types, especially the men with short haircuts and khaki pants. The hippies seem different from other people. They believe that suits and ties are symbols of restriction and conventionality—what they call "straight." In comparison, their long hair, weird clothes, and relaxed attitude are a dead giveaway. It's a different vibe. I identify with the hippies. They're outsiders in this society. I've been an outsider all my life, never really fitting in anywhere, doing my best to avoid attention. But these hippies openly proclaim their outsider status, even celebrate it, revel in being unique and not fitting into the boxes society prescribes. They make a counterculture statement just in their appearance. They're into peace and love.

I'm embarrassed about the suit I wore when I came to Canada. I'm really straight! But then again, I came from the straightest, most uptight place in the world! I wonder . . . *do I belong with them?*

The hippies gather to hear the mind-blowing bands that play in a huge stadium on the east side of the city. Led Zeppelin, Jimi Hendrix, Cream, and the Doors all played Vancouver this year. It's more than just their unique fashion and the great music that awakens my curiosity. The hippies are into psychedelics—drugs they claim expand awareness. I don't understand what they're talking about, but when I overhear them speaking with great passion about their inner discoveries on "Sunshine" or "Windowpane"— the two brands of LSD they seem the most excited about—I take note.

The Naam, a recently opened funky vegetarian restaurant run by Indian women and hippies on West Fourth, serves great vegetarian and Indian meals. It's a magnet for hippies. I linger like an anthropologist observing their customs and norms. The simple and healthy fare is cheap in comparison to other restaurants. A knowledgeable waitress teaches me about vegetarianism and alternative proteins like tofu and tempeh.

A guy by the name of Davy makes custom hippie sandals for a righteous price. He carefully measures my feet and tells me to pick them up in a few days. When I try on the sandals, they fit like a glove! My new sandals have thick rubber soles made from truck tires and strong leather thongs that fasten them securely to my feet. I wear my new sandals out of Davy's leather shop, feeling I've procured an authentic hippie artifact.

My new friend, Jerry, the eccentric yo-yo master.

FOURTEEN

One afternoon, while shopping in a drugstore on Oak and West Forty-First, I almost bump into a guy playing with a yoyo—about my size, wearing a tight T-shirt that shows off bulging muscles. Oblivious to me, he keeps the yoyo going for several minutes at a time, demonstrating amazing tricks, all the while staring into space as though in a trance. We're standing in a drugstore aisle. People are trying to go about their business. I've never seen anyone perform yoyo tricks like this. The guy is amazing. Eventually, he stops, noticing me ogling, and comes over.

"Hi! I'm Jerry. Are you into yoyos? No? You Jewish?" He doesn't wait for answers. "Yeh, thought so, me too. Say, I'm from Montreal. I'm new to Vancouver. I'm going to be a student at Vancouver City College. I'm looking for a roommate."

Immediately, two lightbulbs go off: a far-fetched idea. Maybe I could go to college. I need qualifications to escape the lumber mill. I say, "I'd love to go to college, but I didn't do well in high school."

"Don't worry, man!" Jerry responds. "Just apply. The community college system here in Canada gives kids a second chance. It's like a stepping stone to one of the universities."

A second lightbulb illuminates the possibility of getting away from my uncles. I want to live independently. From age thirteen on, I've predominantly lived apart from my parents. I'm accustomed to my autonomy. Now at almost twenty-two, living with Ernst and Walter is stifling, a throwback to close parental supervision. They've been generous in their ways: Ernst pays the rent on his room faithfully each month, he and Walter provide me with work and money, and Jean feeds me daily breakfast and dinner. Being around their overbearing personalities has worn thin. I'm claustrophobic. I need my space. Ernst's basement room is a dungeon. I still can't understand why someone who owns a mill lives like he's poverty-stricken. I want to be on my own again. I tell this eccentric yoyo master I'm interested in living with him, but I need time to work things out.

I'm not at all sure about getting into Vancouver City College, but I fill out the application. To my surprise, in two weeks, an acceptance arrives in the mail. The college doesn't seem in the least put off by my less-than-stellar high school record.

I've saved some money from working at the mill, and I enter college in the fall semester. Jerry keeps saying that I have to see his place, that we should live together. I still need more time. I want to see if I can handle college-level classes.

I choose somewhat familiar subjects, like sociology and English literature. In sociology class, there's an early assignment. I write about my experiences on the kibbutz. I figure my real-life familiarity will help me. I hand in my paper and wait with apprehension for the professor's judgment. When I get the paper back, a large green *A* jumps off the front page! The prof has also written some very positive comments about my immersion in the socialist structure of the kibbutz, about my courage in volunteering, and what a remarkable learning opportunity my kibbutz experience has given me. This is the first time since age nine—before SACS, before Oudtshoorn, before Wynberg—that I've received an A. I don't remember a previous teacher making positive comments about anything I'd written. Despite a deep-seated belief that I'm an impostor, I find myself enjoying classes.

One class stands out. A young, long-haired professor, who encourages students to call him Sammy, teaches English literature. Sammy is only three years older than me, but he has a master's degree and knows poetry like no one I've ever met.

In class, Sammy creates a relaxed, laid-back atmosphere. He reads from his favorite literature and recites poetry with passion. He encourages us to speak up and not be afraid that our contribution might not be valuable. He finds something positive about what everyone says.

For the first time, I offer ideas without fear. I'm getting turned on to poetry and literature.

The Canadian students are polite and friendly, mellow. The vibe is about as far from Israel or South Africa as I can imagine. Here, it's all about ideas, creativity, innovation, and exploring consciousness. Pushing the envelope. Vancouverites identify with the frontier West Coast spirit—with Seattle, Portland, San Francisco, and LA. A palpable excitement and curiosity fills the air. Vancouver's a great place to let go of the past, to release the constrictions of my South African education and upbringing.

After class one day, Sammy invites me to a party to celebrate the release of the Beatle's new *White Album*. I'm excited about partying with a bunch of like-minded people.

I show up at Sammy's house on a quiet street in Kits. I recognize students from class, but others I don't know. The room is empty of furniture, softly lit, and cushions are strewn casually around the perimeter. A large candle burns in the center of the floor, emanating a soft yellow light and a pleasant aroma. We sit in a circle on the floor. Gradually, things quiet down. Sammy welcomes us and holds up the *White Album*. Everyone makes appreciative sounds. Someone turns the lights lower. A fat joint makes the rounds. In ten minutes, Sammy puts on the first side of the album, and we all listen intently, eyes closed, trying to get the song's deepest meaning.

Wow! I love being with these happy and uncomplicated people, just listening to cool music together. Finally, the album's over. Everyone talks at once.

"Loved 'Back in the USSR'! 'Martha My Dear'! 'Glass Onion'! 'Sexy Sadie'! So cool! Just mind-blowing! Far out!" One woman makes her way around the room, stopping at each person, washing their feet with warm water and soap, and giving them a foot rub! It's wonderful.

One morning after Walter has left for work, Jean and I sit around chatting in her kitchen. I've told her about school, especially Sammy's literature and poetry classes. She asks me whether I'd like to invite him for dinner.

Two weeks later, Walter, Jean, Toby, Sammy, and I sit around the dining room table in Walter and Jean's apartment. Jean has gone all out and made a great chicken orange. After Jean has put Toby to bed, she offers us fresh-brewed coffee and pours a cup for each of us. Walter pulls his coffee cup closer, fumbles for a cigarette, selects one, and puts it between his lips. As he goes through the motions of lighting the cigarette, Sammy suddenly whips out a joint from his breast pocket, grabs Walter's lighter, and without a word, lights it. I can't believe it! He inhales a hit and passes it to Walter like it's the most ordinary thing in the world. Walter reaches for the joint, takes a puff, and passes it to Jean. I'm astonished. Jean takes a good hit, too, and passes the joint to me. Sammy produces a well-worn paperback book and begins reciting a poem by Charles Olson. His voice is slow and droll.

What does not change / is the will to change

He woke, fully clothed, in his bed. He
remembered only one thing, the birds, how
when he came in, he had gone around the rooms
and got them back in their cage, the green one first,
she with the bad leg, and then the blue,
the one they'd hoped was a male . . .

—From *The Kingfishers* by Charles Olson

Sammy has barely gotten through the first stanza when Walter erupts in laughter. He laughs and laughs, tears running down his cheeks. Jean joins in the merriment of the moment, and soon, the four of us are all laughing our heads off. I've never had so much fun with my uptight straight uncle before. It's wonderful to see this very human side of him.

Jean and Walter

Then Walter excuses himself, mumbling something about needing to go the bathroom.

Jean, Sammy, and I sit around the table chatting. Jean's a great sport, thoroughly enjoying every second of this unusual evening. Walter's been gone for ten minutes when I begin to worry.

I head down the corridor to the bathroom. Walter is singing opera at the top of his lungs. Suddenly, the singing stops. I dash for my seat at the table. Walter appears.

"What's that stuff we smoked? Is that pot? It's so overrated. Did nothing for me. Waste of time."

In one moment, our levity goes as flat as a can of stale beer. Walter's back in charge, and it's no longer a fun, relaxed evening. It's not long before Sammy excuses himself, mumbling something about needing to prepare for classes.

The next morning at breakfast, as soon as Walter has left for work, Jean says to me, "I had a great time last night. Sammy's so funny! That was quite a stunt he pulled!"

FIFTEEN
LATE FALL, 1968

"Keep this to yourself. Okay? Not a word to anyone."

"Okay."

"I've got some great mescaline. I'd like you to trip with me."

Wow! Did I hear that right? I'm stunned. Thrilled. Honored. Somehow, Sammy, my professor, now friend, has intuited my secret desire. I've heard hippies talk about mescaline.

They call it "sacred medicine." It's the active ingredient in peyote buttons, which Native Americans have used for thousands of years in their religious rituals.

Sammy and I spend a lot of time together. Recently, he took me to San Francisco and LA, paying for my airline tickets. He said, "I want to show you another piece of the beach." We stayed with his friends. It was fun—a great opportunity to take in hip US cities. I'm grateful. Sammy has taken me under his wing. I'm meeting new people, discovering new worlds.

People have been buzzing about Aldous Huxley's book, *The Doors of Perception*. It's about his experiences using mescaline. It's my first read about the psychedelic experience. Huxley is a *psychonaut*, a psychedelic explorer of inner space. He describes how mescaline unlocks a spiritual dimension usually accessible only to poets, mystics, and holy men.

". . . to be shaken out of the ruts of ordinary perception, to be shown for a few timeless hours the outer and the inner world, not as they appear to an animal obsessed with survival or a human being obsessed with words and notions, but as they are apprehended, directly and unconditionally, by Mind-at-Large–this is an experience of inestimable value to everyone . . ."

In my own small way, I relate to Huxley's words. I've experienced moments of timelessness, of perfect attunement, completely in the here and now. In fact, these are my favorite times: surfing a massive wave, fighting a fish in the breakers, seeing a cricket ball as big as a grapefruit, and knowing in a flash exactly where my opponents will and will not be. Perhaps that's an inkling of what Huxley's describing. I think I have a sense of it. I can hardly wait.

Huxley also has words of caution that sober me: "The man who comes back through the Door in the Wall will never be quite the same as the man who went out. He will be wiser but less sure, happier but less self-satisfied, humbler in acknowledging his ignorance, yet better equipped to understand the relationship of words to things, systematic reasoning to the unfathomable mystery which it tries, forever vainly, to comprehend."

What is the "Door in the Wall?" What will it mean to be "wiser but less sure?" "Happier but less self-satisfied?"

Two weeks pass. I barely sleep the night before the scheduled trip.

It's almost as though I've already begun a journey, though I haven't ingested anything yet.

In the morning, I arrive promptly at Sammy's house. I'm keyed up. Ready for this adventure. We sit around his black kitchen table, an ornamental Chinese lamp hanging over the center. A vase with fresh yellow tulips brightens the room. Two festive green glasses sit on the table. A maroon plate with two large blue pills catches my eye.

"No one will bother us here," Sammy assures me. "I've set up pillows and blankets in the living room so we can relax, and I've got some cool music, everything from rock to ragas. There's water and glasses on the kitchen counter."

I nod. I'm clammy, sweating under my shirt. Sammy must know that he has a nervous traveler on his hands.

We sit quietly for a few moments, and then, without further ado, Sammy offers me the blue mescaline. I swallow it with a few sips of water. Sammy swallows the other pill.

About twenty minutes go by.

Then, an unfamiliar force makes its presence known. It's strong. Stronger than me. I'm trembling. Afraid.

A python envelopes me. I'm writhing in its coils. I'm fighting, but I can't escape. I'm terrified. The python is choking the life out of me. I'm going to die. Why did I take this drug with this madman? What have I gotten myself into? I'm spinning, struggling for control, searching for answers in all the usual places, to no avail.

Then I hear a voice. It's calm and clear. It's my own voice: *Surrender. Don't fight. Allow the mescaline to do its work. Like a medicine. Get out of the way. Open. Let go.*

Every cell of my being gets it. Don't hold on. Just get out of the way. That's it. You don't have to do anything else. Suddenly, I'm immersed in a powerful insight into how fear often dictates my choices and how it's possible to wake up from its tyranny, to operate differently.

I lie down on my back. The mescaline pulsates through my bloodstream to every cell.

No resistance. Just letting go. Opening.

My body is energy. Life force.

I'm aware when fear arises. I taste its bitter chemistry. I remind myself to let go. To relax and let things be. To trust.

I close my eyes. Exquisite flaming red and orange mandalas fill the inside of my head. What a great show! Sammy puts on Japanese shakuhachi flute music. It's pure vibration. Each note shimmers, each a different color. Extraordinary.

I hear. I see. I smell. I know without trying, without conscious effort. I take everything in—in a new way. The yellow tulips on the kitchen table are as bright as sunlight. The curtains are dancing to the music. Everything pulses with life. All interconnected!

Sammy suggests we go for a walk. We step outside. There's an enormous tree in the front yard. I don't know what species. It doesn't matter. It's pristine. Its branches bow and dance with each gust of the wind. They're playing together.

I embrace the trunk, feel the texture of its skin pressed to mine. I slow down, get into tree time, deeper into *treeness*. I'm tuned to its massive, silent strength, its roots deep in the earth.

Eventually, Sammy pulls me away. I don't want to leave my tree. It's perfect. Why go anywhere else? Treeness is enough. We continue walking, everywhere the unfolding energetic miracle of creation. William Blake's words come to me: *"If the doors of perception were cleansed everything would appear to man as it is, Infinite. For man has closed himself up, till he sees all things through narrow chinks of his cavern."*

We walk the streets for hours, avoiding interacting with people. I'm not sure that we could conduct a normal conversation. Our consciousness-regulating valves have been opened wide. We understand each other with telepathic empathy, but we don't want some straight person to become suspicious. Eventually, we head back to Sammy's house. We're coming down. I've never felt as whole and complete in my life.

We talk for hours, and Sammy reads poetry out loud. The last poem is *Dog* by Lawrence Ferlinghetti, the San Francisco beat poet. A few of the lines go through my head as I walk home through the darkness, smiling widely.

> *"The dog trots freely in the street*
> *and sees reality*
> *and the things he sees*
> *are bigger than himself*
> *and the things he sees*
> *are his reality . . .*
> *Congressman Doyle is just another*
> *fire hydrant*
> *to him*
> *The dog trots freely in the street*
> *and has his own dog's life to live*
> *and to think about*
> *and to reflect upon*
> *touching and tasting and testing everything . . ."*

The mescaline journey with Sammy has blasted me into a profound new awareness of inner space, of being, of potential for healing, of psychological and spiritual growth.

I don't know where to start, but I'm ecstatic. I've discovered an inner world, inner knowledge. I am much more than I believed or understood. I'll never be the same. I'm shaken up. I've long carried around baggage that weighs me down—what hippies mean when they say, "heavy karma!"

I've lived in a gray world, but now I've woken from my

colorblindness. I'm dazzled by colors. And once you know color, you know what is beyond black and white. You know there is more to life than you thought. Much more. In biblical days, they spoke about people touched by the Holy Spirit. The analogy comes close. My heart is filled with gratitude to the universe. For the first time, I understand the meaning of the word *spirituality*,

I've been initiated into the movement of young people experimenting with their consciousness, asking deeply existential questions, challenging cultural assumptions, and choosing values and lifestyles that reflect these new understandings.

It's hard to fathom that the ritual I've just partaken in is illegal. But that's not going to stop me. I'll be a psychedelic explorer and outlaw. Seekers are my kindred spirits, brothers and sisters, members of my new tribe. I'm on a journey of awakening. I know with whom I belong.

As the semester continues, I begin to feel more confident about being a student, and I go over to Jerry's apartment, the yoyo guy. His place is located on Broadway near Main Street, a major thoroughfare. We climb the back stairs to the apartment. We enter the kitchen. It's an unbelievable mess. Three or four high stacks of dirty dishes catch my attention. They look like they're about to fall over. The place smells of decaying garbage. Seeing me eyeing the dishes, Jerry quickly reassures me, "Oh, I don't bother to wash any dishes. I just throw the dirty ones away and buy new ones when I run out!"

I take in this information for a few seconds, but then I blurt out, "Jerry, I would love to live with you. You seem like a nice guy, but I just can't live here. Let's find a house. Let's see if we can put together a city commune."

Jerry takes this in stride and suggests we check out a bulletin board at the Naam for listings. In a few days, we rent a house with five bedrooms and a good-sized living room in a quiet area of Kits. We put up a notice that we're looking for roommates. I hope some hippies will see it.

SIXTEEN

It's time to break the news to Walter and Ernst. I wait to broach the subject until Ernst comes to dinner. He and his girlfriend, Barbara, have recently gotten married. One evening, when the full family is sitting around the dining table in Walter and Jean's apartment, I clear my throat and say, "I wanted to share with you. I'm doing quite well at college. I've met a friend. We've decided to rent a house in Kits with some other students. I'll move out at the end of the month."

At first, an awkward silence greets my declaration.

Then Ernst begins sputtering, "What? This is the gratitude you show us! Moving out! How are you going to make money? Who is going to pay for your education? Not me! Your mother will be very unhappy when she hears that you are moving away from the family. Just when you're getting settled!"

Before I can respond, Walter joins the fray. "I told your mother you're hanging around Kits with a bunch of dope-smoking hippies! She thinks you're rubbish."

At that point, Jean steps in, trying valiantly, though unsuccessfully, to calm Walter and Ernst. I tune out. Nothing I might say will convince them that my new direction has promise. I guess they feel they've failed to rein in their wayward charge. I can't wait to get out.

Our Kits communal house attracts a small group of fellow hippies. Everyone keeps up a semblance of student life during the day, but the real action takes place at night—getting high and listening to the latest rock music. Sammy's old girlfriend, Jane, moves in. She's a fellow poetry lover. I'm glad to have a like-minded female member of our fledgling community. Nigel, an introverted piano player and fellow student, also moves in. By the looks of things, he and Jane are becoming a couple. Another housemate, Tony, is a well-spoken Greek immigrant with an attractive accent. Tall and handsome, with dark hair and deep brown eyes, he has an intense and mysterious air.

"I'm an orphan," Tony tells us. "My uncle lives here in Vancouver. He's also from Greece. He gives me an allowance to go to school."

I met Tony in Sammy's class. We struck up a conversation when I saw him repeatedly rolling a coin on the sidewalk and calling out "Heads!" or "Tails!" just before it lost momentum and toppled over. Tony called it right most of the time! It was uncanny.

Intrigued at how he could beat the odds so consistently, I asked him how he did it.

"When I drop acid, I can tap into a part of my mind where I see the heads or tails before the coin comes to rest," he tells me.

A few weeks after we've moved into the communal house, Jerry and I take our first acid trip. It's a warm day, and we lie on Jericho

Beach, hidden from other people by huge driftwood cedar logs. In the distance, snow-topped peaks surround us, and cloud formations of cosmic chariots chase across the sky. At sunset, radiating, garish-gold and ruby-red cosmic rays streak across the heavens in a dynamic display of mighty grandeur. It's deeply moving. I'm at one with the universe and simultaneously aware of my utter insignificance.

Soon, more trips follow, each journey opening up new spaces, new experiences, and discoveries, reinforcing the desire for the next trip. I'm becoming an experienced explorer of inner space.

Jerry and I have both done well enough at City College to apply to Simon Fraser University (SFU). We're both accepted, he in the sciences and me in the humanities. Secretly, I know I'm an academic impostor. It's almost impossible to shrug off that I'm a Latin nineteen-percenter.

In the meantime, I'm trying to keep lines of communication open with Ernst and Walter. They don't have a clue about what's happening with me, but my longer hair and increasingly hippie-look broadcast my changes. Not in ways that necessarily meet their approval.

Ernst and Barbara buy a house a few miles from the SFU campus. It's convenient for Barbara who lectures in SFU's English Department. I don't know Barbara well, but I like her fiery temperament, her good looks, quick smile, and mischievous green eyes. She's much younger than Ernst, accustomed to voicing her own opinions. I don't get how they got together.

One unusually hot day soon after I've begun at SFU, I nonchalantly walk the campus. I take off my shirt and bask in the sun. After a while, I meander into the faculty lounge. In keeping with SFU's reputation as a progressive learning institution, the faculty lounge has been opened to students. I saunter into the lounge and immediately notice my new "aunt" Barbara. She's talking to a studious-looking man. I wander over to say hello. Barbara looks too young to be my aunt. She sees me making my way over to her, out of the corner of her eye. A slightly mortified look comes over her face.

I'm in my shorts, bare-chested. On my feet are Davy's handmade leather sandals. I've allowed my hair to grow out. Now my long curly locks and beard give the impression of a hippie holy man, an unkempt Jesus look-alike. I don't think anything of being shirtless. It feels natural in the heat of the day to wear as little clothing as possible. But Barbara is embarrassed. "Uhm . . . this is Professor Holtzman," she stutters, introducing me to her brainy-looking companion. "Professor Holtzman, this is my, uhm . . . nephew. He's new to SFU." The professor looks over his glasses like I'm unwelcome vermin.

He mumbles something, averts his eyes, shuffles his papers, stuffs them into his briefcase, and makes a beeline for the door. Barbara lets go of her embarrassment about my sudden bizarre appearance in the faculty lounge.

"Ernst would love to see you and show you our new house. He's quite proud of it. He says it's a big step up from his cell in the basement of that apartment building." I take this information in. It's hard to believe that Ernst lives in a real house and wants to show it off to me.

Barbara changes the subject. "I met your friend, Jerry. He's also new to SFU. Seems very sweet. Smart too. Probably good at science. Why don't the two of you come to stay with us for a few days? We have plenty of room, and it's close to SFU. Come next week!"

Ernst and Barbara's house is situated on a large, neatly manicured lot on Burnaby Lake. Ernst has installed a park bench where he admires the view and feeds the birds. The house has five bedrooms and several bathrooms, and the large living room is filled with couches and soft, comfortable chairs. Framed paintings decorate the walls. I can't help marveling at the difference between this veritable palace and the basement hovel I inherited from Ernst upon my arrival. In his new castle, Ernst seems content, his feet on a hassock, smoking incessantly, waxing eloquently, and arguing with anyone who will sit with him into the wee hours of the morning.

Ernst is bright and overbearing, but I enjoy his lewd sense of humor and his gruff generosity. Barbara, like other straight people, doesn't have a clue about the experimentation going on behind the scenes but makes up for her naivete with a genuine fondness for the hippie ethos—the cooperative living, the eccentricity, the free-spiritedness. She even likes the bizarre costumes that have increasingly become the norm in Kits. "Quite a scene down there these days! I used to live in Kits, but now a lot of freaks have moved in!"

Ernst, on the other hand, doesn't like the whole hippie thing, with all this interest in psychedelic drugs. And pot is *verboten*—forbidden. He calls hippies "freeloaders" and tries to persuade us that we're on a dead-end path. He loves being a provocateur.

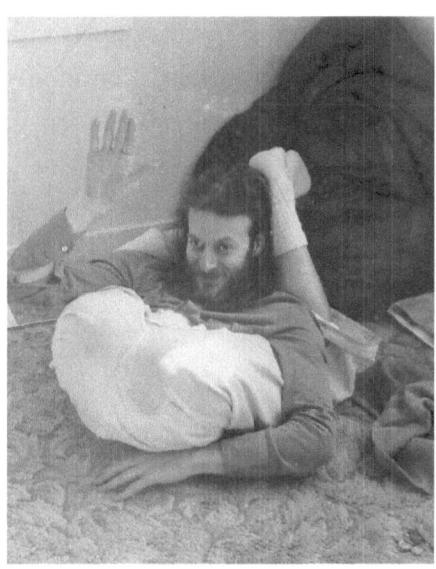

Jerry, the yogi, circa 1969

By this time, Jerry and I have gotten into yoga. Jerry taught himself *asanas* or postures from a book. I watch him and then get into it myself. Having been an athlete all my life, I enjoy exercising and stretching in this new way. We've both made tremendous strides. In the beginning, some of the postures were difficult for me, even painful, as my damaged shoulder was an impediment and I hadn't stretched systematically before. But I want to learn this ancient spiritual discipline, and my enthusiasm overrides my pain. Gradually, my flexibility and strength increase.

Doing yoga every morning has become a daily ritual. On the first morning at Ernst and Barbara's, we look around for a good place to practice. In one of the smaller lounges, we push aside the furniture, close the door, take off all our clothes, and begin practicing our *asanas*.

Being stark naked, without the constrictions of clothing, adds to our sense of freedom. We joke that we are *Naga Babas*, from an ancient sect of naked Indian yogis.

We begin with sun salutation, a series of twelve postures that flow into one another, each movement synchronized with our inhalations and exhalations. I'm amazed at how yoga is opening my body, relaxing my tight physical and psychological armor. After practicing various postures for about an hour, we conclude our session with a headstand, as naked as the day we were born, balanced upside down, our penises and testicles hanging freely. The door opens. There's a momentary silence. Then a loud shriek. Barbara's cleaning lady! From my position upside down, I see the look of absolute horror on her face. She turns and beats a hasty retreat.

Jerry and I waste no time getting dressed and leaving for SFU.

In the early evening, we hesitantly return to Ernst and Barbara's house. We're not sure what to expect. Ernst seems his usual self, pontificating to no one in particular about the latest with Israel and the Arabs. Barbara feeds us dinner and is friendly enough, but I can tell she's holding something back.

When we finish eating, she finally gets to it.

"You two freaked out the cleaning lady this morning! Imagine the poor dear walking into a room and finding two long-haired and bearded men, standing on their heads, upside down, stark naked. Naked yoga! I've never heard of such a thing. And, last week, you waltzed into the faculty lounge practically naked too. You looked like a wild man. I was mortified!"

Jerry and I don't defend ourselves, and we all move into the big living room. Barbara places a fancy cake with mounds of snowy white icing on the coffee table. I eye it hopefully, but Barbara's in no hurry to serve it. Instead, she and Ernst begin a spirited conversation about Canadian politics. Things come to head when Ernst sputters, "Pierre Trudeau is nothing more than a pot-smoking liberal. By God, his wife is a hippie!" I don't think Pierre Trudeau is a pot-smoking hippie. He's young at heart, and a lot of Canadians adore him with almost cult-like fervor. The press call it *Trudeau mania.*

"Pierre Trudeau will bring change, and it's so necessary!" Barbara huffs. "He's a man with vision! He's smart. Charismatic. I'm proud of him! "

"Jesus, Barbie!" Ernst sputters. "You're just another one of those Trudeau crazies!" My eyes meet Jerry's. At this point in our psychedelic evolution and our yoga practice, being mellow is where it's at. Peace is cool. Arguing is nowhere. Ernst doesn't stop. He provokes Barbara. I don't know if he's acting more brazen than usual. Barbara matches every line he throws out with piercing wit.

"You're just an old-fashioned conformist! Ernst, you're so straightlaced!" Barbara tells him.

"And you're just a hippie like them!" Ernst replies, pointing at Jerry and me. Suddenly, Jerry reaches over to the coffee table, picks up the plate with the white cake, and in one swift and irrevocable movement, dunks his head deeply into it. His whole face disappears into the frothy white icing.

Everything stops. Jerry calmly uses his hands to wipe the white icing from his eyes and mouth. Ernst sputters in utter disbelief. For once, he doesn't know what to say. Barbara laughs uncertainly.

"Guys! Guys! Arguing is nowhere!" Jerry preaches while the icing drips from his beard. "Don't you see? Love and peace are where it's at!"

One weekend, Jerry, Tony, and I visit Charlotte and Perry who've moved to a farm in Abbotsford, about an hour outside Vancouver. Charlotte and Perry are newly minted back-to-the-landers who're trying their hands at subsistence farming. On Saturday, we work in the vegetable garden most of the day, and in the evening, we smoke dope and listen to Perry's collection of psychedelic rock. He's into some incredible English groups like Jethro Tull and Pink Floyd.

Tony seems a bit out of sorts. He keeps getting up and going outside. I tune into Tony.

He doesn't look good. Something's off. "You okay, Tony? Anything bothering you?"

Tony just looks at me blankly. Everyone notices that something's up with him, but no one probes further. Eventually, we hit the sack.

Early the next morning, Tony wakes me up.

"I'm heading back to Vancouver. I have to see my uncle. Some friends are coming to pick me up now." It's odd that Tony's taking off, but if he has stuff to do, so be it.

Tony's friend shows up in a two-seater convertible with his girlfriend, but somehow, Tony squeezes in behind the seats. They drive off with him staring at the sky.

Late in the afternoon, the phone rings. Charlotte takes the call. It's Jane from the Kits communal house. Suddenly, the color drains from Charlotte's face. She slumps into a seat and silently hands me the phone. I put the receiver up to my ear and hear Jane crying on the line.

"Jane, what's up? Why are you crying?" There's a long silence.

Then Jane replies softly. I can hardly hear her. She's trying very hard to control her emotions. "It's Tony. He came back here from Charlotte and Perry's.... He went upstairs to his room. He was quiet.... Then, a loud bang shook the whole house! I ran up the stairs, but when I got there, it was too late. Tony had gotten ahold of a hunting rifle.... He shot himself in the heart. He's gone!"

Oh, my God. I don't know what to say or do. I've never had a friend commit suicide or die before. It's hard to understand why someone would choose to take himself out of life, and so violently. Especially Tony. He's been such a kind presence, such an integral part of our scene. I remember hearing his laugh and looking in his eye when he predicted the coin toss. I'm devastated. I won't ever hear his soft voice again.

Back in the Kits house, we all walk around in a kind of daze. Tony's suicide doesn't seem real. It's like a bad dream from which we'll shake ourselves awake.

I wonder if Tony had a mental breakdown. Some people react badly to psychedelics. Perhaps all the acid Tony took somehow pushed him over an existential edge. There are a few accounts of trippers suffering schizophrenic breaks and sensational reports about psychedelicized people "flying" to their deaths off tall buildings. They call them *casualties of the sixties.*

Being in the Kits communal house is a constant reminder of Tony and how he ended his life. It's a real bummer. The place is haunted. No one wants to continue living in the house. Jerry and I find another house across town, on East Fourth Ave. We move there with four friends.

SEVENTEEN

The East Fourth house has a new spirit. It's a beehive of activity and parties with friends and friends of friends. We smoke dope every day and listen to records like rock connoisseurs. On weekends, we take a psychedelic together. Often, a dozen people participate. Exactly what we take depends on what's available. Although prized, mescaline is difficult to find. The chemicals for manufacturing it have been restricted by the Canadian government. Probably because it can be smuggled easily, LSD—acid—is readily available. A dollar a hit.

One Saturday night, a group gathers, and we drop Owsley acid. It's been smuggled into Vancouver from California. Owsley Stanley is a notorious hippie chemist, widely rumored to make the purest acid. We're thrilled to have enough for everyone.

Santana's "Soul Sacrifice" fills the house with hypnotic conga drum rhythms. Carlos Santana blows us away with his amazing guitar work. People trip in various rooms, their doors open, a sense of unity connecting us all. I go to the bathroom to take a leak. The bathroom door is open. Charlotte's in the bathroom with Wayne, an artist who often paints under the influence of acid. Charlotte is standing directly next to Wayne. They're both gazing intently into the bathroom mirror. Wayne has regressed. In the mirror, he resembles an ape. The very shape of his head has transformed. I watch in utter fascination. In a quiet, reassuring voice, Charlotte encourages him. "Wayne, just try to relax all the muscles in your face. Good. Let's try to move toward Homo erectus now." Wayne slackens his face muscles and, with great focus, manages to relax his brow.

"Good, good, Wayne. Now, let's work on your posture. Stand up straight. Okay? Now focus on your jaw and draw your lower lips back toward your neck. . . . Yes! Moving toward Neanderthal." I don't know how Charlotte has developed her evolutionary expertise, but Wayne trusts her and follows her instructions.

"I think you will soon evolve to Homo sapiens again!" Charlotte says, now with more confidence.

Almost in slow motion, he metamorphosizes back into the Wayne we know. He turns his head from side to side, examining himself carefully in the mirror.

"I couldn't have gotten back without your help, Charlotte."

He seems none the worse for wear for someone who's just traversed millions of years of evolution in less than an hour.

The East Fourth Ave house starts going through changes. The once lighthearted vibes now turn heavy. Lots of hippies—some we know, and some we haven't seen before—increasingly frequent the house. A few have strayed from psychedelics into narcotics, specifically heroin.

Vancouver is notorious for easy access to heroin. One guy sets up camp in our living room, shooting up and nodding out. I'm repulsed. The whole point of psychedelics is about waking up—tuning in, not nodding out.

One of my roommates has become a big-time dealer, regularly importing ten thousand hits of acid from Seattle. Smaller-time dealers come and go from his room at all hours.

It's dangerous. Vancouver's tough narcs will get wind of what's happening in our house.

I'm paranoid. Workmen show up to repair the street. They're wearing ear mufflers to dampen the sound of their jackhammers. I'm concerned they're part of a narcotic squad, listening to our every word, gathering evidence. It's only a matter of time before we're busted.

I find solace in one place. Banyen Books, a New Age bookstore, opens in the heart of Kits on West Fourth, specializing in books on meditation, yoga, Buddhism, Hinduism, Kabbalah, Sufism, Christian and Jewish mysticism, Vedic astrology, palmistry, psychedelics, numerology, Ayurveda, and many other psychological and spiritual topics. Meditative music plays softly in the background. The aroma of incense wafts to every corner of the space. In this temple-like vibe, people sit around reading and meditating. A small sign in beautiful calligraphy announces:

"All paths lead to the same place."

Stained glass window custom-made by the author for Banyen circa 1974

I'm drawn to this new bookstore. It's a peaceful place. It reflects the emerging interest in spirituality in the psychedelic counterculture.

The seekers at Banyen are excited about life. They're learning and growing, and their enthusiasm fuels in me a yearning for deeper meaning and understanding. After my difficult life in South Africa, the possibility of psychological growth and spiritual change fills me with hope. I want to change. To grow. To lessen my load. To find peace. In the accepting atmosphere of Banyen, my self-conscious Jewish identity has all but disappeared. One's religion doesn't matter as much as one's inner spiritual path.

One of Banyen's books is a science-fiction novel called *Stranger in a Strange Land* by Robert Heinlein. I identify with the hero, Valentine Michael Smith, an earthling born on Mars. Michael has never seen another member of his species until he visits Earth and learns what it means to be a man. I feel like a stranger in a strange land myself. Part of Michael's Martian culture is summed up in the word *grok*. To *grok* something means to take in a person or an experience completely. You *grok* them with your whole being. I want to grok this new world I'm discovering and leave my old world behind.

One afternoon, Sammy hands me a cassette recording of a lecture recently given at UBC.

"Just listen to this tape. Take your time. It's about a westerner's amazing journey to enlightenment in India." I put the tape into my old cassette player.

A calm, well-spoken, American male recites the lines of a poem by Zenren-Kushu. "The wild geese do not intend to cast their reflection. The water has no mind to receive their image."

A silence follows, which, even on the cassette's tinny speakers, seems to invite contemplation. I'm all ears.

The speaker is Dr. Richard Alpert, a former Harvard University psychology professor.

Alpert describes his dramatic life change in 1963, when a fellow Harvard professor, Timothy Leary, gave him psilocybin, the active ingredient in "magic mushrooms." Like the Native American ritual use of peyote, magic mushrooms have been used for centuries by the Mazatec Indians in Mexico.

Alpert's journey on magic mushrooms affected him profoundly. He touched an identity beyond his various roles in life. He claimed he'd learned more in one mushroom session than in years of training to become a psychologist.

Alpert and Leary subsequently initiated the Harvard Psilocybin Project to research psilocybin's potential as a spiritual and psychological catalyst. Participation in the project was open to Harvard graduate students, but the administration forbade undergraduate participation.

Harvard's Psilocybin Project achieved dramatic results. In one of the studies, 167 students participated, and 95 percent of them reported that the experiences had changed their lives for the better. Their enthusiasm and the reports of Harvard's newspaper, *The Crimson*, quickly infiltrated the larger Harvard community, coming to the alarmed attention of the administration and concerned fellow professors. Alpert, Leary, and their collaborators were accused of blatant scientific bias—of irresponsibly taking psychedelics with their subjects. Research required neutrality. Leary and Alpert had violated this cardinal scientific rule. The final straw came in 1963 when Harvard fired Alpert for breaking his promise not to give psilocybin to undergrads. Leary was fired shortly after when he didn't show up to teach. The Harvard Psilocybin Project reincarnated at Millbrook, a large New York country estate, where the psychedelic experiments continued unfettered by academic restrictions.

By the midsixties, Timothy Leary had become famous with his cryptic "Turn on! Tune in! Drop out!" This little aphorism gave a middle finger to the establishment. It's so simple, so subversive, so revolutionary. So threatening. I knew from my own psychedelic experiences the truth of Leary's other notorious aphorism: "To learn how to use your head, you have to go out of your mind." Cute as Leary's messages were, they didn't satisfy my hunger for long. Like others who had experimented with these powerful drugs, I sought an explanation, a deeper lens through which to understand the spiritual yearning that psychedelics evoked.

After Harvard and Millbrook, Alpert traveled through India with an American yogi, Bhagavan Das. Alpert was carrying a bottle of White Lightning—each pill 305 micrograms of pharma grade LSD-25 made especially for Alpert's Indian enlightenment experiment by Owsley Stanley, the genius underground chemist. When they met yogis and *sadhus* along the way, Alpert doled out the acid to test their enlightenment. After encounters with several holy men, *sadhus* and yogis, all had failed Alpert's psychedelic enlightenment test.

Eventually, Bhagavan Das guided Alpert to the foothills of the Himalayas and introduced him to Neem Karoli Baba, a Hindu guru whom people called *Maharaji*—Great King. Soon after arriving, Maharaji blew Alpert's mind with an accurate description of his mother's recent spleen cancer and her subsequent death. Alpert was stunned. Here he was, in the Himalayas, far from America. How did "this little old man with a blanket" know his mother's history? It was uncanny. Then, Maharaji demanded "the medicine"—the White Lightning Alpert had been handing out. Not satisfied with the single pill Alpert offered him, Maharaji demanded three pills—915 micrograms of the purest acid—enough to thoroughly blow even the most experienced tripper's mind. Maharaji popped the pills and sat around twinkling all day, showing no signs of having been affected by the massive dose.

Alpert, arguably one of the most experienced psychedelic explorers on the planet, could only "Wow!" He realized the old man was the real McCoy. He had found his guru. He wept.

In keeping with Hindu spiritual tradition, Alpert was given a new name—*Ram Dass*—Servant of Ram, an incarnation of God. Richard Alpert was now Ram Dass.

Maharaji directed Ram Dass to study and practice with a master Himalayan yogi by the name of Baba Hari Dass. Some twenty years before, this yogi had taken a vow of silence.

Though he grew up with yogis in the jungle, Hari Dass was fluent in six languages and could read and write several more. He taught students by writing on a small chalkboard.

"When a pickpocket meets a saint, he sees only pockets."

"The world with desires is an illusion or ignorance; without desires, it is truth, love, God."

"A yogi searches for God in the world and says, 'This is not God . . . this is not God,' and rejects everything."

"As soon as he finds God, he says, 'This is God . . . this is God . . . this is God.' He begins to see God in everything."

Ram Dass spent months in retreat under Hari Dass's supervision. Step by step, the sophisticated Harvard psychology professor learned the ancient principles of *Ashtanga*—eight-limbed yoga, a comprehensive path for achieving enlightenment.

I listen to Ram Dass's three-hour lecture through to the end. Then I listen to all three hours again. Ram Dass's journey speaks to me. As a college student, I've heard many lectures, but this—if it can be called a lecture—blows everything else away. I tell Jerry about it. We huddle in his room with the door closed, away from the hubbub in the house. He's as taken as me. We listen together over and over, till we've heard it dozens of times.

We play the tape to anyone who shows even a smattering of interest.

Ram Dass is a perfect messenger, a Pied Piper for the spiritual yearning many of us are feeling. He claims that following a spiritual path will lead to a permanent high without the aid of psychedelic drugs.

At the end of the semester, Jerry says, "Things are pretty intense in the house. Let's get out of Vancouver. I'll show you Montreal."

Getting away from the East Fourth house sounds right. I'm certainly up for exploring Quebec. The French Canadians I've met are very friendly, quite different from their reserved English compatriots.

EIGHTEEN
WINTER 1970

We pile our belongings in an old VW van and head across Canada. The underpowered van struggles to maintain fifty miles an hour on the highway. The further east we drive, the colder it gets. The heater is no match for the bitter temperature. Ice fogs the windows. To avoid our feet getting numb, we take turns driving for an hour at a time. The road is so straight and empty, we figure we might as well place a brick on the accelerator to keep it flat against the floorboards and push the old van to its max.

Now, sitting cross-legged meditation-style, wrapped in Mexican blankets, we drive across the prairies, chanting *Om* until its vibration transforms the freezing van into a sacred temple. When we aren't chanting, Ram Dass's voice on the cassette tape keeps us company.

Every time we play it, something new reveals itself.

"Just be here now!"

"Here. Now . . . when *then* becomes *now*, you'll have super consciousness and know exactly what to do."

Finally, after a week on the road, we arrive in Montreal. We've slept in the freezing van. We're cold and hungry. We head to a district near McGill University and rent a room in a student house.

Our money's running low, so we get jobs as janitors at a nightclub—the Black Bottom—in a seedy part of Montreal. The Black owners think it's cute that long-haired White boys are cleaning up. Flashy gangster types arrive in their shiny Cadillacs with New Jersey number plates. A Black guitarist in one of the bands asks me for some acid. I hand over a tiny transparent sheet of high-quality acid—windowpane—I've stashed in my wallet, wondering how he's going to play the guitar on such a whopping dose. He's possessed. He holds the guitar like it's on fire, plucking notes that send electric flames into the atmosphere. He sounds pretty good to me. We usually leave the club around 4 in the morning and walk back to our pad in the cold snow.

In a few weeks, Jerry comes up with another of his bright ideas. "Let's ditch the Black Bottom. We have a few bucks now. Let's go visit Swami Vishnudevananda. Everyone calls him Swami Vishnu for short. His yoga ashram is an hour outside Montreal. He wrote a great yoga book with lots of photos. Let's see if we can stay there and get into yoga more deeply!"

I'm intrigued. Learning from an Indian yoga master would be a unique opportunity to further explore the spiritual path, now the most important thing in my life.

The snow lies deep in magnificent valleys on the way to Val Morin, but we're disappointed to learn that Swami Vishnu is away, establishing an ashram on Paradise Island in the Bahamas. We're shown various photos of the swami, who is dedicated to promoting peace all over the world. In addition to being a yoga master, Swami Vishnu is a pilot. His plane has been painted with trippy colors by Peter Max, the famous psychedelic artist. The swami has flown over various world hotspots and been buzzed by both Israeli and Egyptian jets along the Suez Canal. He's also "bombed" India and Pakistan with flowers and peace pamphlets.

The yogis running the ashram are young people like us. The swami will be back in a few weeks. We're invited to stay. In exchange for room, board, and yoga classes, we'll clean the ashram and help with maintenance. We won't be paid, but it will be a good experience in what they refer to as Karma Yoga, selfless service. We're happy to be in the ashram, eating great vegetarian fare, warm for the winter, and practicing yoga and meditation.

When Swami Vishnu returns, we're quite disappointed with the real person compared with the svelte yogi we've seen in the photos in his book. Now the swami has turned middle-aged and rather pudgy. He's irritable, stomping around the ashram and shouting angry instructions. Maybe he knows a lot about yoga and has a cool plane, but I find it hard to approach him. He's authoritarian and uncool. He leaves again after just a few days. We aren't able to meet with him. None of the devotees mind that we stay on.

A few months go by. Both Jerry and I steep ourselves in yoga. We practice for four or five hours every day. There isn't much to do in Val Morin, so I listen to the tape of Ram Dass's lecture over and over. I want to meet Ram Dass—the only source in my world who seems to grok the spiritual yearning awakened by psychedelics. I begin fantasizing about inviting him to Montreal to give a similar talk to the one on my tape. Someone at the ashram mentions that Ram Dass's father lives in Franklin, New Hampshire, relatively close to Quebec.

I write to Ram Dass, in care of his father in New Hampshire. Wings on a prayer, I lay everything out—how I'm an immigrant from South Africa, that I have been introduced to psychedelics, have lost interest in school, am learning yoga and meditation at Swami Vishnu's ashram, and how deeply his story has touched me. Finally, I ask whether it might be possible for him to give a talk in Montreal.

To my surprise, a reply arrives in less than two weeks. Ram Dass would be happy to do a lecture in Montreal. Would I set it up? Enclosed are two small black-and-white photographs, one of Maharaji, the sage who sailed through Alpert/Ram Dass's acid enlightenment test, and the other of the silent teacher, Baba Hari Dass, who taught Ram Dass advanced yoga. We're thrilled.

Jerry and I decide to take an acid trip with the photos of the two gurus. We stick them on a wall at eye height. An hour or so after dropping, we stand close to the photos. In seconds, they transform into vibrating, breathing beings. Involuntarily, we take a few steps back. This encounter is unlike anything either of us has experienced. We don't understand it, but it doesn't matter. We stand before the silent yogi Hari Dass. He's elegant and simple and radiates.

Maharaji remains a toothless, grizzled old man wrapped in a blanket.

I rent a hall at McGill University with a seating capacity of 1,500. It's many more seats than we need, but it's better to have more space than too little.

Ram Dass arrives in a classic silver Jaguar. With its sleek silver body and faded red leather seats, it's a remnant of his past. When he was a Harvard professor, he owned a collection of classic cars and a Cessna plane. He comes from money. I'm a little intimidated.

Ram Dass steps out of the Jag with a dazzling smile. He's tall with a bearded, pixie-like face, and long thinning hair tied in a ponytail. He's about forty, slim, and dressed entirely in white. He incessantly moves prayer beads between his fingers. He looks me right in the eye.

"Can we get on the radio to advertise my talk?" he asks me. "I could do a mini version of my bigger schtick; then people would have a taste of what I'm offering."

I hadn't thought of a radio program to advertise the talk, but it sounds like a great idea. Someone gives me the number of Mitchell Marcus, a hip radio announcer, popular with Montreal's freaks and misfits.

The next afternoon, Ram Dass, Jerry, and I head to the radio station. Ram Dass brings a tamboura, which he strums from time to time on the air, its melodic and hypnotic sound tuning us all to the same frequency. He talks in a relaxed way, slowly unfolding his message. At some point, he begins chanting *Sri Ram, Jai Ram, Jai Jai Ram*. Over and over. He urges Jerry and me to chant too. Jerry and I have never heard Hindu chanting before, but we join in, doing our best to stay on key.

"Chanting is a path called Bhakti Yoga, the yoga of devotion," Ram Dass explains to the invisible radio audience.

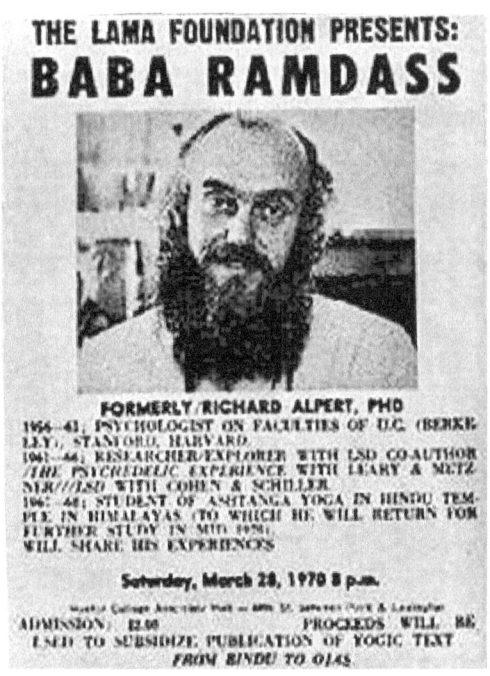

Ram Dass poster circa 1970. Courtesy of Jon Vasu Seskevich

In the evening, an hour before the lecture, hundreds of people loiter outside the auditorium at McGill. They've heard us on the radio. More and more people arrive. The auditorium is packed. The fire marshal refuses to allow any more inside. Hundreds congregate on the sidewalk outside.

"See if you can get this hall again for tomorrow night," Ram Dass says with a big grin.

He begins the talk. He holds the space with a mixture of silence and speech. He is charming. Funny. Irreverent. Knowledgeable. Wise. Inspiring. Soon, the entire auditorium is eating out of his palm. His journey to the secret Himalayas is an analog for the psychedelicized spiritual yearning all of us feel. The atmosphere is charged with the excitement of possibility.

The next day, Mitchell, the hip radio guy, plays segments of the previous night's talk. That evening, the auditorium is again packed to the rafters. It's clear that Ram Dass is a kind of magician. He is turning earnest psychedelic-seekers onto Eastern spiritual teachings. I'm happy.

I've helped this really cool thing happen in Montreal.

The next morning, we say our goodbyes to Ram Dass. We're still intoxicated with the previous two night's happenings.

"Are you interested in studying with the silent yogi Baba Hari Dass in India?" Ram Dass asks Jerry.

Jerry smiles. This is just the thing for him. India. Studying yoga with a real master. And we had such an amazing connection with Hari Dass on that acid trip.

Ram Dass turns to me. "You're good at setting up these talks. Would it interest you to set up more for me?"

Wow! Did I hear that right? If Ram Dass recognizes some useful talent in me, that's a big compliment. Still, I'm disappointed that he hasn't seen fit to send me to India with Jerry. Am I not pure enough? Am I too worldly? Not ready for a spiritual teacher? Why has he chosen

Jerry for India and not me?

But I let go of these feelings of inadequacy and focus on the worldly task I've been given. I create a strategy for a series of talks spaced over a few months that Ram Dass will give in Toronto, St. Louis, the University of Michigan at Ann Arbor, and Vancouver.

Each of the talks attracts hundreds of seekers, eager for Ram Dass's message. Without any doubt, Ram Dass is the most eloquent person I've ever met. It's deeply moving to sit with hundreds of like-minded people who imbibe his every word.

At the University of Michigan in Ann Arbor, after the lecture, students petition Ram Dass to stay and teach yoga. Ram Dass demurs but proposes that Jerry and I teach a yoga class together. Over 150 students sign up for the six-week course. Our training at Swami Vishnu's ashram serves us well, and we're a good team. When the class finishes, Jerry leaves for India, with promises to write. I head back to Vancouver. I'll meet Ram Dass there for the final talk.

NINETEEN
FALL 1970

Returning to Vancouver, I rent an apartment on West Fourth and begin teaching yoga classes. Yoga and meditation have become the central focus of my life. I'm not interested in going back to university. The apartment's large living room with black hardwood floors makes an excellent yoga studio. There are few, if any, yoga teachers in Vancouver, so the two classes I offer daily are filled with students eager to learn the ancient discipline.

Ram Dass arrives in Vancouver. This is his second trip, and it draws a big crowd. He stays over at my studio, charming as ever.

Over the next few months, Jerry and I correspond. He's living in a hut in the foothills of the Himalayas. Baba Hari Dass has given him a spiritual name—*Anand Dass*—Servant of Bliss. Hari Dass calls him "A.D." I'm envious. My buddy has been blessed to study yoga with a master in India. He even has a new spiritual name. In Montreal, I tried to get a visa for India, but the Indians rejected my South African passport. No doubt Mahatma Gandhi's experiences as a young lawyer in racist South Africa before the turn of the twentieth century had influenced their attitude. Despite having a first-class ticket, Gandhi was thrown off a train because he wasn't White. Apartheid's karmic tentacles have reached into my spiritual life, cutting off my fantasies of a journey to the mystical East.

I ask Jerry if he would pass on a note for Hari Dass. Would he take me on as a student even though I live in Canada? Several weeks later, an aerogram arrives from India. In small, precise handwriting, Baba Hari Dass informs me he will soon be moving to California. I should meet him there. This news is stunning. I will finally meet the same master who has instructed Ram Dass and my friend, A.D. India is no longer a problem. I can get to California. Magic is alive, and destiny has taken a fortuitous turn.

A month later, I write to Hari Dass in California asking permission to visit him. He invites me to meet at the home of his US sponsor, a professor at the University of California.

I hastily arrange with friends to accompany me to Sonoma County. My former housemate, Nigel, with whom I've shared Ram Dass's talk, is eager to meet Hari Dass. Another acquaintance, Lynne, a philosophy student, offers his VW van for the drive. I hope it's more powerful than the decrepit van A.D. and I drove across Canada last winter, a million years ago.

A middle-aged woman dressed in white with a pleasant face and gentle demeanor greets us at the front door of a weathered wood-clad house near the ocean. She introduces herself as *Ma Renu* but tells us to call her *Ma*. "Please call Baba Hari Dass *Babaji*," she suggests and shows us into a nearby room.

Leaning against the wooden headboard of a large bed sits Babaji, magnetic in white cotton robes that complement his gleaming mahogany complexion. I recognize him from Ram Dass's grainy black-and-white photo, but in real life, he's far more striking. Smiling broadly, he gestures for us to sit with him on his bed. His hair, a pile of dreadlocks stacked directly on top of his head like a large beehive, looks strangely elegant, making him appear much taller.

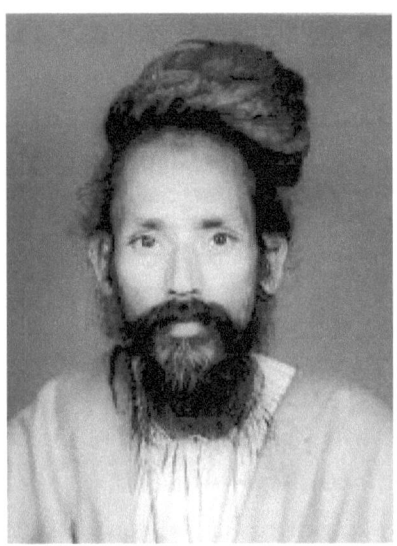

He quickly scribbles something on his small chalkboard and points it in my direction. I read, "You are Gary. A.D.'s friend. You wrote to me in India."

I nod and bring my two palms together in the Indian way of greeting. I sit cross-legged on the bed directly opposite him. Nigel sits on a corner of the bed, and Lynne is on the floor nearby.

The small chalkboard hanging around Babaji's neck initially captures my attention, but it quickly recedes into the background as we interact with him. The pace of his writing slows down the conversation, compelling us to pay attention, effortlessly bringing us into the here and now.

"Babaji, why don't you speak? Why have you maintained silence all these years?" I ask.

Babaji picks up the small chalkboard and writes, "When I was young, I had much anger. I practiced silence as a discipline. Now I prefer silence."

"But, Babaji," I say. "In the Western world, it's not practical to be silent, even if we are angry. We have to interact with lots of people, and in this culture, they would think it's weird if a person didn't speak and wrote on a chalkboard to communicate!"

Babaji nods as though my observation is particularly sage. Then he writes, "Silence is not for everyone. But a yogi can practice a day of silence a week. It calms the mind."

Then he flips the chalkboard and writes, "People waste much energy by speaking."

He silently mimics people jabbering away like a bunch of cockatoos. We laugh, and so does Babaji.

Periodically, when a natural silence ensues, I find myself lapsing into self-conscious embarrassment. I'm sure Babaji can see into my mind. He just sits there. Silent. Making no pretense at relating. I find his comfort with not engaging both refreshing and disconcerting. I want something to happen—an interaction to escape into. I'm desperate to fill the void with something familiar.

I can't think of anything to say, so I close my eyes and try to meditate. My efforts are soon greeted by the most embarrassing thoughts and sexual fantasies, one after the other. A real nightmare. I groan. *Aspiring seeker meets guru, and all he can think about is sex!* I open my eyes but dare not look at Babaji. I desperately try to control my wretched mind, but my efforts only make things worse. Instead of calming down, my mind races.

Across from me, Babaji's breathing stops. He enters some unfathomable state. In contrast, my breathing is constricted. I'm embarrassed by my obvious *un*enlightenment. After what seems like an eternity, Babaji begins breathing again. The sound of the chalk on the small chalkboard breaks the silence. He thrusts the chalkboard toward me.

"Your mind is out of control."

Then he erases the sentence and writes, "There are yogic exercises that can help. I will show you."

He demonstrates a series of four breathing exercises. We practice them to make sure I absorb every nuance. His insight into the condition of my mind is on the money. I'm grateful he hasn't mentioned my particular fantasies. Over the next few hours, as the silences grow longer, my mind continues to wander into territory I would much prefer to keep private.

Eventually, Babaji writes on his chalkboard, "How many times have you taken LSD?"

"I'm not sure anymore, Babaji. I've lost count."

Babaji takes this in and writes, "You learned everything you needed on the first trip."

This is shocking. My psychedelic experiments have been incredibly meaningful. After all, Babaji told Ram Dass, "LSD is like a Christ in America awakening the youth." Ram Dass broadcasted this important message to thousands of psychedelic seekers. It made perfect sense. But here and now, Babaji is giving me a different message.

"Drugs can damage the nervous system. Takes time to heal. But yogic purification and breathing can help. Ayurvedic herbs too."

I have so many questions. Babaji patiently explains the principles of yogic breathing and the ancient Indian medical system of Ayurveda.

Five hours on Babaji's bed are interrupted only by our questions and Babaji's answers. Despite my periodic bouts of mind-wandering and embarrassment, I want to sit on Babaji's bed forever. There's a feeling of having reached an important destination, of no place further to go, but we say our goodbyes and head directly back to Vancouver. The time flies like we're traveling on a magic carpet.

TWENTY

DEAR DAD/MOM

I hope you are well. I haven't written in a while, but I thought to let you know where I am and what I'm up to. At the moment, I'm living on a farm on Cortez Island between the mainland of British Columbia and Vancouver Island.

It's a remote place, but I'm here with my friend A.D. who just got back from India. I'm taking a break from university for a while and learning yoga and meditation and about Ayurveda, the ancient Indian healing system. We get up early in the morning and practice our yoga and meditation. I'm learning a lot and enjoying it. There's a big vegetable garden here, and I'm learning about organic farming too. Since getting into yoga, I've become a vegetarian. It's a bit harder to get protein, but my body seems to be adjusting to my new diet, and I feel well. I've met some very interesting people and had many adventures since leaving South Africa.

Anyway, I hope this letter finds you in good health.

GARY

When I write to my parents, I try to be honest and avoid saying anything that might be too controversial. I never mention hippies, psychedelic drugs, or grass; God forbid, that would be way too much information, an insurmountable cultural and generational barrier. How can I adequately explain the mind-blowing changes in my life since I left South Africa four years ago? I'm a different person. In any case, neither writes back. Mom stays in touch with Jean, and occasionally, I get a message from her that Mom knows I'm alive and kicking.

A.D. and I are living on a farm on Cortez Island at the invitation of one of my yoga students. Ed proposed individual yoga instruction in exchange for a retreat cabin on his farm. Ed's in his late thirties, a psychologist who's become a Rolfer.

Soon after we move to Ed's farm, we make friends with Ed's brother-in-law, Jack. He begins attending our morning yoga sessions. This mountain of a man with a friendly freckled face and long brown hair is a pleasant addition to our tiny spiritual community.

I continue writing to Babaji. He always replies promptly, giving me guidance on yoga practice, meditation, and how to live a more pure and focused spiritual life. A relationship is building. I ask Babaji to give me a spiritual name. Having a spiritual name signifies one's initiation on the path. But for me, it's more than that. The name my parents gave me is endowed with all my negative family history and my South African karma. A spiritual name will mean a new beginning, a rebirth.

Babaji requests my birthplace, my birthdate, and the time of my actual birth. I send off the information and wait for the arrival of a new name—one that will express my deepest identity. The letter arrives. My spiritual mentor proposes the Sanskrit name, *Surya Dass*. I can't help myself. I can't relate to this name. *Surya* is just too foreign sounding. I write Babaji that I'm sorry, but I just can't use it.

He writes back, "Use Ravi Dass. It's the same as Surya Dass."

Somehow, Ravi Dass sounds more palatable. Babaji explains that Ravi Dass was a fourteenth-century Indian saint who stood against caste-based oppression. He was a Nelson Mandela of his time. He immediately begins referring to me as "R.D."

After five months of our simple existence on the Cortez Island farm, the weather begins to change. It's becoming colder and rains almost every day. Winter looms. Ed takes off for New York City to attend enlightenment training with Oscar Ichazo, a Bolivian spiritual master. Oscar has developed a methodology called the Arica Training, specifically designed to streamline the path to enlightenment for Westerners. Ed promises to let me know if the training lives up to its hype. Although my relationship with Babaji has been going well, I'm curious about other spiritual paths. I look forward to hearing Ed's report from New York.

With the change of weather, staying in our unheated cabin has become untenable. We're cold. It's become difficult to practice yoga. I propose a trip to see Babaji in California, where the weather is warmer. A.D. agrees. Jack says he'd like to meet Babaji too. We build a cabin on the back of Jack's old Ford pickup so the three of us can travel together.

I've saved some money from my yoga classes in Vancouver. After stopping in to see Babaji, I intend to jump on a plane and head to Maui for the winter. I long for the warmth of a South African summer, and Maui's climate is similar. It will be great to practice yoga in a beautiful warm setting.

Babaji now lives in a cabin in the woods above the city of Santa Cruz, California. We arrive in the early evening after three days on the road. We're excited to see Babaji; A.D. hasn't seen him since India, and though this is only my second face-to-face meeting, we're welcomed like old friends.

Several hippie-yogis sit cross-legged, meditating on cushions in a semicircle around Babaji. Just as we're joining the group, Babaji writes a cryptic message on his chalkboard. He points it toward me. "R.D, have you met Aparna yet?"

I hesitate for a moment. "No. Who's Aparna?"

With a big grin, Babaji writes, "You know her."

"Her?"—my mind spins. *Who's he talking about?* "No, Babaji, I don't know Aparna."

Babaji looks at me, smiles mischievously, and scribbles, "You know her."

Now he holds the chalkboard up so all can read the three words. He shakes with laughter at my protestations, instantly making me the object of everyone's amusement.

This is not how I imagined the session with Babaji would unfold. I thought we'd sit, quietly meditate, maybe ask occasional questions, and contemplate the holy man's answers.

Someone asks a question, but I barely hear it. I'm preoccupied. *Who is this Aparna person? Why is Babaji so insistent that I know her? And why does he think it's so funny?* I rack my brain, but no one comes to mind.

Babaji continues answering questions, but then, an hour or so later, he writes, "You know Aparna." He shows the chalkboard to A.D.

A.D. turns and says, "You must know her. Babaji would never say anything that wasn't true."

Babaji smiles. My anxiety races. Now and then, Babaji teases me again, laughing with his big white teeth. Soon, the whole room is giggling like tipsy patrons at a bar.

Finally, at about midnight, as we're taking our leave, one of the other yogis hands me a note with an address in the city of Santa Cruz.

Babaji nods and writes, "You will find Aparna there." Then he laughs again, slapping his leg in glee.

Jack drives us down from Babaji's cabin in the mountains into the city of Santa Cruz.

A.D. keeps shaking his head. "You must know her!" I'm more than a little curious about who this Aparna person will turn out to be.

By the time we get to the address on the slip of paper, it's 12:30 a.m. A light's on, so we don't feel too badly about waking up the household. A young woman answers the door. She's a bit portly, and I secretly hope that she's not the Aparna I'm seeking. A.D. immediately blurts out that Babaji has sent us. She smiles and invites us in. Just mentioning Babaji's name works like magic. We knock on a strange door, after midnight, mention Babaji, and are welcomed. A.D. can't contain himself. "Does Aparna live here?"

The young woman answers, "I think she's still up. I'll get her."

Two very long minutes later, a beautiful blue-eyed woman with long blond hair walks into the room. She's wearing a white dress and greets us with a knowing smile.

"Hi, I'm Aparna."

I've never seen Aparna before in my life, of that I am certain. This is a woman I will not easily forget. Before I can say anything, A.D. points to me and asks, "Do you know him?"

Aparna looks at me and shakes her head. "No."

A.D. shrugs, pulls out his sleeping bag, and prepares to bed down on the living room floor. He doesn't have to ask permission. We're guru brothers and sisters. Jack chooses to sleep in the truck.

For me, the evening is just beginning. Aparna brews some herbal tea, and we sit at the kitchen table whispering while everyone sleeps.

Aparna is the same age as me, twenty-five. She tells me about her childhood. She'd been an oddball in her little town in central Massachusetts, a budding bohemian in a straight time and place. She was very involved in her church youth group and, through that, got into the Civil Rights Movement. When she was a teenager in 1963, she'd attended Martin Luther King's March on Washington and the Selma Marches in 1965. She'd taken a year off college to live in Roxbury, a Black neighborhood of Boston, one of the very few White faces there. While I was making my way out of South Africa, she was actively involved in fighting racism in America.

"I became a hippie at Goddard College in Vermont," she tells me. "We were a bunch of freaks in the woods, and we did a lot of acid and other psychedelics—it was a safe place to be—a very fun time of my life. At Goddard, I was able to study what interested me—palmistry and astrology—and it's also where I got into yoga and meditation. Two years ago, I met Ram Dass and learned about Babaji from him.

Since then, I've been writing Babaji letters. I've been wanting to come to Santa Cruz to meet him ever since."

I'm entranced by Aparna. Something about the way Babaji teased me all evening has cast a spell on me. She is gorgeous and unassuming. Obviously smart, and a natural feminist. But there's something much deeper that makes me feel close to her. Though we come from completely different backgrounds, we share a spiritual connection. Our paths have big overlaps.

But, so far as Babaji insisting that I know her, I take this as his weird way of introducing us—like an Indian holy man *shadchan*—a Jewish matchmaker on steroids.

Aparna and I are both still wide awake at 4:30 in the morning. We've created a magical cocoon in this strange kitchen, whispering our stories to one another while everyone else sleeps. I know I want to spend more time with Aparna. It's obvious that we're just beginning to get to know each other. I pluck up my courage.

"Would you be interested in coming with me to Maui? We could avoid the winter and practice yoga in a warm paradise."

I haven't planned this trip to Maui at all. I've simply conjured a romantic dream of going to a utopia for the winter. Sharing it with this wonderful woman, with Babaji's stamp of approval, seems like a great idea.

"Let's see what the I Ching advises," Aparna responds. She disappears for a minute and returns with a well-worn copy of the ancient Chinese oracle.

The I Ching is also my go-to whenever any major decision must be made. Someone at Banyen introduced me to it early on. The oracle contains unerringly dignified wisdom, and I've come to use it as a kind of inner compass to guide my actions. The ritual of obtaining a reading slows a person down. It becomes an exercise in mindfulness. Seeking the oracle's advice in a moment like this is natural to me, and the fact that Aparna is also into the I Ching confirms we're on the same wavelength.

"Let's agree on our intention before we start," I propose.

Aparna nods and says, "Should we go to Hawaii together?"

She takes three Chinese-looking coins out of a small colorful pouch. We focus on our question for a few moments. Then we take turns throwing the three coins, carefully recording each result. On the edge of our seats, we wonder, *What will the oracle tell us? Is this "youthful folly," as it sometimes indicates?*

It takes a few moments to look up the hexagram. We scan the text, and immediately, one line stands out: *"It furthers one to cross the great water."*

Wow! That's clear. We look at each other and smile.

TWENTY-ONE

We've landed in Maui. The sun has set. It's dark. The fragrances in the breeze are the only hint of the world we will discover in the daytime. We find our way to a beach. It's too dark to make anything out. We bed down in a level sandy area. When we wake at first light, we realize we've been sleeping on a gravel road, an inauspicious beginning.

Someone tells us about some hippies living in a church in Haiku, an off-the-beaten-path village some miles away. We hitchhike to the hippie church. Recognizing us as fellow spiritual seekers the residents offer us the vestibule to sleep in, on the condition we put away our bedding during the day. We stay at the church for a few weeks, and then one of our new friends tells us about a secret campsite in a forest nearby. The owner has gone back to the mainland, and it's cool for us to use it. Things are falling into place.

The campsite is in a flat clearing. It has everything we need—a good-sized tent, a Coleman stove, storage areas, firepit. We carry containers of water from the church. Our diet is simple—oatmeal for breakfast, lentils and brown rice for our main meal, and mangoes and guavas, which grow wild. I learn that Aparna is the best cook I've ever met. She turns our simple vegetarian meals into delicious feasts with aromatic spices she finds at a small local health food store. We practice yoga and meditate twice a day, sharing our spiritual bond and getting to know one another.

We have our first argument. Aparna is a straight shooter and takes no prisoners. When she trains her guns on me—when her eyes turn from their usual ocean blue to glacier blue—it's trouble. I have a lot to learn.

We've been camping here for six weeks. I brought some windowpane acid, hoping Aparna and I will take a trip together sometime while we're on Maui. That would be amazing bonding. I propose the idea. Aparna tells me she stopped taking psychedelics when she got into yoga and meditation, but she'll make an exception to join me.

On the designated morning, we get up early, do a yoga session together, and meditate. We ask for protection and guidance on our journey. Then we drop the acid.

Though we haven't known each other long, I feel it's important that she know my background, know where I've come from, know my sadness. Well into the trip, I begin to share the pain of my family's disintegration, the split-second decision to intervene with my parents, and how it went violently awry. I've never opened up about my past to anyone, but the acid has brought my wound to the surface. It pours out in an incoherent jumble. Aparna listens with great intention and focus, but it's all too much for the limited conceptual capacities of her brain on acid. She keeps repeating, "I can't catch the train. It's going too fast."

Nevertheless, she's groks that I grew up with violence and

emotional abuse, that my relationship with my parents is complicated and strained. She tells me, "I'm so fortunate. My parents are very loving. Maybe you'll meet them one day."

We hear about a nine-day silent *Zazen sesshin* at the nearby Diamond Zendo. We enroll along with about thirty other participants, some with shaved heads who look like serious Zen students and a few other long-haired hippies who look more like us.

Two days into the sesshin, I'm wondering why for the life of me I've chosen this torture in the name of my spiritual development. The sixteen hours a day of meditation—facing a blank wall while attending only to your breathing—is interrupted every thirty minutes by the ritual Zazen walk. The sesshin has become completely, utterly, ridiculously monotonous. I'm going to die of boredom.

If your meditation posture—ramrod straight spine—leans even slightly to the left or right, a monitor creeps up behind you. He bows, and you are expected to bow in return before he whacks you on the shoulders with a short paddle. Then he bows again, and you bow in gratitude for his abuse. This ritual is supposed to wake you up, but it pisses me off. What a crock! The Japanese and the South Africans have one thing in common: beating people into compliance. A few times, I contemplate tripping the malnourished bald little fucker when he shows up behind me, doing his little bow before clobbering me.

Once a day, we meet with the roshi, a big-bellied, inscrutable Japanese man dressed in a black kimono. He draws a line on a piece of paper and asks me, "Where are you? Here or here?" He indicates one side of the line, which I assume means enlightenment, and the other side, which I take as ordinary consciousness. Every day, my body language telegraphs my pathetic answer, "I don't know, Roshi. I don't know."

I struggle for the entire nine days. This approach to enlightenment is like climbing a vertical wall without any footholds. Aparna and I are not allowed to speak or make eye contact. Somehow, I make it to the ninth day. On the last morning, there's a renewed intensity in the zendo. It's our final session, our last chance. A half-hour before lunch, the roshi enters and slowly walks around, his hands on his potbelly, his eyes all-seeing. The strain in the zendo goes through the roof as he dawdles by the hungry and keyed-up meditators.

The roshi comes upon one earnest young meditator, stands in front of him, and yells at the top of his lungs, "YOU MUST KILL YOURSELF ON THE MAT!" The young meditator begins weeping on his cushion, cowering in confusion, and then howling loudly. The tension in the zendo blows the roof. It's unbearable. The roshi turns and yells at the rest of us, "KILL YOURSELVES ON THE MAT!"

Now the young meditator's weeping and howling reaches a new crescendo. He's completely defeated, broken down to an indignity I hope will never happen to me, shaking and moaning. I'm faking one-pointed focus as hard as I can. Everyone is doing the same. Then the roshi strikes a gong and announces the end of the sesshin. What a fucking relief.

Finally permitted to speak after nine days, I ask Aparna how things went for her. "Well, I found it boring after a day or so, and the roshi's instructions didn't help me either, so I made up my own meditation. I summoned everyone I know and surrounded them with light. When the roshi asked me about my progress, I told him what I was doing, and his mouth dropped. He stammered, 'That's not what we're doing here.' I laughed. I was having fun!"

I'm amazed at Aparna's silent rebellion. I tried my best to do the Zazen as the roshi prescribed. It never crossed my mind that I could just do my own thing. The results of my strategy have been nine agonizing days. Aparna is amazing. She's taught me an important spiritual lesson: *Don't be afraid to use your noodle!*

One evening, we're sitting around our campsite. Millions of stars twinkle down at us in the clearing. We chat about the future. I tell her that I want to be with her, but I need to go back to Vancouver. I explain that I can legally work there, that I have friends and family there. If we get married, she'd be able to get a work permit too.

Aparna looks me directly in the eyes for a few long moments and then says, "I want to be with you too. Let's get married."

We return to Santa Cruz and make arrangements to see Babaji, to get his blessing for what both of us believe he instigated. Though we've been blasé about tossing around the word "marriage," we're both aware that taking this step is uncool. Conventional. Straight. Hippies simply live together. What love won't hold together won't be held together. But in this case, the practical necessity of being legal in Canada trumps hippie custom. We're sellouts for a good reason.

On the day when Aparna and I hop onto Babaji's bed to get his blessing, we sit as far apart from one another as we can without falling off. Secretly, I have some doubts. Have I jumped too soon? Did Babaji trick me? There are other gorgeous women around, and I haven't risen above lust. Aparna looks like she's having some misgivings as well. For ten agonizing minutes, we sit like this, barely daring to glance at one another or Babaji. The scratching of Babaji's chalk breaks the silence.

"I knew the two of you would marry when you came here a few months ago."

"But how did you know, Babaji?" We're incredulous.

Babaji shrugs his shoulders, grins mischievously, and scribbles, "Someone told me."

We laugh. We know Babaji's putting us on.

He turns to Aparna and writes, "Why are you so unhappy? You are getting married."

She frowns. "But Babaji, I thought I was supposed to be a celibate yogi?"

Babaji looks at her and scrawls, "You were deluded. Be a householder yogi."

That settles that. We relax.

Aparna calls her parents to share the news. She holds the receiver between us. I listen.

"Hi, Mom! Get Dad on the other line. I've got news. How are you? Yes! I'm wonderful. No, I'm in California. I'm getting married! His name is R.D. . . . he's from South Africa . . . South Africa. Yes, we met about three months ago."

Aparna's Mom asks, "Are you pregnant? Do you have to get married?"

"No, Mom. I'm not pregnant . . ."

Her Mom sobs, suggesting heretically, "Why don't you live together for a while?"

"Mom, we already lived together in Hawaii for more than two months in a tent. The wedding is the day after tomorrow. Would you and Dad like to come?"

Aparna's dad pipes up, "We'll send you money."

"Thank you. Mom, Dad, I love you."

With real affection and muffled sadness, they say, "We love you too."

Then, I call Mom.

"Hello," Mom answers groggily.

"Hi, Mom! I . . ."

"Do you know what time it is? It's 2 a.m. How inconsiderate!" The phone clicks and goes dead. I have no chance to apologize for waking her up or to explain why I've called. The difference between the two calls is stark. I write brief letters announcing our marriage and send one to Mom and the other to Dad.

Two days later, the wedding ceremony takes place in the living room of the house where we met three months earlier. About ten people, including A.D., Jack, and a few other seekers, gather in a circle. Aparna looks stunning in a white dress she's transformed from lace curtains.

For me, she sews a light green wool robe with a big Sanskrit Om embroidered over the chest. Jack, who once considered becoming a minister, has a Universal Life Church license to conduct weddings, and he facilitates the ritual—as Hindu style as a few idealistic spiritual types can throw together. We need prayers, a *yajna*—sacred fire—and blessings.

We begin with a prayer to Lord Ganesh, the elephant God of beginnings and good fortune, the remover of obstacles. We improvise a sacred fire, throw twigs into a Chinese wok, and light them. Jack reminds us that fire symbolizes the transformation of energy. I hold onto Aparna's long dress, and like a poor semblance of an Indian wedding, we step slowly around the flames seven times, throwing grains of rice into the wok. Then, in the vague likeness of Hindu conventionality, we wish each other a long and healthy life along with the proliferation of children. Jack signs the marriage certificate.

It's official. We're married!

A few days later, we hitchhike the thousand miles to Vancouver. I'm returning as a married man with nothing in my pocket and little idea about the future. Our only worldly possession is Aparna's sewing machine. She's lugged it from Massachusetts to New Mexico, California, and now British Columbia.

TWENTY-TWO

We find a cheap basement apartment in Kits within easy walking distance of the beach. Aparna and I get part-time jobs at a health food store next door to the Naam. We aren't making much money, but we're good at living simply. Aparna never complains about how little we have. She always makes do with what's available. I admire her practicality. She tells me she learned it from her dad and living in New England. That's all very well, but I want to make more money.

I continue sharing my Ram Dass lecture with friends and acquaintances. My story of being his road manager provides extra creds, as does the fact that I've met the silent yogi Ram Dass speaks about in his talks. Dozens of people hear the three-hour tape and want copies. This brings up the idea of copying and distributing the tape. My lawyer friend, Sid, also a Ram Dass fan, says the talk is in the public domain, and I should bootleg and distribute it far and wide.

Turns out that a vinyl record is the best way to go. The talk is over three hours in duration and will require a three-record set. The record company demands cash on the barrel. I scramble to get the money together. The three records are packaged in a box, which we call *Here We All Are*. A California spiritual book wholesaler begins distributing *Here We All Are*.

Ed, my friend from Cortez Island, calls from New York. He's been attending Oscar Ichazo's Arica Training in New York. I'm curious about it. I wondered how it went for Ed. Ram Dass told me he had considered attending Arica, but he had gone back to India instead.

"Wow, man! All I can say is you have to come to New York! This is a tremendous opportunity. Arica is the fast track to enlightenment. Oscar understands Westerners better than any Eastern guru."

Something's changed about Ed. He's more confident than I remember him.

"Look, Arica's conducting another training starting in six weeks. You and your new wife should get in on this. Just get to New York!" Then, as if to sweeten the invitation, he adds, "There's a car in Victoria that belongs to one of the Arica people. He needs it driven to New York. The training is three grand a person, but don't worry, something will work out."

What a call. Here we are in Vancouver, working in a health food store, being humble yogis, when we get called to a spiritual training in New York City. According to Ed, "Arica is the highest thing that's ever happened." It must be karma. Good karma, because even our ride to New York City has been laid out. We could live with Ed for a while. We could hang around the Arica scene and see what will happen. It sure sounds like an incredible opportunity for intensive psychological and spiritual training. Something powerful is going down in New York. As for the money. Who knows? Something will work out.

I salivate at the idea of experiencing the Big Apple. I've dreamed of visiting it since childhood. Aparna's also intrigued and adds, "My parents live about four hours from New York. We can visit them, and you can meet them too. It'll be good to see them!"

After three days on the road, we drive into Sturbridge, Massachusetts, the tiny village where Aparna grew up. Her parents' stone house stands out from the otherwise nondescript wooden houses on a quiet middle-class street. "Isn't our house cool?" Aparna asks. "My dad and his brothers built it themselves from fieldstone. I was four when we moved in."

We walk into the kitchen of the stone house. Aparna's mom, Mabel, a sprightly woman with sparkling blue eyes, throws her arms around me and hugs me. Aparna's dad, a short, unassuming guy, also smiles and warmly shakes my hand. He tells me to call him Carl.

Although I can't deny their warmth, Aparna's parents look pretty straight. And they call Aparna "Sandy." I wonder how long it will be before they make comments about my beard and hair. In anticipation of heading east, Aparna cut my hair to shoulder length, and I trimmed my beard, but I haven't compromised that much. It's not difficult to see the underlying hippie.

"We're so happy you're here!" Mabel says. She seems to mean it.

I begin to relax. Maybe I could just be myself with these people. Time will tell. They're part of my family now. Wouldn't it be great if Aparna's parents turned out to be as kind and accepting as she claims? What a change that would be.

We hang around Carl and Mabel's for about a week. They're both first-generation American Swede Finns—Swedes who lived in Finland for hundreds of years, maintaining Swedish as their language. Both of their families of origin emigrated to America. Carl is a research engineer at American Optical. His evenings are often taken up with community activities—school committee, church committee, library committee, and chores—like fixing the bell in the church belfry. Although he doesn't brag about it, he holds thirteen patents, including one for a crucial part in television picture tubes and another for early lasers. "He's a very bright man," Aparna tells me.

Mabel stays home—keeping up the house, speaking to her many friends on the phone, and baking. She's happy to have us around. Every evening, the four of us eat together, a mix of Aparna's delicious fare and Mabel's overcooked veggies. Her delicious apple pies, however, more than compensate for any nutritional deficiencies lost in her limp green beans.

Carl and Mabel's easygoing acceptance makes a stark contrast to my parents. They're Christians who believe in being good and doing good, in loving their neighbors. Although I make no secret of my Jewishness, they take this in stride and even seem to like me. They worship their daughter. This is a loving family. I hadn't experienced anything quite like it. Now I'm a part of it. After a week's stay, we head for New York, relaxed and up for whatever will come next.

Ed sets us up in a small room in his apartment in the Orwell House, an upscale red brick building on the corner of West Eighty-Sixth, across from Central Park. Jack, Ed's brother-in-law, who joined A.D. and me in our Cortez Island yoga sessions and performed our wedding ceremony four months ago, has just arrived from California and plans to attend the training.

In 1972, the economic recession resulted in an overabundance of housing in Manhattan. Upscale apartment buildings—like the Orwell House—have become surprisingly inexpensive, especially if eight adults share a four-bedroom place. Over time, more and more Aricans moved into the Orwell House. Now, about 120 live in the majority of the building's eighty-nine apartments. Aricans pop in and out of one another's living rooms, making the Orwell House a kind of upscale urban commune. The uniformed doorman in the lobby no doubt has made massive adjustments as these weird Aricans take over the building.

On our first evening, we're invited to an Arica party in a large apartment in the Orwell House. Within seconds of walking into the party, it's clear we don't belong. We're simple yogi hippies—it hasn't been that long since we were living in a tent on Maui, without plumbing. This scene almost bowls us over.

A live band blasts electric guitars and synthesizers out of massive speakers. A spotlight focuses on several guys playing African congas. People snake around the apartment, writhing to the beat in spandex. Heavily made-up women bop around holding long cigarettes and glasses of champagne. People are stoned on something, not necessarily grass. We've walked into a full-blown, 1972 New York happening: loud, hedonistic, wild.

The scene is the opposite of what we've strived for. Wearing simple clothes, we stand out. Someone refers to us as "the yogis," a moniker that, in this circle, is not a compliment. But we've made a big investment in getting to Manhattan, and this is no time to turn back.

Oscar periodically addresses the entire Arica school, and we will meet him in due course. An aura of mystery surrounds Oscar. All we have to go on are the superlatives of the Aricans and Ed's enthusiasm. After this buildup, I look forward to meeting Oscar, the *Western Guru*.

Arica appeals to an upscale, well-heeled clientele, and its dress code is a real departure from the casual vibe of most spiritual scenes. To fit in with this more sophisticated big-city crowd, I shave my beard, and Aparna cuts my hair quite short. This is the first time my wife has seen my bare face. We are both relieved that she isn't disappointed. Then she measures me and sews beautiful Arica-style shirts and even seventies style pants. They're the fanciest casual clothes I've ever owned. I feel self-conscious about wearing such flowery duds. Aparna also transforms herself from a gorgeous flower child into a chic seventies fashion plate with a short shag haircut and updated, urban clothes.

After settling in, we meet with the Arica admissions people to discuss the training fee. We can't afford the price tag, but Ed encourages us to work something out with them. I have one ace up my sleeve. I've contacted the Record Club of America, whose headquarters are in New York. I'm sniffing around to see whether they might be interested in disseminating *Here We All Are*. Ram Dass is an underground sensation, and they are very interested.

The Arica musicians have also produced an album. It's titled *Woosoo*. I listen to the record. I think they're pretty good. But what do I know? Nonetheless, a brainstorm comes: introduce the *Woosoo* album to the Record Club of America.

The Aricans are enthusiastic. "If you sell *Woosoo* to the Record Club of America, we'll give you the training in exchange!"

That sounds like a good deal. I contact my guy at the Record Club, who's still hoping to land the Ram Dass record. He agrees to add *Woosoo* to their list. My training fee is waived. I get in touch with Ram Dass. He wants no part of the deal. The Record Club of America sounds like a sellout to him, and besides, he's soon going to put out his own recordings. Still, the Record Club includes *Woosoo* in their next catalog.

Ever resourceful, Aparna sees the need for childcare and begins caring for Arica kids in Ed's apartment. She will be credited for caring for the Arica children in exchange for the training, but she will have to work for several months to pay off the fee. In comparison, it seems grossly unfair that my entire fee will be waived for less than five minutes of work. Maybe I should have driven a harder bargain for both of us, but that opportunity has slipped away.

The initial training will extend over a period of three months and consist of a strenuous physical regime, psychological work, study of Oscar's psychospiritual theories, and individual and group meditations.

Early on, we're put on a high protein, low carbohydrate diet, and as the months pass, many look healthier and trimmer. Arica's an intensive training, with enlightenment as its ultimate goal. We're expected to be available for a minimum of twelve hours a day.

The training is held at a ballet studio in the west seventies on Amsterdam Ave. The trainers are an odd mix of young, sophisticated big-city types, therapists, Big Sur hippies, and musicians. They all studied with Oscar in Arica, Chile, and came to New York City to open *The School*, a training academy for the dissemination of Oscar's teachings.

Our fellow trainees are a ragtag mix of some forty people. Most are in their twenties and thirties, several from Big Sur, and a cadre of straighter middle-aged empty nesters wanting to make up for lost time.

One morning, we're practicing "psycho-calisthenics," a mix of Canadian Air force exercises and yoga. The Rolling Stones' "Brown Sugar" pumps up the vibe. To give instructions, an Arica trainer abruptly pulls the needle from the record in the middle of the cut. We go from loud, frenzied movement to silence.

"Hey, man! You can't just yank the needle off the record! That's the Rolling Stones! That's sacrilegious!" a long-haired mountain man dissents.

The trainer ignores the interruption, demonstrates the correct movement, and places the needle in the groove again. The class returns to the psycho-calisthenics.

After two minutes, the trainer again lifts the needle. We halt in mid-position.

Mr. Mountain Man shouts, "I told you, man, you can't do that! Yanking it in the middle of the cut is sacrilegious!"

The trainer, by now visibly perturbed, condescends and tries to calm the ruffled long hair.

"Harry, I hear you. I understand your attachment. But our purpose here is higher than the Rolling Stones, higher than rock 'n' roll."

Once more, he puts on the record player, and we return to a series of rapid calisthenics.

Out of the corner of my eye, I notice some movement on the second-floor balcony. There, Mr. Mountain Man, Harry, stands, balanced on the banister, holding a garbage can. He waits for the unaware trainer to lift the needle, and then with careful aim, he torpedoes it down. The garbage can smashes the record player to smithereens.

In the ensuing mayhem, Harry yells, "I told you, man! This is the Stones! It's sacred art!"

At that moment, the difference between the West Coast hippies and East Coast spiritual seekers becomes evident. The imports from Big Sur cheer, "Right on, man!" The East Coasters stand quiet, mouths agape. I'm not sure on which side I belong.

One day, we're finally told that Oscar will address the entire school at midnight. This will be our first time meeting this famous Western guru. Everyone gathers in the large meditation hall known as the *Green Room*. Here, we meditate in preparation for Oscar's appearance at midnight. Finally, the clock creeps up to midnight, but there's no Oscar. We continue sitting.

One in the morning comes and goes.

Finally, at 2:05 a.m., a balding, mustached man with dark brown eyes, wearing a black samurai kimono, strides over to a chair on the low stage. He begins speaking. He's intense and earnest, but I can barely understand a word. His thickly accented Bolivian English defeats me.

Over the next months, the training accelerates, and eventually, every waking moment is completely regimented. On Sunday mornings, we meet in Central Park and practice an elaborate walking meditation while holding heavy rocks. New Yorkers must think we're members of some weird stone-worshipping cult. On some level, maybe we are.

The new Arica trainees are invited to meet one-on-one with Oscar, a process that takes a few weeks. When my turn arrives, I walk into the room where Oscar sits, this time dressed in conventional Western clothes. He focuses his laser-like eyes on me. I gaze back.

After a minute of being locked together, he breaks the trance and informs me, "You don't see me. You see your father."

It's clear that the interview is over. I leave, puzzled. I certainly have some stuff to work out with my father; that's true. Mostly, I have a frustrating sense that the gulf between us is too wide to be traversed. Being so far away from one another ensures our issues will remain calcified. I'm sad about it and probably project those issues somehow. Maybe I even unconsciously evaluate men I meet in the shadow of my relationship with Dad. But anyone who'd read a little Freud could make that statement.

Still, Oscar's teachings have had a profound influence on many people, including my friend Ed. He's as enthusiastic as ever. Through the training, he's come out of the closet and is finally living his life as a gay man. We're happy about his awakening, but we don't see much of him anymore. We're on separate paths.

Eventually, the entire school is divided into two groups. The *A* group are the high potential, the beautiful and wealthy people, and the *B* group are the trainees with less potential, the losers. Aparna and I find our names on the B list. A couple of the trainers let me know that they're eyeing Aparna for the A group—if only she'll let go of her silly attachment to monogamy. Then, she would become a member of Arica's inner tribe where attractive women are in short supply. Aparna isn't interested. I'm relieved.

After about three months, a meeting of the entire school body is called. Rumor has it that an important announcement about our future is going to be made. It's all very hush-hush and mysterious, which adds to the anticipation. A senior trainer steps onto the stage and announces, "Beginning next week, each of you will receive a thousand-dollar monthly stipend. This will allow us all to continue with the training." A stunned silence follows. Then people clap and cheer. To us, this is a windfall. But we remain frugal, living simply, true to our yogi roots.

We have an ally in the only other person with a yogic background, a cheery guy named Phil, who wears *mala* beads Ram Dass gave him. Phil returned from India. He's into Sathya Sai Baba, a contemporary Indian saint, famous for manifesting objects out of thin air. Like us, Phil finds the Arica culture too materialistic, far from yogic simplicity. We are all there for the ride, to see what will unfold in this training. In a short time, we become great friends with Phil.

With Phil and two other couples, we take over the lease of a Tibetan diplomat's apartment at the Orwell House. One evening, while settling into the new apartment, Aparna takes my hand and tells me she's pregnant. I'm thrilled to be starting a family with her, but the implications of fatherhood are vague. I just know that I don't want to be an uptight reactive parent. I certainly don't want to beat my kid. That's for sure. I want to engage my kids with respect—not talk down to them or assume I know more because I'm an adult. I don't have a clue how that will translate into reality. Babies need resources. That means money. I'm about to be responsible for a small person who will depend on me for everything. *How will I make a living?* For the time being, Arica rewards our procreation by upping Aparna's stipend by another $225 a month.

A few weeks later, we're given a message with strict instructions: "This is a special meditation from Oscar. Do it at exactly midnight, and the entire school will become enlightened."

At the stroke of midnight, we all begin Oscar's prescribed meditation. I focus and follow the instructions. It's done in an hour. I assess the impact. *Is this enlightenment?* I don't feel different from before. I hear Aparna rustling. "Do you feel anything?" She shakes her head.

"No, feels about the same to me," she says.

We go into the hallway, and soon, Phil and our apartment mates come out of their rooms.

No one is aware of anything particularly different. We go to bed, puzzled. Nothing happened.

Everyone agrees. How weird that Oscar made such big claims about this meditation.

The next morning, Aparna tells me about a dream she had.

"I dreamed I did Oscar's enlightenment meditation and got pelted with money!" She laughs.

Her irreverent dream stimulates my doubts. Although we've learned several helpful exercises and techniques, we're out of place. One day, Aparna says, "Maybe we can take a break. Get some perspective. Let's go visit my parents."

So, we make an appointment with Oscar's right-hand person. This person has short hair and wears a military shirt. Their reputation is as tough as nails. I get right to it. "We're having some doubts about the school. We'd like to take a break and get some perspective."

"There's no doubt! You're out!" The response comes without hesitation.

Though the conversation hadn't gone exactly as we'd planned, we leave in a hurry, elated at our newfound freedom. We skip through Central Park like two happy kids, ecstatic to have been cut loose from a scene that hadn't felt right from the beginning. Neither of us gives any thought to the $2,225 stipend we're walking away from. We leave immediately for Sturbridge.

As a welcoming gift, Carl builds a bed for us from an old Ping-Pong table. He and Mabel are happy to have us. They're easy to be around—the most tolerant and accepting people I've ever met. They truly believe in "live and let live." They have faith that things will work out. After the pressured, judgmental atmosphere of Arica, being with Carl and Mabel is refreshing.

We settle into the stone house. Soon, the issue of making a living arises. Sturbridge is a small place. Everyone knows each other. A former classmate of Aparna's offers me a job as a bartender in his Italian restaurant. We need the money, so I take the job knowing nothing whatsoever about mixology. The waitresses help me up to a point, but after one irate customer pours my drink down the sink, I know the time has come for me to quit. In a few days, I get another job as a janitor at the local high school. I start at 11 p.m. and work until about 3 a.m., a similar schedule to my old janitorial job at the Black Bottom in Montreal.

Carl and Mabel take off on a trip in their camper for a few weeks. We're in charge of Carl's elderly father, who is quite senile. When he sees me dressed in my overalls and a small-peaked cap for my janitor job, he assumes I work on the railroad. He regales me with stories about his travels by train as a prohibition proselytizer in the old days. His long-term memory seems good. When Aparna shows up with her protruding belly and bare feet to say goodbye before I leave for work, the old man becomes agitated.

"He's going away to work on the railroad, and he's leaving her here with me. How can she take care of a baby? She doesn't even know to wear shoes!"

TWENTY-THREE

An aerogram arrives from Mom. She'll be coming to the States for a visit during the Christmas holidays and would like to spend some time with us. Hearing from Mom is unexpected, and we're excited. This will be her first visit to North America, and she'll meet Aparna for the first time.

An Arica friend invites us to stay in his house near Boston while he's away. It's a big house surrounded by a forest with trails. A carpet of sparkling white covers everything.

Mom will delight in this classical New England white Christmas vibe.

With Mom's imminent arrival and Aparna five months pregnant, fatherhood is on my mind—my own impending fatherhood and my relationship with my father. It's an old wound, scarred over but unhealed. The continuity between generations is not intact. I'm sad.

He's so far away in every sense.

I decide to try something out of the box to move the ball further up the field. I don't have Dad's home phone number. All I know is that he and Eve live near Clifton Beach. I can't bring myself to call his business. The ghosts of my past make it unpalatable. Besides, it's the weekend. I don't want to wait until Monday.

I call the international operator and blurt out a single run-on sentence: "I'm trying to reach my father in Cape Town . . . not a word in seven years . . . about to become a father myself." The operator listens to the anxious male voice from Boston. She softens her professional presentation. "Hold on, dear, I'll help you." She contacts the South African operator. A businesslike male says, "There's only one Harry Fuchs in the directory," and provides the number to the international operator. She stays on the line to make sure I reach Dad.

The male voice that answers the phone is unfamiliar. It's not Dad.

"Yes," the voice informs me. "I've heard there's another Harry Fuchs—no relation—but I don't know where he lives or his number." The operator thanks the man and tells me to hold on.

"Do you have any relatives who might have your father's number?"

I rack my brain. I quickly decide that contacting Penny will be too much of a hassle. Too much explaining. Instead, I say, "Well, there is an old family friend who will surely have Dad's phone number." Traute! She's Eve's mother.

Mom's friend. The operator connects to the South African operator again for Traute's number. She calls the number and tells me to speak directly to Traute.

"I won't charge you," she says.

"Hi, Traute! This is Gary. I'm sorry to call you out of the blue, but I'm looking for my Dad's phone number. I'm calling from the USA. I haven't talked to him in years."

"Mein Gott, Gary!" Traute says in her thick German accent. A long silence follows. I can hear Traute wheezing on the line. My operator ally is still listening in.

"Ma'am, are you there? Can you please give us Mr. Fuchs's number?"

Traute comes back on the line. "Yes, I'm here, but I can't give out his father's number."

"Why not? He just wants to speak to his father. He's calling from the United States."

Another awkward silence. Then Traute says, "His father is very ill. I don't want to upset him."

"For God's sake, ma'am, it's his son! He just wants to talk to his father." She's outraged.

"I'm sorry. I can't give you his number. Goodbye."

The operator stays on the line and consoles me. "I don't understand why this woman won't give out your father's number. It's not right."

Despite the operator's kindness, my attempt to reach Dad through Traute is a failure. I'm disappointed. I chalk it up to karma—residual bad karma between Dad and me. I don't know about Dad being too ill to receive a call from me. I don't know what to think about what Traute said. I don't even know if it's true. But her refusal reinforces the sense of being locked out.

Rejected. Othered.

Mom arrives with the white Christmas carpet covering the ground. It's New England winter at its most pristine. Bright sunny days and crisp air. Mom's happy to see me. It's been five years since we saw one another. She and Aparna seem to be hitting it off well. After a few days of rest and catching up, we pile into the Volvo station wagon that comes with the house and head for Vermont.

Mom loves Vermont's landscape. She says the rolling hills remind her of Austria. In Stowe, we stop at the Trapp Family Lodge. The Von Trapp's emigrated from Austria to the US in 1940. I'm reminded of that fateful night when Mom and Dad saw *The Sound of Music*. I flash back to that terrible night, to the violence, to Dad leaving. If Mom is having the same memories as me, she's hiding it well.

Back at our friend's house outside Boston, Mom is relaxed and enjoys taking walks on the snowy paths around the large property. She's invigorated by the cold air and sunshine, so different from South Africa and so similar to her childhood in Austria. One day, I lead her to a beautiful clearing in the woods. I decide to be more open with her about my lifestyle.

"Mom, I've got some really good marijuana. Would you like to try some?"

"Well, I don't know. Maybe I'd try it. Can we stay out here, though? I like being in the snow," Mom responds without judgment.

I hand her my pipe and light it for her. Mom's been a smoker for years, and she accepts the pipe like an old hand. She takes three or four hefty tokes. Within minutes, she's singing in German and skipping down the snowy path like a happy kid. I'm thrilled to see her so uninhibited and happy. This is the Mom I love.

"I'd like to paint or draw," she says. "Do you have any paper and crayons, maybe?"

I walk back to the house and find a sketchbook and some colored pencils. I head back to Mom. She's sitting on a rock, eagerly awaiting my return. She takes the sketchbook and begins drawing the scene around her. I take off, happy that our visit is going so well.

About an hour later, Mom returns to the house. She hands back the sketchbook and colored pencils. She says, "You remember my old friend Toffee from Cape Town, the psychiatrist? He moved to Great Neck, New York. I want you to make an appointment with him. He's the one person who can help you. He's known you since you were a little boy."

I'm taken aback. An hour ago, Mom was a happy camper. "No way, Mom. I'm not sick. I don't need psychiatric help. And if I did, I would never go to Toffee. For years, I thought he was after you. He always visited when Dad wasn't around. There was something weird about that. I never trusted him then, and I don't trust him now."

"You're in no position to make a judgment about whether you are well or sick," she asserts. "You are on drugs."

Mom looks quite stricken, like I've just refused the medicine that's sure to cure me. I don't argue. There's no point. Mom arrived with this plan—no doubt fueled by Ernst and Walter. There's no way I'll consider talking to her friend, Toffee, the shrink. After a while, she stops mentioning it.

On Christmas Day, Carl and Mabel welcome us into their warm stone house for the holiday. They're happy to meet Mom. A large Christmas tree decorated with colorful ornaments and brightly wrapped presents dominates the living room. It's about as Christian a scene as can be imagined, but the loving atmosphere soon dissolves my conditioning about Christmas and Christians. Carl's a bit of a flirt and charms Mom with stories about his early life as a farm boy in Sturbridge. Mom's surprised that a man who's come from such a humble background has become an accomplished researcher and inventor. She likes clever people and is quite taken with him. When Mabel hands her a wrapped present from the base of the Christmas tree, Mom is delighted with her gift, *The Sturbridge Federated Church Cookbook*.

A few days later, Mom leaves for Vancouver with a bit of a doorknobber. "I'm going to discuss with Walter and Ernst whether it might be a good idea for me to emigrate to Canada. I'd like to be closer to them, and you as well."

TWENTY-FOUR

Aparna is approaching nine months in her pregnancy. In Sturbridge, she's had great medical care from her uncle's partner, a fellow obstetrician. Her parents expect us to have the baby at the local hospital. Aparna's adamant. "I want to have this baby at home, not in a hospital."

Homebirths are rare in 1973, and Carl and Mabel are concerned. We get along very well with them, but we have spirited differences about two things: Carl has strong opinions about nuclear power—he's all for it and we're instinctively against it—and both Carl and Mabel think home birthing is irresponsible and dangerous.

Carl consults with his brother, Eddie, the obstetrician who delivers most of the babies in the district. "She's healthy. It's no problem having the baby at home." This relieves their concern to some extent, but the subject keeps coming up. They're nervous about our rather casual attitude. In the hippie subculture, increasing numbers of women are having their babies at home. We want to be with our loved ones in a relaxed atmosphere. Doctors and hospitals are only necessary when there's an emergency. In any case, midwives are preferable and know more about birthing than most doctors. Responsible medical backup is important, but it's backup.

Finally, we consult with the only doctor we know who delivers babies at home, Hector Prestera, an Arica graduate. Hector agrees to deliver the baby if we come to New York. Phil is open to the idea of a home birth. He invites us to stay at his new apartment on West Eighty-Third near Broadway.

In the weeks before the baby's due, back in Manhattan, we run into Aricans every day.

Several of them exclaim, "Wow! You guys look great! What have you been doing?"

We accept the compliment without going into details. The reality is I'm a failed bartender and a successful late-night janitor in a high school. Still, we both look better than when we were striving for enlightenment, exhausted and disenchanted.

By mid-March, Aparna's due any day. I arrive back at Phil's apartment late one evening and implore Aparna, "I'm so tired. Please try not to have the baby tonight!" About an hour later, Aparna wakes me up. "I think I feel contractions."

"Really?" I mumble. "Sure it's not your imagination? Maybe try to sleep."

She takes my hand. "Really. I feel a trickle of water. Put your hand between my legs."

I obey.

Without warning, the bed is flooded with a gush of water.

I jump up, escaping the flood.

She laughs. "I told you."

Whatever stupid comments I made about being tired are quickly forgotten.

Now Aparna's in a mode I've never seen before. Ever the yogini, she rides the contractions like a champion surfer rides waves. She sits on her haunches, rocking back and forth, her breath and being in tune with the universal mother, with nature's eternal birthing rite.

Soon, about fifteen Aricans show up. They're here to witness the birth. In Arica, home births are a public gathering, a sacred party.

I hold Aparna's hand. She looks into my eyes. We connect. She's completely amazing, meeting each contraction without fear. Without warning, she bolts upright and throws her hands over her vagina. One of the Aricans, a nurse midwife, comes over to examine her and then calmly goes to the telephone. I hear her say, "Hector, if you plan on presiding over this birth, you better hightail it over here."

Hector arrives and calmly directs the event, slowing down the action.

Aparna gives birth to a gorgeous girl, a tiny, little being. I've never experienced such joy.

The birth has been so natural, so obviously the way babies ought to be brought into this world. Witnessing my own daughter's birth is an amazing experience—deeply spiritual, forging an unspeakable bond with mother and baby. I whisper the mantra *Om* into our baby's ear. I place her in Aparna's arms. Our little one looks at every person surrounding the bed. She focuses, assessing each one. Satisfied, she turns to Aparna's breast and nurses.

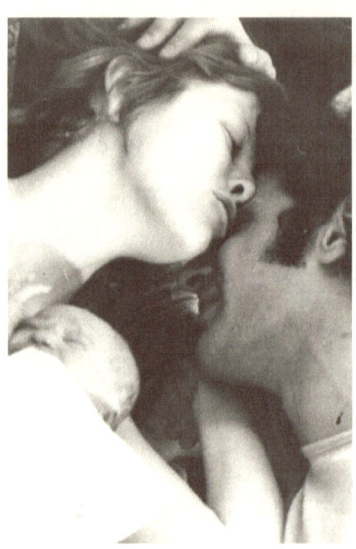

Everyone melts away. We're left to care for the baby girl. She's beautiful and perfect. We name her Kavanah, the Hebrew word meaning intention of the heart, the state of mind found in spiritual devotion and creative endeavors.

About a week after Kavanah's birth, we're invited to rejoin Arica—on the condition that we perform some remedial meditations. Arica wants to establish centers in various cities around the country. We hadn't intended to rejoin Arica, but with our expanded family, the prospect of receiving a stipend again is tempting. Stability has become much more important.

I think of creating an Arica center in Vancouver. Aparna likes the idea. I know Vancouver, and I have landed immigrant status in Canada. I'm the only Arican who can work in Canada without a work permit. I also know Vancouver's spiritual scene. As an Arica trainer, I will have a legit teaching gig at a higher level than the funky yoga classes I previously offered.

Arica approves a center in Vancouver and agrees to provide seed funding. A few trainers indicate that they might show up once we're settled. Jack, the man who acted as clergy at our living room wedding, is interested. Phil says he might show up too. Minimally, we'll get free plane tickets back to Vancouver.

Before we leave New York, Rabbi Schlomo Carlebach—the singing rabbi—invites me to take a *mikveh*—a ritual bath—with him. Sid and Lindy, who knew him, had introduced us when he came on a tour to Vancouver. I liked Reb Schlomo. I loved the joyous spirit he evoked as he got everyone to sing together. He and Reb Zalman were the only two rabbis with whom I felt an affinity. I'm honored Schlomo has invited me for a ritual bath.

After we've immersed ourselves several times in the mikveh, Schlomo, draped in a towel, beads of water running down his face, looks me right in the eye and says, "*Nu*, what's with you? *Really. Really?*" I tell him about my toxic relationship with Dad. He recommends I make an appointment with a rabbi of his acquaintance. Aparna accompanies me. I tell the good rabbi the story. Aparna adds a few details I've forgotten. The rabbi listens thoughtfully.

"It's good you came to see me," he says. "I can tell you are in pain and want to heal this wound. We rabbis have a procedure when two disputing parties are physically distant from one another. I can contact my rabbi counterpart in Cape Town. He will convey your message of goodwill to your father. That is the best I can do to help you."

Leaving the rabbi, I have some fresh hope that something positive might come as a result of my visit. I can leave New York knowing I've left no stone unturned about healing my karma with Dad. But, with time, I will understand that this indirect method of communication will not bear fruit.

TWENTY-FIVE

We lease a big house in Shaughnessy, one of Vancouver's upscale neighborhoods, and offer our first forty-day full-time training. Ten participants show up.

Then a vision comes to me: outdoor training in the summertime in a remote area, a tent community where people will live together cooperatively and do the training. We could use a circus tent for classes and set up a communal kitchen and bathrooms. The training would be enhanced by everyone living together twenty-four seven. Everyone thinks my idea is brilliant. I'm introduced to Bill Wine, who owns a large piece of land in Rock Creek, in the southern Okanagan Valley, a desert area about three hundred miles east of Vancouver.

Bill asks for a nominal fee for leasing the land and wants to participate in the training. Jack can build anything, and he checks out the Rock Creek land. He returns with his assessment. "Look, it's pretty remote—a long dirt road to get there. Very hot and dry. Parts of the land have been clear-cut, and a fire swept through the area a few years ago. It's still pretty barren and unattractive, but it'll work. There's a creek we can pump water from. I can build a kitchen and shower area and set up gas stoves and refrigerators." This is an upbeat report from Jack, who's very quiet and usually says only what's necessary.

I place ads in the *East-West Journal* and *New Age Journal*, the only two national periodicals read by the crowd we believe are our target audience.

> *Experience the Forty-day Arica Enlightenment Training in an outdoor community. Sleep in your tent or camper. Remote British Columbia desert location. $175 includes tuition and meals.*

Jack spends over a month preparing for the event. He builds an amazing plumbing complex, pumping water out of the only creek on the land, supplying showers for thirty people at a time, and running water for the kitchen. He creates food preparation areas and installs industrial gas cooking stoves and refrigerators.

Aparna and I arrive to see the spot where we'll teach "the highest path to enlightenment mankind has ever known." Aparna checks out a barren field, a broken down barn, an abandoned chicken coop, surrounded by a forest of clear-cut stumps, the remaining ravages of a lumber company's rape of the land. She thoughtfully observes, "This is the ugliest land I've ever seen."

Within a day, the teaching staff, our fellow New York Arica trainers, arrive with their Gucci luggage. Jack shows them to their army tents.

Over 150 people sign up from all over North America, and even a few from Europe. They show up in caravans, colorful VW vans, campers, converted school buses, or with packs on their backs stuffed with small tents. A small village of tents and RVs begins to take shape. This is the biggest turnout for an Arica Training, ever.

Jack calls for volunteers to erect the huge circus tent that will serve as our training center. Working in unison, twenty people lay the massive tent flat. They raise the tent and secure the various poles and beams. It stands tall and proud, a funky spiritual beacon in the desert.

Just as we're about to begin the training, a white delivery truck drives up and stops in a cloud of dust. The uniformed driver gets out of the cabin, goes to the refrigerated back, and emerges with an enormous bouquet—the type suitable for a fancy wedding. He calls my name. It's quite surreal. I can't believe anyone would send me a huge bouquet here in the middle of a remote desert. But the flowers are indeed for me.

Arica headquarters in New York sent them to congratulate me for dreaming up this forty-day, communal training in the desert. Someone in the New York office intended to be thoughtful, but Bill's farm is no place for fancy bouquets. Maybe they thought that Rock Creek was some kind of resort, but we're in the middle of nowhere. A huge bouquet of flowers is off-the-wall.

Finding enough pots for the flowers proves difficult.

The community works quite smoothly. Jack's genius in setting up the shower and water systems makes being in the hot and dusty desert tolerable. Aparna, with the help of a rotating crew of participants, manages the preparation of three vegetarian meals for two hundred people every day. We even have a day care run by Margaret, a tall, fresh-faced woman from Boston. By the looks of things, she and Phil have taken a liking to one another. While Aparna and I teach classes and see to the smooth running of our outdoor community, Kavanah's in loving hands.

Classes are held in the circus tent. We leave the sides open so breezes will cool us off while we do the vigorous Arica exercises. The participants are well-fed and clean, enjoying the training. The scene resembles a well-functioning commune, a kind of temporary kibbutz.

When we aren't working, we hang out with Phil and Margaret in the hay barn. We hadn't been good social mixers in New York, and we don't make any particular effort now. For me, much of the spirit had been killed back in New York when all 150 of us in the school had been classified into A and B groups. Secretly, Aparna, Phil, and I—the original yogis—took pride in being in the B group. It was a badge of honor of sorts—like being hippies in a straight society.

Thirty-five days into the training, Phil, Aparna, and I are summoned to an urgent meeting of trainers at a motel in Osoyoos, a small town about twenty miles from Bill's land. We're told to drop everything and just show up. We haven't left the tent community since arriving there some six weeks earlier. The directive surprises us, but we drive over to Osoyoos. We show up as instructed. About ten A-group Aricans are gathered in chairs set up in a semicircle. As the three of us walk in, they abruptly stop talking. The three empty chairs facing the group are where we're supposed to sit. Phil, Aparna, and I take our seats and face the group. We're greeted with unsmiling stares.

Jack is the designated spokesperson. "We've decided that the three of you must circulate," he says in a monotone. Circulation is a euphemism for being fired from Arica.

The three of us sit there silently for a few seconds, look at each other, shrug, stand up, and walk out.

Phil, ever the cheerful optimist, notices a Dairy Queen and says, "Let's go get a peppermint milkshake."

At first, we're shocked at the abrupt expulsion. What a power trip. What a crude ritualized rejection. I'm pissed, disappointed, and relieved all at the same time. Pissed because these jerks would never have dreamed of a communal training under a circus tent in the remote desert. The powers that be in New York had sent flowers of congratulation only to have their underlings fire us for not fitting in. I'm disappointed in Jack's betrayal. Clearly, he's put allegiance to Arica over his friendship and our history. I mean, shouldn't a friend like Jack, the guy who married Aparna and me, have given us at least a heads-up? Something like, *Just so you know, friends, here's what's coming down* . . . Part of me wants to retaliate with my own power. Being the sole signature on Arica's Vancouver bank account, I could withdraw the money that the Rock Creek venture has brought in. But I don't want a cent. I sign the account over without a word. Deep down, I'm relieved. I don't want to spend another second in Arica or have anything further to do with the organization. The power trippers have done us a favor. We don't fit. We never did.

TWENTY-SIX

The next day, back in Vancouver, I run into A.D. on the street in Kits. I haven't seen him in the almost two years we've been in Arica. We've lived through tumultuous times together. I love him like a brother. But before we can catch up, he blurts out, "Babaji's coming to Vancouver tomorrow! It's his first visit to Vancouver!"

This news is amazing. We've been in New York for almost two years, much longer than we anticipated, and we haven't seen Babaji since our wedding. How strange that he's coming to Vancouver the day after Arica tossed us out. Uncanny. If we had stayed until the end of the Arica Training, we would have missed his visit to Vancouver.

The next morning, we head over to see Babaji. He's sitting on the floor in Sid and Lindy's living room in Kits, on a simple cushion, surrounded by a small group of people. Smiling and radiating, his dark complexion and long black hair contrast with his white robes. I remember how much I love being around Babaji. He's the opposite of materialistic. He doesn't use money and owns only a few personal possessions. He left home when he was eight years old and has spent his entire life steeped in practicing and teaching the *dharma*. But he's more than just a yogi. He's fluent in six languages. On his path, he's learned architecture and facilitated the building of temples in the Himalayas, building walls, working side by side with devotees. He's an exotic artifact of ancient mystical India, an inimitable ambassador of East to West. We're buzzing with excitement.

Babaji writes on his chalkboard. A.D. reads it aloud. "My friend in India asked me what do Western yogis like?"

He waits a few seconds. Then he turns the small chalkboard over and writes, "I told him they like ice cream!" Recognizing the truth of this North American yogi weakness, everyone cracks up.

Babaji's mischievous sense of humor is contagious and sets us at ease. After the intensity of the last few years of Arica, of all the changes in our unsettled and insecure existence—including becoming a family—just sitting with Babaji feels reassuring. He's like a beacon beaming the way on the spiritual path. I tell him a little about our Arica excursion. He gets a kick out of the claims to rapid enlightenment. "People will believe anything. Nothing is more important than regular *sadhana*—spiritual practice."

Then Babaji reaches for Kavanah. She settles comfortably on his knee and plays with his chalk. After a few minutes, he takes up his chalkboard and writes, "She is very smart."

Seizing the moment, I ask him, "Babaji, would you give her a spiritual name?"

"Her name is Manju."

We rent a sunny apartment in a run-down Victorian mansion on Spruce Street, on the edge of an upscale neighborhood near Vancouver

General Hospital. At some point, the landlord converted the big house into thirteen small apartments, with a communal bathroom on each of its four floors.

After living on Spruce Street for a few months, the landlord offers me a job as caretaker. In exchange for collecting rents, we can stay in our apartment for free. I grab the opportunity.

Manju becomes the resident munchkin. Since she was four months old, she's greeted strangers with an enthusiastic "Hi!" They stop in their tracks. Mouths agape, they exclaim, "That baby talks!"

We're still in the same apartment when Manju says her first sentence. "I like it." She's not yet a year old. She wanders the apartment and the world, inspecting everything with care, and declares, "I like it!" Sometimes a thoughtful murmur. "I . . . like . . . it." She practices different intonations and cadences.

One day, I arrive home to find A.D. following her around the apartment. Every time Manju says, "I like it," A.D. echoes her tone but says, "Oh, wow, I like it." By the end of this tutorial, Manju has mastered hippie-speak. She now says, "Oh, wow, I like it," with variation and devotion. A.D. is proud.

I write to Babaji that I've become the caretaker of the Spruce Street house. He answers, "Slowly fill the house with yogis."

We begin hosting regular *Satsang*, spiritual gatherings, on Sunday mornings in our living room. In the beginning, six or seven people show up for the weekly event. Like us, these are spiritual hippies who've heard about Babaji and are interested in yoga. Gradually, these Sunday Satsangs grow. We meditate, chant, and read passages from various Indian holy books or a letter from Babaji. With more people, our chanting evolves into what we call *rock 'n' roll kirtan*, featuring musicians on guitars, drums, and cymbals, while everyone dances and chants in Sanskrit. We joke that we're either going to levitate the house or fall through the floorboards. It's a lot of fun.

Gradually, old renters become more and more uncomfortable with the comings and goings of long hairs with beards who make a ruckus on Sundays. Nothing they can do. I'm the caretaker. One by one, they vacate the house. I fill their apartments with spiritual seekers, most of whom are Babaji devotees. The big old house begins to resemble an ashram.

A.D. moves into a studio on the top floor with an eccentric named Narendra, a tall, skinny Argentinian mathematician with a heavy accent. Narendra jokes, "You and I should form a society: the brotherhood of people from bad countries—me from Argentina and you from South Africa!"

Early in the summer of 1974, Babaji stays with us for ten days. I've kept a studio apartment vacant for him. Aparna will cook his meals. Soon, word gets out that Baba Hari Dass—the silent Himalayan yogi Ram Dass has spoken about and now written about in his newly published book, *Be Here Now*—is staying on Spruce Street. Dozens of curious yogis and spiritual seekers descend on the house.

We sit with Babaji on futons and cushions on the floor of his room. Most of the time, we are quiet, meditating, but people ask questions. I sometimes sit next to Babaji and read his chalkboard to the assembled group. This role demands being completely present, in sync with the silent man's transmissions, an opportunity for learning.

The days with Babaji pass quickly. Sometimes the vibe is lighthearted, sometimes more serious. One morning, a stranger sits with the group. Eventually, he speaks up. "Babaji, I'm going to prison for dealing dope. How can I survive in jail?"

Babaji looks at him intently for several seconds.

"Treat prison as an opportunity for *sadhana*. Find freedom in your mind, and you will not be imprisoned."

When someone complains about difficulties in his life, Babaji responds, "Nothing is easy." I contemplate this for a second and blurt out, "But Babaji, it's easy to pee!" He laughs at my quick comeback but then adds, "Not easy to pee if you can't." He has me on that one.

Even this simple response awakens the truth that life often involves suffering and that what one person takes for granted can be a source of great difficulty for others. I love getting Babaji to laugh at my jokes, while at the same time imbibing his wisdom.

I get a job as a part-time mailman at the Kits post office. For a college dropout with a wife and baby, being a mailman isn't a bad gig. It fits my lifestyle and gives me a certain flexibility, and being a mailman is a step up from being a night janitor at the Black Bottom or the high school in Sturbridge. Aparna begins pursuing a master's degree in teaching at SFU. She's heartbroken about leaving Kavanah—who we now call Manju—with a babysitter five days a week, but she feels that she needs the credential to earn a living.

Jean often invites us over for Sunday brunch—feasts of bagels, lox, hummus, tahini, and scrambled eggs. Walter and Jean love making a fuss over Manju. Their son, Toby, is now about seven, and they're thrilled to have a new baby in the family. One visit, while everyone gets down to the business of eating, Walter steers the conversation around to his favorite subject. "The situation in the Middle East is very bad again. The Israelis got caught with their pants down in the Yom Kippur War!"

This refers to the recent Israel-Arab war of late 1973—when Egypt and Syria had preemptively attacked an unsuspecting Israel. Walter had himself fought in the Israel Defense Forces in 1956 against the Egyptians in the Sinai, and he loved to hold forth to a captive audience.

After taking up an inordinate amount of airtime with inane details, Walter finally takes a breather. He reaches for some pickled herring. Jean seizes the moment and asks, "Would anyone like more tea or cake?"

Jean's attempt at hosting upsets Walter. He gives her a withering look and slams both of his hands down on the table. The plates and silverware shake. We're all as meek as mice.

"Quiet, Jeanie! The master is still speaking!"

Jean looks over at Aparna with a smile. They connect. They recognize they're kindred spirits. Both cool blond shiksas with good senses of humor, a powerful antidote to the madness of King Walter.

When we're safely out of earshot, Aparna and I laugh our heads off.

After my postal route, I often spend afternoons at Banyen. I read about spirituality and marriage and family life, what Babaji calls "being a householder yogi." Becoming a husband and father has broadened my spiritual search beyond that of a solitary seeker treading the path to enlightenment.

My time at Banyen influences me in another way. Banyen publishes an occasional journal called *More Light!*—an extensive review of noteworthy New Age spiritual books. It's packed with inspiring quotes and cool graphic arts. Banyen's review journal gets me thinking about doing something similar for the Satsang. We could publish our own yoga journal, an informal newsprint magazine dedicated to various aspects of yoga, meditation, and the spiritual path. I propose the idea to Babaji. He encourages me to do it. So, A.D., Narendra, and I begin writing articles for the first edition. I focus on householder yoga, how to deal with problems in relationships as opportunities for growth and change. A.D. writes introductions to the eight limbs of yoga and about the principles of Ayurveda, India's ancient healing system. Narendra writes an article on self-inquiry, an introspective method for finding one's true identity. Lindy, who we now call Sharada, creates beautiful graphics that we intersperse to highlight themes and break up the text. Gradually, we accumulate enough material for the first edition. I learn printing layout. In early 1976, *Dharma Sara: A Journal of Yoga Sadhana* is published. It's great—funky yet informative.

Aparna and I devote ourselves to creating a vibrant center in Vancouver. We renovate space on West Fourth—suitable for fifty or sixty people to participate in yoga classes. On Sunday mornings, we hold busy Satsangs with people singing and dancing. The energy of the *rock 'n' roll kirtan* rocks the new venue. Aparna is the perfect Satsang lady, just the person to welcome new people into the scene.

TWENTY-SEVEN

Mom emigrates from South Africa to Vancouver in mid-1976. She has reasons for wanting to leave South Africa, the country she adopted as a young woman and where she had her children. It had always felt foreign and unwelcoming to her. She hadn't remarried and recently ended a sad love affair with a prominent Afrikaner, a married man. My sister, Penny, and brother-in-law, Benny, have been married for several years now and are busy raising their two small children. Penny and Mom's relationship has remained strained. Here in Canada, her fourth country, Mom will again make a fresh start close to her two brothers, who are important to her. Of course, I'm also in Vancouver with my young family, but I get the impression that Mom hasn't emigrated to be with me or us.

Mom rents a small apartment in Shaughnessy, the suburb adjacent to Kits. She's sent all her furniture and worldly possessions from Cape Town to Vancouver in a large shipping container. When she receives notification that the ship has docked, I rent a big truck and drive down to the warehouse to pick up her things. At the port, the supervisor explains that there's been a bad storm somewhere between Cape Town and Vancouver. The container with all Mom's belongings has been lost at sea.

I search for a way to break this shocking news to her. I'm scared to be the messenger of such bad information.

At first, Mom's in denial. "You must have gone to the wrong place. They made a mistake. There must be some misunderstanding."

Mom is arriving with some small savings, but she's not a wealthy woman. Walter and Ernst will help her, but their generosity is not boundless. She will need to work. It's hard for her to face that everything she owns in the world has been lost, that everything she's collected and saved to create her new home is at the bottom of the ocean. But after a while, the truth sinks in. She has insurance, but only for a small fraction of the actual value of her belongings. She adjusts, trying to find joy in the new *tchotchkes* she finds on East Main Street, but not without what she calls—*a bittere gelegte*—a bitter laugh at the mysterious twists and turns of life. When I tell her that Babaji says losing her belongings at the bottom of the ocean "means a new beginning," she scoffs and says, "What a cold fish! How does a penniless monk know about belongings? He doesn't even have a pot to pee in!"

Even as a woman in her fifties, Mom is still beautiful and magnetic. People are drawn to her effervescent personality. Back in Cape Town, she had an entourage of admirers—her sewing students and many friends would often come calling. But that was a public face. She was different at home; in private, she sometimes lapsed into depression.

A honeymoon phase of Mom's Vancouver reunion with Ernst and Walter begins. What a sight to see these three together—the older sister reunited with her younger, now middle-aged brothers, in yet another new country. The three siblings have not lived in the same city since World War II and speak with nostalgia about their childhood in Graz.

"Remember the time before the Nazis, before Kristallnacht, when Papa was well-to-do and owned three men's clothing stores? Everyone knew him. Even the chief of police was his customer. He had a motorbike with a sidecar. He taught us about the Austrian Empire and Afghanistan. And remember Maxie, our pet monkey? And our governess?" They hanker for the old country, for a time that seems magical in their memories. Ernst, a diabetic, frequents a Viennese café for Austrian coffee and apple strudel. In a weak moment, Walter admits that he—also diabetic—does the same.

The three fall into a groove, bantering and bickering in a mixture of English and German, sprinkled with Hebrew and Yiddish. From the word go, crude insults are normal fare. Ernst knows Arabic and Russian vulgarities, and he delivers them theatrically, exaggerating each lewd syllable, causing us all to laugh out loud. I can see how Mom developed her voice. With brothers like Ernst and Walter, if you want to be heard, you have to speak up, make your opinions known, or risk being ignored. Mom will not allow herself to be sidelined by her younger brothers. Not then, not now.

On Sunday afternoons, after Satsang, Aparna and I take Manju to visit Mom at her new apartment. Mom lights up around Manju, but she won't be a babysitter. She pays attention in small spurts, gushing her emotions. But she still acts like children are to be seen, not heard, and taken care of by others. From the outset, arguments punctuate our visits. As soon as I make any sort of comment, Mom starts. "What do you know? You're a nobody. Don't think because you're married and have a kid that you know something now."

I hate Mom's attitude, her judgments, her insults, and her aloof entitlement. These visits are depressing. Mom has things to say about all aspects of my life, from my appearance to my lousy career, my weird religious cult, my strange food, and my lack of respect and ambition. I've also married a shiksa. Both of her brothers had done the same, but somehow that doesn't count.

Aparna's not a sycophant, and Mom doesn't like it.

"She might be a good wife," she says as though Aparna's not sitting right there. "But she's a lousy daughter-in-law. I would never have chosen her." Hadn't I seen Dale Carnegie's *How to Win Friends and Influence People* on her nightstand?

TWENTY-EIGHT

After two years of living at the Spruce Street house, Sid (now *Sudarshan*) and Lindy, (now *Sharada*) invite us to live with them communally on a farm in Abbotsford, about an hour from Vancouver. They're one of the few couples in the Satsang who also have a child. Their daughter, Daya, is two years older than Manju.

The Abbotsford farm offers us the opportunity to experience living in a small back-to-the-land spiritual commune while still being close enough to Vancouver to maintain our link with the center there. I'm insecure about giving up my mailman income and moving to the country, but Aparna has completed her master's and gotten a job teaching in an elementary school. So, at least for the time being, money isn't an issue. With the landlord's consent, A.D. takes over the caretaker role. He moves into our apartment.

The farm has a large main house where Sharada and Sudarshan

live, a few barns, and several run-down sharecropper shacks. Two other couples also live on the farm. One couple, Stew and Isha, have converted one of the run-down shacks into a cozy home. Another couple, Frank and Anuradha, from Saskatchewan, have renovated a big old-school bus into a deluxe hippie RV. Frank has also built a good-sized workshop in one of the barns where he makes cedar toys. The land is covered in acres of raspberries, which grow wild except for the month of July when migrant workers descend to harvest the fruit.

We move into one of the larger shacks on the farm—a real *pondok* in South African parlance. It has a functioning indoor toilet, which is a blessing, but the whole place requires significant cleaning, clearing out, and painting. Undaunted by the problems, we set to work to make it into a home. Aparna finds a classic woodstove, and we install it in a central spot. With her decorating eye and hands-on ingenuity, a transformation begins to unfold. We line the rooms with cedar shakes and build a floor with cedar planks, all from Walter and Ernst's mill. Now the little house smells like a big cedar chest, and the woodstove turns the previously cold and damp space into a warm and pleasant home.

I build a playhouse bed for Manju in the second bedroom. She loves to climb the ladder and play on the top platform. She's comfortable on the farm, shuttling back and forth between our little house and the main house where she plays with Daya. Sharada is particularly fond of Manju.

Manju's a precocious kid, surprising us with wisdom far beyond her years. Once, when Aparna and I are locked into an argument, she toddles up to me, lifts herself to her full height, pats me on my thigh, looks me right in the eye, and says, "Daddy, I'm a person too!"

In the heat of our argument, we've ignored Manju entirely. Now I look down at her. I recognize the being behind the eyes, the small person who asserts that she's not just a little kid who can be conveniently ignored; she's a fully aware being, an equal member of our little family.

The look in her eyes—the deep intelligence and knowledge—will always remain with me.

Manju's made her presence known. In one unexpected moment, she has challenged my conditioning about children and what it means to be a father. A huge gift.

Manju shows dramatic artistic talent even before she turns three. She has Plasticine for mushing around, one of her available "toys." We're impressed when one day, sitting in her high chair, she sculpts Snow White and all the Seven Dwarfs. Her hands are small, but she creates figures with confidence, like she's accustomed to working with the material. We realize this is a person with remarkable artistic talent. We feed her encouragement and every conceivable art material we can afford.

After fixing up our little house, I spend part of my time on the commune trying to become a back-to-the-lander. I buy a chain saw and chop wood for our stove. But fully dedicating myself to the practical aspects of living on a communal farm is a shoe that doesn't fit. Though I enjoyed my time on Givat Brenner working in the kibbutz gardens and orchards, now, years later, I find that I don't love working in the garden, chopping wood, or preparing communal meals. Living communally in the countryside sounded attractive, but the excitement has worn off. The intimacy of our new relationships is more difficult than I imagined. Although I think of myself as extraverted, I can't help feeling stifled living in such close quarters with the other Satsang members.

My relationship with Sudarshan, whom I consider a friend, has become strained. While we willingly relocated to the farm, there's something weird in the dynamic of a communal living situation where one family has a much nicer house than the rest. It hardly feels like we're all on equal footing. It makes me more determined to make more money. I'm tired of being a bottom. The nagging question is . . . how?

Penny and her husband, Benny, come to visit from South Africa. I haven't seen Penny in eleven years. She's never met Aparna or Manju. We've lost touch.

She and Benny have been married for a decade, have two kids, and live in a nice house with a swimming pool in a prestigious suburb of Cape Town. They're doing well. They're as straight as a summer day is long. I'm apprehensive about meeting them after all this time. In a way, I'm coming out. Penny and Benny have known me in an altogether different incarnation, a much younger one. At thirty, I'm not the same person they knew in South Africa. I'm still emerging. In worldly terms, I've been unsuccessful. No doubt Mom has filled them in on the basics from her perspective—a college dropout, taking drugs, sucked into a weird cult, and now living in a hippie commune.

I stand on the farm's driveway awaiting Penny and Benny's visit. I have a good view as their car arrives and slowly rolls down the driveway toward me. I see Penny's face through the car's open window. She looks a little older than I remember, and her expression is frozen in horror as she sees firsthand the funky farm and the sharecropper *pondoks*. Penny isn't a good actor. Her disbelief at the low station to which her brother has fallen is clear. We muddle through the afternoon, and they sleep over in Sharada and Sudarshan's much more acceptable house.

Early the next morning, out for my usual walk, I meet Penny

and Benny—also out for their morning constitutional. Somehow the subject of yoga comes up in the conversation. "You know, old *Boet*," she says, using the colloquial Afrikaans for "brother" she's used with me since we were kids. "Many years ago, I also got into yoga. I found it helped me relax, to get beyond my problems. I had a wonderful teacher. She was like a therapist to me. You weren't the only one who had a tough childhood, you know."

"Yes," I agree. "We went through a lot together. How are things with you and Mom these days?"

"Well, the truth is things have never been good between Mom and me," Penny responds. "All my life, Mom thought making me a dress was love, but that's not love. I've never felt that she loved me—just for me." I get where Penny's coming from. I remember the strife.

"And Dad?" I ask. "How are things with him?" I'm curious about any news. Other than a brief note wishing us well on our marriage, I haven't heard from Dad at all. He hasn't responded to any of my letters.

"We've kept things peaceful with Dad by keeping our distance," Penny says. "He and Eve are very involved with their new family. They have Eve's two sons from her previous marriage and their daughter, Candice. She's a very sweet and pretty little girl, almost the same age as our daughter, Loren. The two of them are cute together, but it can be difficult with Eve. Dad is always complicated. Last year, when I had my thyroid op, I never heard a thing from Mom, but Dad called—the first time in years—and wished me well."

I'm flooded with memories and feelings of my Cape Town youth.

"And South Africa?" I ask.

"The economy seems okay," Benny answers. "But my business is close to downtown, and there are many more demonstrations since your day. Now, I see groups of demonstrators in Adderley Street doing the toyi-toyi, the African National Congress protest dances. They sing political slogans, and hundreds dance together. You wouldn't believe the energy—it's awesome, and it's frightening at the same time. It could be a sign of what's to come. We're keeping our eyes on the situation, but already, Whites—especially the educated ones—are exiting in droves."

"Enough about our family and politics," Penny says. "It's too depressing! The past is the past. Let's get off this and go do a yoga session. That's a much better way to start the day!"

So, we head to the yoga room in the main house and practice together. Penny's very flexible, and it's fun sharing our newfound commonality. Though we've drifted apart over the years, I feel a rekindling of the bond I've shared with my feisty little sister since early childhood.

Keeping up writing and publishing a regular yoga journal has proven to be too much. I've underestimated the amount of work and expense involved. We decide instead to publish a book with our material. This will be a one-time effort, and we won't have the pressures of deadlines. I begin working in earnest on the Satsang's new book—*Between Pleasure and Pain: The Way of Conscious Living*. I believe our writings will put the Satsang on the map. I learn every facet of the book publishing process, from writing to layout to printing and distribution. My enthusiasm and elbow grease pull the Satsang's publishing project along. The effort gives me purpose, and I spend many days alone, focused on writing or laying out the book's pages in preparation for printing. I've learned many new skills and become familiar with the world of publishing.

Shortly after Penny and Benny's visit, Carl and Mabel visit us at the commune farm. They're amid one of their cross-continent trips.

Manju's three. Mabel and Carl are delighted to see her. They stay for a month, and despite the countercultural stereotypes about straight parents, they fit in. Carl himself grew up on a farm and is comfortable fixing things and working in the gardens. Mr. Fixit on the farm is a welcome addition. Mabel plays with Manju for hours and helps with meal preparation. They love the communal meals. In some ways, they're better commune members than Aparna and me. Aparna's parents are special people—steady, reliable, and kind, good people who love their daughter, adore Manju, and wholeheartedly accept me. Whatever my karma with my parents, having Carl and Mabel on my team has changed my familial karma for the good.

After a year, the Abbotsford farm commune dissolves. Sudarshan and Sharada, the glue holding the scene together, announce they'll be moving to a new farm in Aldergrove. Sudarshan makes clear that our family is not invited. He says the new farm will be a family compound. Sharada and her brother have come into some inheritance and want to live together as a blended family. Despite the rationale, we feel rejected and more aware than ever of our lower-class status.

We put out word that we're looking for a new home. Call it good karma, but Ariela, an Israeli friend who types for me, tells us she's moving out of her cute hobby farm in Surrey, much closer to Vancouver. We jump at the opportunity. Our new little farm comes with goats, chickens, and two roosters that scare Manju when they fight for dominance. I chase them away, yelling in Afrikaans, "*Voetsek!*" much to Manju's frightened delight. When one of the roosters comes at Manju, claws bared, she kicks it full force in the chest. He flies through the air, squawking ever after to keep his distance from our little samurai.

The Satsang's new book—*Between Pleasure and Pain*—has finally been published. It's satisfying to see the finished product. I'm proud of it, but now I'm obsessed with an idea I've been quietly working on for years. It's called *The Marriage and Family Book: A Spiritual Guide*. I've become the Satsang's make-it-happen publisher—writer, editor, designer, and layout artist. The Satsang's publishing efforts have flourished under my leadership, but I want *The Marriage and Family Book* to be independent of the Satsang. I want it to be my own expression. I begin dreaming of approaching a real publisher in New York when the manuscript is ready to show.

TWENTY-NINE

In the beginning, building Babaji's Satsang in Vancouver enthused me and filled me with purpose. With time and more people, politics has emerged. Things are changing. I've invested enormous energy to put the Satsang on the map. Now there are well-organized retreats where hundreds learn yoga at beginning, intermediate, and advanced levels, meet privately with Babaji, eat great vegetarian meals, and enjoy themselves with fellow yogis.

Between Pleasure and Pain has reached far and wide. The Satsang is popular.

Competing agendas have emerged. A blaming and shaming culture has developed. I blame myself, and others blame me for my anger and shakiness under pressure. Everyone has a direct line to Babaji via first-class mail.

Too often, meetings about the smallest details turn tense and competitive. It's as though deciding where to host Sunday Satsang will determine the fate of humanity. It's absurd, laughable, but I fail to see the humor. The Satsang has become my life purpose. My relationship with Babaji is the source of my spiritual value. I dread these meetings. I have a bad habit of speaking my mind, even when I know I'll pay the price. My impatience and frustrated outbursts are met with whispered speculations about my level of enlightenment. I hate this spiritual judgment. I'm deeply committed but not always the picture of a calm yogi. By temperament—like my father, mother, and uncles—I have a short fuse. Like many South Africans, I'm competitive and brash, outspoken. When I feel I'm right, I can be self-righteous, aggressive about getting what I want. In language I will learn later, my *emotional intelligence* is limited. And the Canadians tend to be milk-toast mild and conflict-phobic while holding on to their position without budging an inch. No one compromises or even listens with openness and compassion.

As an emerging group, we don't have a clue about group dynamics. We don't know how to articulate goals or settle differences. It's a kind of free-for-all, all of us writing to Babaji, looking for the all-wise Daddy to bless us with his approval. We're a dysfunctional family, "Guru brothers and sisters" vying for approval. We're not even friends. We're trapped in sibling rivalry with siblings we haven't known for very long and don't like. Significant tensions have built up.

Eventually, Babaji weighs in. "Ashram politics are the worst."

The next summer, Babaji comes to Vancouver. We hold a public *darshan* at Sudarshan and Sharada's new farm. I invite Mom to the event, wanting to introduce her to Babaji and share a glimpse of what

I've become so dedicated to.

A crowd of about eighty people gather in a small meadow on the farm. People sit on the grass in front of Babaji. Dressed in pure white as usual, he sits on a cushion playing with three or four kids. They climb all over him. Babaji loves kids, and they love him. He has all kinds of ways of alluring them—from candy to magic.

Yogis from all over BC have come for their annual Babaji fix. It's a cool scene. People who haven't seen one another since last year's retreat hug and laugh together.

Mom shows up and sits cross-legged on the grass like everyone else. In her elder years, Mom's bright auburn hair and silk scarf stand out in the crowd. Things quieten down.

We sit in silence for minutes. Gradually, one by one, people begin asking questions.

A woman asks, "Babaji, I feel afraid of life sometimes. I don't know why. How can I overcome my fear?"

Babaji writes, "What is fear? Fear is the brother of anger. When you accept fear, you will understand why you are afraid." He pauses and looks at the woman.

Then he continues, "Anger is a weapon for self-protection. Sometimes to protect us from our guilt." The woman begins crying.

An earnest young man asks, "Babaji, is doing yoga postures a complete path?"

"Yoga is more than just standing on your head!" Babaji laughs.

"Yoga *asanas* are not only physical. *Asanas* are a trinity of mind, breath, and movement. The slower the movement, the more mind, body, and breath will be in tune. It is a meditation. A perfect yoga."

"Babaji, I know meditation is important, but sometimes I don't feel like meditating. I just want to relax with a cup of coffee and read the paper. What should I do?"

Babaji quickly scribbles, a big grin on his face. "Kick yourself!"

Everyone laughs.

As the day unfolds, I let Babaji know that my mother has come to see him. He asks me to point her out, then writes on his chalkboard, "How are you?" and points the question at her. Mom's surprised that Babaji has addressed her directly. She answers in her signature breezy way, "Oh, fine, thank you."

I watch the interchange carefully. I notice Mom's automatic answer, her fake smile. This may fool some people, especially people who don't know her, but Babaji sees right through the façade. He just nods and continues taking questions from other people.

After the *darshan* ends, most people leave, and only the core Satsang group remains. It's a good opportunity to ask Babaji about Mom while his interchange with her is still fresh in his mind. "Babaji, what should my attitude toward my mother be?"

He immediately picks up his chalkboard and writes, "You must protect yourself from her."

Yes, that rings true. I've been trying to do that instinctively for years, but Babaji's directness shocks me. Nevertheless, this is a great opportunity. I plunge ahead. "What about my father, Babaji?"

Babaji makes no response for several seconds. Then he takes up his chalkboard and writes, "Your father is like a Hitler."

This description hits me like a ton of bricks. Babaji has just met my mother whose family has suffered so much under Naziism, and now he compares Dad to Hitler?

I'm ashamed that a holy man has likened my father to Hitler. I'm mortified that he's pronounced this in front of the entire group. Who wants Hitler for a father? Not me. But what's Babaji really saying? Does he mean that Dad is authoritarian, rigid, autocratic, controlling?

Before I can respond, someone in the group says, "That explains a lot about R.D."

Babaji writes, "R.D. = much anger, much love."

I'm reeling. I'm unprepared for Babaji's uncensored perceptions of Mom, Dad, and now me, words that everyone hangs onto like they're hearing the Gospel from Jesus. I'm exposed as a person with "much anger." The "much love" part doesn't balance things out. My mother's manipulative, my father's a fascist, and I, myself, an angry guy. I just want to hide, but I can't.

Narendra, my eccentric Argentinian friend, says, "R.D. has always loved me." That friendship reaches back before the Satsang, yet he's outnumbered, and I cannot be consoled.

Four hundred people sign up for Babaji's annual retreat, held for the first time in the Okanagan valley at Camp Hatikvah, a Jewish kids' camp Aparna and I found. The evening before the retreat, about twenty Satsang members arrive to prepare. Soon after Babaji arrives, he writes, "400 people arriving tomorrow. Vibes are bad. You will scare people. Do *Vamana Dhoti*."

Babaji's term—*Vamana Dhoti*—refers to a purification method we've learned as a part of our yogic training. It's a technique that yogis practice to purge and purify. Traditional *Vamana Dhoti* requires one to drink a quart of water mixed with a teaspoon of sea salt and bicarbonate of soda. This noxious mixture facilitates vomiting of the stomach's toxic impurities. Babaji modified this physical yogic purification rite into a psychological antidote for contaminated ashram politics. His Vamana Dhoti is about purging our emotional and interpersonal issues with one another, in one intense session. The intention is that we air out our differences and be ready to move forward free of the toxic weight of our challenges with one another. Think *group primal scream*. Newly cleansed, we will be free to host a large number of people.

As Babaji turns to leave, someone says, "Have a good sleep, Babaji."

Aparna laughs. "He's not going to sleep. He's going to watch everything that happens here from his room in the inn." Babaji swivels and glares at her.

I drive Babaji to the inn where he's staying, about two miles from camp.

As soon as I return, the group launches into the session. In the blink of an eye, things deteriorate. As the person in charge of the retreat, I receive a good helping of verbal bile.

"You're so full of shit! You don't act like a yogi!"

"You're an asshole! You manipulate everyone so that you can be closer to Babaji!"

"Yeah, R.D. You're out for yourself!"

And so on. I'm shaking. Vulnerable. Holding back tears.

Then Sudarshan weighs in. "You've held the reins of the retreat for the last three years. I'm taking charge of the next retreat!"

Sudarshan's power grab and the group's criticism leave me feeling isolated and unappreciated. I'm in charge for now, but I'm alone.

The psychological and emotional vulnerability the *Vamana Dhoti* process demands would be difficult in any group setting—even with the guidance of an experienced group therapist, but no one in the Satsang has any training in group dynamics. We're unskilled at articulating our issues, giving and receiving constructive feedback, or any of the basics necessary for healthy communication in a group. The session is an eruption of anger, blame, justification, spiritual judgment, and fear. I'm trembling. I don't feel safe. I don't trust these people. They're so angry. They don't like me. I hate these sessions. I hate how I handle myself under the pressure. I'm unsure of my place in the group. Unsupported. Unappreciated. Rejected.

At dawn, after a few hours of sleep, I drive over to the inn to pick up Babaji. He's standing outside his room, waiting for me. He's writing on his chalkboard. "When Anandi said you manipulated, why did you hide?"

I'm blown away. How does Babaji know what Anandi said last night?

"I don't know, Babaji. She wasn't very specific."

"You were hiding." He taps the chalkboard a couple of times to emphasize his point. He doesn't need to speak. He projects certainty. The truth is, I'm not sure what he means. I was "hiding"? I didn't think there was any place to hide in that god-awful group. *Jesus, I'm a basket case! He's right. Fuck!* I don't know. Seems like no matter what I do, I'm wrong. He hasn't commented about Sudarshan taking over the next retreat. Perhaps he's secretly encouraged him to challenge my leadership. One never knows what Babaji's saying behind one's back. But then again, he makes fun of people's foibles in front of the group too.

In a few minutes, we arrive at Camp Hatikvah. The devotees surround the car, eager to receive Babaji. He immediately begins giving feedback to people about their behavior during the session, pointing out specifics about what they said, when they cried, or when they lost their tempers. He doesn't let anyone off the hook. Everyone is awestruck. We've never experienced anything like this before. How can Babaji know what happened during the *Vamana Dhoti* session? So specifically? This is an apparent display of clairaudience, a form of telepathy. He can sit two miles away and tune in to our interactions.

Aparna asks him, "How do you know?"

"It's not a high *siddhi*—yogic power. It's like watching TV." He leaves it at that.

Babaji's telepathic display has reinforced my faith in him as an advanced yogi. But the *Vamana Dhoti* session has only added to my insecurity. I don't feel cleansed or peaceful. I'm humiliated and ashamed, a spiritual failure. I'm hurting.

I teach yoga classes in the mornings. It takes my mind off myself for a few hours. I love yoga, but I'm wounded.

In the afternoon, Babaji organizes us into canoe jousting teams. A person perches on a canoe gunwale, waiting to knock the enemy—equally precariously balanced on the gunwale of another canoe—into the water. Everyone inevitably falls in. Babaji kills himself laughing.

He teaches us stick dancing, an Indian martial art form that's easy to learn and great for coordination. Everyone loves having fun. Playing is a part of Babaji's teachings. Formal practice—*sadhana*—comes first, but playing is also important, and Babaji is like a big kid. He loves it when we laugh and carry on.

In the evening, after dinner, the entire community gathers in the camp hall. The atmosphere is lighthearted. The core group puts on skits about seeking and the spiritual scene. Some of the skits are hilarious. With the energy of 400 God-intoxicated yogis chanting and dancing, accompanied by an impromptu band of guitars and drums, the camp hall rocks like a Stones concert. I can't help being concerned that we'll go through the rickety floorboards. No one seems to care. They'll leave camp, and I'll have to explain to Camp Hatikvah what happened.

Despite the core group drama, the retreat turns out to be a great success. The attendees all speak with enthusiasm about next year's retreat.

Back in Vancouver, I continue my research into the spirituality of marriage and family life. In addition to Babaji, I interview many of the spiritual teachers who come to Vancouver. Reb Zalman Schachter-Shalomi spends a day with me and provides a progressive Jewish perspective. When Stephen Gaskin, the popular hippie guru, comes to town, I sit with him and his group, discussing their large commune's lessons about relationships and natural childbirth. Pir Vilayat Khan, the Sufi teacher, takes me under his shawl and blesses me and my work. I write to various spiritual teachers, requesting contributions from their perspectives. I collect dozens of articles and interviews. I compile a substantial manuscript. I send it off to Schocken Books in New York. They published Martin Buber's wonderful book, *I and Thou*. I figure I may as well aim high. I don't know about agents or the protocols for getting published—what you're supposed to do, the right way, etc. I just send my manuscript with a letter describing my concept for the book.

Two months later, Seymour Barofsky, the executive editor at Schocken Books, calls.

"We'd like to publish *The Marriage and Family Book*!" he says.

"We can give you $1,500 as an advance against future royalties."

I can hardly believe what I'm hearing, but I reply, "That's great, Seymour, but it cost me $1,500 just to type up the manuscript."

Without skipping a beat, Seymour replies, "Well, we'll give you $3,000. How's that? We'll publish spring '78."

Well, that's very fine. Schocken is the only publisher to whom I've sent the manuscript. This is my first foray into the world of books as an independent entity, separate from the Satsang and Babaji's oversight. I like the freedom of doing my own thing without having to gain anyone's approval. But it's a bit complicated. Though Babaji's teachings command a prominent place in the book, he will see that he's only one of dozens. Babaji always honors the universality of different approaches, but I get the sense that he thinks the yogic path is superior. What do the eclectic contents of my book say about my allegiance to yoga and to him?

THIRTY

We're back at Camp Hatikvah. It's late summer 1978. Two years have gone by. It's the last day of another wildly successful retreat. I'm in charge again. Sudarshan held the reins for a year but then admitted I was better at organizing the retreats and requested I take back the leadership role. There seemed to be some support for me taking over again, and I was easily had. But the country-city divisions in the Satsang have calcified.

Some good things have been happening with my publishing endeavors. *The Marriage and Family Book* has just come out. It's beautiful, full of inspiring pieces about relationships from the perspectives of different Eastern and Western religions and spiritual paths. Every page has gorgeous photos of nature, couples, kids, or teachers. There's a lovely shot of Babaji smiling. We're in it, of course, and Manju. There are great photos of A.D. and Kalpana's wedding in a Hindu temple. I'm proud. Banyen features it in their window. And more publications are on the horizon. Schocken has contracted for two books. Aparna has written *Yoga for Pregnancy and Birth*, and both of us are well into *Ways of Being Together*—a guide for couples.

I've found a big old house near Kits that will make a great communal Satsang center. It has room enough to hold Sunday Satsangs, a day care that will employ three or four Satsang women, a large yard, and lovely apartments for a core group of city dwellers. Never mind that Sudarshan and others are looking to establish a country communal yoga retreat. A.D. and his wife, Kalpana, and a few others have indicated they want to be a part of the new city scene.

Aparna, Manju, and I will be boarding a plane for a month-long visit to Aparna's parents and to meet with Seymour Barofsky at Schocken Books in New York. We'll leave for Boston directly after the retreat. We'll move into the new center when we get back.

I have an appointment to see Babaji before he leaves for California. It might be several months before I see him again. He's waiting for me, standing in the doorway. He doesn't invite me to sit down. He writes and thrusts the little chalkboard toward me.

"The problems in the Satsang are your fault."

I'm in shock. My stomach cramps. I'm off-balance, lightheaded. I instinctively try to defend myself. My words come out weak and unsure. "How can the problems in the Satsang be all my fault, Babaji? I'm sure I play a role, but there are a lot of us involved." I'm vulnerable, but I'm also indignant. Babaji insists.

"You can't take much," he writes. He's angry, convinced that he knows the truth. Babaji has never unleashed this stone-cold judgment on me before. He's an omnipotent disciplinarian like childhood authorities in South Africa. I've been here before. Only this isn't South Africa with an anti-Semitic bully, a stupid teacher, or a dumb army officer. We're at a spiritual retreat, and this is Babaji—the person I've elevated to the highest throne. And he's being contemptuous.

Then he writes, "I don't care if you stay or if you go."

The entire exchange has taken no more than two minutes, but a psychic two-by-four has slammed into me. The Satsang's problems are my fault. I'm of no value to Babaji. He doesn't care whether I stay or leave. His indifference is frightening. Suddenly, I'm on my back foot, alone and teetering. After knowing Babaji for seven years, he's finally come out with his real thoughts about me. I'm less than a slug to him.

I leave him without another word, like a dog who has displeased his master, my tail tucked between my legs, holding back tears. I stay alone for hours, confused and ashamed. I don't say anything to anyone, not even Aparna.

I'm shaken up. I'm depressed. I want to hide. What am I doing with my life? Where have I come from, and where have I landed? What's really important to me? Who am I? The Satsang and Babaji are my life.

I begin entertaining secret thoughts about leaving the group. But where would I go?

Where would *we* go? What will Aparna think?

Aparna, Manju, and I fly to Massachusetts. I'll relax in Carl and Mabel's stone house. I'll sort things out. We'll return to Vancouver in time to move into the new urban commune with our fellow Satsang members.

PART THREE: KISMET

Call it kismet—fate, *bashert*, destiny, ordained, meant-to-be, grace, Providence, the hand of God—whatever—but things sometimes happen for mysterious deeper reasons.

Kismet's origins found in Turkish, Arabic, and Hebrew—a portion or allotment.

A musician must make music, an artist must paint, a poet must write, if he is ultimately at peace with himself. What humans can be they must be.
—Abraham Maslow

THIRTY-ONE

We arrive in Boston on a gorgeous, blue-skied autumn day, the air crisp and clear, the leaves a riot of color. I've never experienced a New England fall before. I'm in love with the beauty and graciousness of the season. New England's sunny fall weather is welcome after Vancouver's gray dampness. It lifts my mood.

Being with Carl and Mabel strongly contrasts the judgment and pressure of our Vancouver lives. The stone house Carl and his brothers built is a kind of sanctuary, simple and uncomplicated. We stay in a small ground-level apartment below their garage—one bedroom for Manju, a living room with a sleeper bed and a stone fireplace, an eat-in kitchen, and a bathroom, cozy with lots of light. We take walks and eat. Mabel sets out cake, cookies, pies, and tea three times a day, every day, like clockwork. We sit around their kitchen table—eating, talking, and laughing. As the five of us come together, we bond as an extended family. I feel at home. I'll never tire of Mabel's apple pies. Still smarting from Babaji's rejection, this simple family acceptance means a lot to me. My family-of-origin dinner table memories are punctuated with tension, arguments, putdowns, and violence. No such shadows enter here.

Then, one dinner, Carl tells us about some difficulties he's having at work. I'm on the edge of my chair, listening to his explanations about a cutting-edge eyeglass manufacturing technique that he's developed. He claims his process will completely disrupt the prescription eye market. "We can make lenses in four seconds. But the pencil pushers have Jewed down the budget for my new technology."

Jewed down your budget? Is this the moment I've secretly dreaded? To find out that my Christian father-in-law is anti-Semitic, deep inside a Jew-hater?

"You know, Carl," I say. "I'm Jewish, and it hurts me when people speak about Jews in that way. My mother escaped Naziism by the skin of her teeth, and I was bullied as a boy because I'm Jewish."

From the look on Carl's face, I see he's mortified.

"I'm so sorry! I never thought of it like that."

Carl is a thoughtful and sensitive man, conscientious about doing the right thing. This incident has affected him. He's ashamed.

"I believe God is love, and love is God," he says. I believe him. He's a good man. He accepts me without judgment.

I still haven't shared any details about Babaji's condemnation with Aparna. That's my shame. He once cared enough to bring us together. But now he's singing a different tune. "I don't care if you stay or go." The words are colder than ice. Over and over, they rattle around my brain. I'm boxed in. On one side, he doesn't care if I stay in the Satsang. On the other side, he doesn't care if I leave. What have I done to deserve this rejection? How is it all my fault that the Satsang has problems? I justify. I'm racked with self-pity. I'm angry. I want to be appreciated, accepted, loved by this man.

Over the last five years, the Satsang has grown enormously. I've been a leader from the get-go. Have I taken too much power? Am I too abrasive? Is my lack of wholehearted support for the rural yoga center behind this? Is it an ego trip getting published by Schocken in New York? Have I gotten too big for my britches? Is it ashram politics—*the worst politics*—as Babaji himself said? Is he scapegoating me? Blaming me for the dysfunctional group dynamics?

As for the Satsang, I have mixed feelings. I'm resentful of the endless criticism. I crave appreciation. The group has been my primary focus. The Satsang serves my spiritual needs and provides a community of Babaji devotees, yet I can count the friends among them on less than one hand. Now, the life I've worked to create in Babaji's name is riddled with politics and dysfunction. Still, I hang onto hope. We'll return. The communal house will be a place of belonging. I'll once again be valued in Babaji's eyes.

Two weeks into our Sturbridge visit, A.D. calls from Vancouver.

"The Satsang has had second thoughts about moving into the communal house. We've canceled the lease."

We're both shocked. It's most unlike A.D. and the other yogis to make a rapid decision without warning the two of us, the project's champions. I sense Babaji's hand at work. Once Babaji disapproves of something, that's it. Done. Over. He's scuttling the house. A.D.'s call is Babaji's second rejection in the past month.

Aparna's reaction surprises me. "If they don't want that house, if they don't want to live together and create a new center in Vancouver, then there's no reason to go back."

Finally, one evening, a few nights after A.D.'s call, after Manju's tucked in bed, as Aparna and I sit by the fireplace, I confide in her.

"I've been meaning to share with you what happened with Babaji at the retreat," I begin.

"Yes." Aparna waits and listens.

"Honestly, it was a heavy meeting. I'm still confused by it. Babaji said the problems in the Satsang were my fault. He didn't care if I stayed or if I left. I'm still reeling. I can't figure out what I did to make him so angry. And now, A.D. tells us they aren't interested in sharing a new Vancouver commune house anymore. . . . I'm pretty sure Babaji's behind it."

Aparna looks at me thoughtfully. By the fire, in the house that her family built, surrounded by love and security, there's no rush to get someplace else.

"That must have been painful. I know what you put into building that scene. I was there," Aparna says.

I'm grateful to hear her reassurance. She had also put in a lot and been a close witness to what had come down.

"I told you when A.D. called, I don't want to go back," Aparna says. With my revelation, Aparna's resolve is redoubled. "There's nothing to go back to. Not Babaji. Not the Satsang. I'm sorry, but not your family either. I'm done with Vancouver."

"Living here with my parents, I feel free and confident. I craved Babaji's approval. I fell into an insecure, infantile mentality." She imitates a begging child. "'Please, please love me.' It must have been irritating. It's not Babaji's fault. I just wasn't one of his favorites." She laughs before saying, "Babaji is the judgmental father I never had."

I have to agree that there isn't much to go back to, but it's not so simple for me. Vancouver has been my home for ten years, my entire adulthood. It's where I've cut my teeth outside of South Africa. I'm at a crossroads.

Even now, hurt and humiliated, I follow my habit. I write to Babaji and express my uncertainty about my life's direction. In less than a week, a response arrives. It's brief.

"It is better to move toward something than away from something else." And then, as if to confuse matters more, he adds, "Everyone says Aparna is the best Satsang lady."

"Now he wants us to come back. No way." Aparna snorts. "He was always looking for someone to take my place. Girija, Anuradha, anyone but me. I was ignored and unappreciated." Aparna's clear. I'm still struggling. Babaji's cryptic koan about moving toward something versus moving away from something intrigues me. What's the truth of that for me? Vancouver is a beautiful and happening place, but making a living there has never been easy. At least for me.

For the first time, away from the Satsang, we have the opportunity to put our creative energies into our own projects. We're having some success. *The Marriage and Family Book* is out. Schocken have contracted with us for two more books. They're making nice noises about another idea—*The Complete Guide and Cookbook for Raising a Vegetarian Child*. This gives me a sense of purpose and direction. It's the closest thing in our world to "moving toward something." Slowly, as we focus on our futures, Babaji's strong influence and the Vancouver Satsang's tentacles begin to lose their hold. I'm coming to see how I've ceded my power to Babaji, how I've set myself up to be hurt and disappointed. How his rejection is opening up new possibilities.

We make arrangements to visit Seymour Barofsky at Schocken and meet with an agent who's interested in representing us.

Connie Clausen is known for her success as an editor. She's the brains behind two bestselling books—*Watership Down* and *Jonathan Livingston Seagull*. Now Connie's a literary agent. She's the archetype of a brash New Yorker—charismatic, opinionated, always on the lookout for a new hit. She's taken a liking to us, like we're cute long-haired flower children who know nothing of the ways of the world and deserve her protection and guidance. She isn't wrong.

Her first intervention is unexpected. It resonates like a gong in a meditation hall.

Connie looks at us with her slick New York brusqueness. She says, "Your names—Gary and Sandy Fuchs. So 1950s . . . Fuchs—Fucks! Terrible! Change them."

Aparna said she'd like to stop using the spiritual name—Aparna—given to her by Babaji. She'd like to be called "Nina," the name Carl wanted to give her when she was born. Carl had deferred to Mabel and agreed to the more common name, Sandra, but in the end, everyone called her Sandy, and Carl invariably remarked, "Sandy's a dog's name."

Aparna has never called me Gary, always by my spiritually-sanctioned nickname—R.D.

A year ago, I approached the Kabalarian Society in Vancouver. They specialized in analyzing peoples' names according to numerology. Their analysis of my names uncannily pinpointed several aspects of my history—divorce, alienation, emotional trials. They claimed that continued use of my name, Gary Fuchs, would basically lead to a load of further bad karma. Based on numerological principles and my birthdate, they proposed several names that would offer more propitious karma. I didn't feel comfortable presenting myself as Ravi Dass, though Schocken had insisted we use our spiritual names for *The Marriage and Family Book*.

Now that we've decided not to go back to Vancouver, I'm again making my way in a new country—the United States of America. Like many who have arrived on these shores, I want a fresh start. I pull the one Kabalarian name that had resonated. "Connie, how about the names Michael and Nina Shandler?"

"Oh, yes!" Connie jumps. "Michael and Nina Shandler! Much more modern."

The writing team of Michael and Nina Shandler is born. We

begin a highly creative phase, researching our various projects, writing, editing, rewriting, etc.

There are moments of loneliness in Sturbridge, but so much is happening with our publishing endeavors that those feelings are fleeting. The possibility of a breakthrough fuels our enthusiasm. We both like the creativity involved in manifesting a book from idea to finished manuscript. We're on a roll. Schocken contracts *The Complete Guide and Cookbook for Raising Your Child Vegetarian*.

I'm researching nutrition and couples' communication for the books in the pipeline, but much of the load falls on Nina. Our new books involve subjects in her area of expertise—yoga for pregnancy and raising vegetarian children. We've been vegetarians for years, and Nina has a lot of ideas about how to make vegetarianism attractive and appetizing for kids. In addition to writing, a lot of her time will be spent in the kitchen. I've always admired her as a culinary artist, and I now experience Nina's mad scientist side. She goes at it like a witch brewing secret potions, mumbling recipe details to herself.

Amid her culinary fervor, Nina pitches Connie some more book ideas: *Holiday Sweets without Sugar, Homemade Mixes for Instant Meals the Natural Way*, and *How to Make All the Meat You Eat from Wheat*. Only one day passes before Connie calls back.

"Rawson Wade Publishers wants all three books!"

We're thrilled at this validation.

I talk to A.D. periodically. He lets us know that the Vancouver Satsang has significantly dwindled since we left. Several of the original core group members have moved to Salt Spring Island and are establishing a yoga center there. I'm not altogether surprised to hear that things hadn't gone well in Vancouver after we left. I feel some vindication. We're both competent and dedicated, and replacing us would be difficult. But I'm not tempted when A.D. asks if we'd consider returning to Vancouver. A.D.'s my friend. I appreciate his loyalty. But I have mixed memories of life in Vancouver. Things are happening for us here on the East Coast.

We appreciate having a peaceful haven at Mabel and Carl's house to get back on our feet after five years in Vancouver, but we're also clear that this is a stop on the way. We don't want to live with Carl and Mabel permanently. Sturbridge is the New England equivalent of a South African *dorp*—a more genteel version of a one-horse town. It's a perfectly nice village, even charming, but the New Age hasn't touched down here. While Manju fits in—loves taking the yellow school bus to kindergarten and has a sweet group of friends, Nina and I do not belong. Our difference—long hair and beard, Nina's long flowered skirts—mark us. It's like we've stepped off the cover of *Time* magazine declaring our membership in an outlandish counterculture. Of course, Nina has never conformed to the all-American nature of her lovely small town. In her high school yearbook, other girls declared their favorite things: football, cheerleading, senior prom, Elvis. Nina proclaimed her love of mystics, beatniks, and Kahlil Gibran. As for me, I feel as conspicuous as a fur-hatted Hasid in Nina's hometown. Needless to say, we have no intention of idling in Sturbridge indefinitely. With the advances on five books in our future—meager as they are—we begin considering our next move.

THIRTY-TWO

We begin scouring the territory west of Sturbridge in search of a new home. Carl announces, "You two belong in a college town." *College town*—what's he talking about? I'm a college dropout whose only visible means of employment is as a janitor. Sounds off to me.

Our reconnaissance trips take us to investigate a Sufi community and meet a children's book author. On both trips, we pass through Northampton, a small city with a vibrancy we hadn't seen since Vancouver. There's something about this place. When we walk down Main Street, we see other people who look like us—cleaned-up hippie types with shorter beards. Gone are the robes and beads, but bell bottoms and Nehru shirts remain. We make eye contact and nod in recognition. This town has possibilities.

That spring, I drive to Northampton. I've heard about a New

Age bookstore there called Beyond Words. As I enter the store, a bespectacled guy with long hair and a beard smiles at me.

"You're Ravi Dass," he says.

I'm very surprised that someone knows my spiritual name.

"You look just like the photo on the cover of *The Marriage and Family Book*. Welcome to Beyond Words! I'm Jeff."

Incredibly, my book has reached this corner of the world in America. Beyond Words has a similarly eclectic spirit to Banyen in Vancouver. Later that day, I meet Jeff's wife, Dee. We are kindred spirits. Spiritual book freaks. Soon Aparna, Manju, and I begin shuttling back and forth between Sturbridge and western Massachusetts and our new friends.

Manju will be starting first grade in the fall. Nina researches schools. Northampton schools are straight-rowed buttoned-up institutions. She's looking for progressive, child-centered, open education. A Northampton administrator scoffs. "For that, you go to Amherst."

Amherst, one town away from Northampton, from the look of it, is more of a country town with rolling hills and farms. Nina falls in love with one particular street. Call it kismet, we rent an old farmhouse on that very street.

Only after we've settled do I realize that Amherst is a company town, and the industry is education. All life revolves around the town's three colleges—the University of Massachusetts, Amherst College, and Hampshire College. As Carl predicted, we've landed in a college town on steroids.

Our new home is close to downtown Amherst but surrounded by farms with rolling meadows and the Holyoke range in the background, pastoral prettiness that at first doesn't resonate as home. It's just not dramatic like Cape Town or Vancouver. It's modest and unassuming with a quiet beauty. It will take a little time to get accustomed to this gentle scene. Amherst is known as the *People's Republic of Amherst*, a dig at its liberal and socialistic values. It's on the Boston and New York

City circuit, a mecca for music, theater, education, and spirituality. An eclectic and tolerant *all paths lead to the same place* vibe permeates *the Valley*, as people call the area. Like Kits in Vancouver, it's easy to meet people. It's not long before we're surrounded by a whole set of new friends who gather at our house to eat, take long walks, and hang out.

Still, an insecurity lurks. These new folks are different from me in one glaring way—they're educated. All have undergraduate degrees. Many have master's degrees. They're social workers and psychotherapists. I'm not sure how our book gig will pan out—whether we'll ever earn a living from writing.

"I'm pregnant," Nina tells me early one December morning. I'm thrilled and secretly scared. I'll be a husband with two children and a precarious means of income. Money continues to be tight, but we're muddling through and enjoying our writing projects. I must admit I'm more settled and happier than in Vancouver.

At a memorable feast, Jeff and Dee introduce us to a lanky hippie doctor named Barry. He and his girlfriend, Mariam, help women have babies at home. Barry's the most laid-back doctor I've ever met—a renegade Yale graduate, a doctor who knows about herbs, Ayurvedic medicine, and meditation. He's met Babaji in California. Barry and I have much in common.

He's a sacrilegious Jew too. We enjoy joking and laughing together. He shares his grandmother's admonition about life. *"Don't look for poifekt—you von't find."* He and Mariam promise to deliver our baby when the time comes.

At about 3 a.m., on a hot humid night in late July, Nina wakes me up. "I might be starting labor." She's calm and centered. About every ten minutes, she breathes deeply with each contraction. She suggests we take a bath. We relax together in our antique claw-foot tub.

As we head to our bedroom, she says, "The contractions are quite mild. I think I'll take a nap."

"Before you do, maybe I should check your dilation," I say.

Nina lays on the bed, legs splayed, knees up. I put my ring and index fingers on her vagina. I spread it open. I feel the hair of our baby. My eyes bulge. I say, "I need to call Barry."

Soon, Barry and Mariam arrive. I've also called our new social circle. Six couples, hoping one day to have a home birth, encircle our wood-framed bed. They meditate in silence. Manju, now seven years old, dressed in her fanciest outfit, her hair in pigtails, sits like a small adult on a cushion near the bed, ready to welcome her new sibling. It's not long before Nina gives birth. Barry's large hands cradle the tiny newborn, who bursts into pink life and gurgles her first sounds in this world. A girl!

The birth of our baby is a deeply spiritual experience. We're overjoyed. We call the baby girl Sara, Sanskrit for essence, and also after the biblical Sara, wife of Abraham. She's beautiful, pink, and chubby, and her disposition is sweet and easygoing. She coos contentedly as she suckles milk for the first time. I whisper the sacred mantra *Om* into her ear, just as I'd done with Manju. We're a family of four. I love being a dad and pray again that I will be a kind and loving father and that I'll be able to support my family.

A week after Sara's birth, Mom visits us in Amherst. I love seeing her delight in holding the one-week-old Sara, arguably the cutest baby in the world. We're completely absorbed in this miracle in our lives. But soon, what started with warmth and happiness deteriorates into dissatisfaction. We simply aren't paying enough attention to Mom. "I've come all the way from Vancouver, and you're ignoring me."

It's true. We're in love with newborn Sara. We've made no particular effort to entertain Mom. To make matters worse, it's sweltering. Our old farmhouse doesn't have air-conditioning. We're unaware that the spare bedroom upstairs, where Mom sleeps, is even hotter than the downstairs. We've put Mom in an oven to bake.

The heat and lack of attention soon make a difficult situation intolerable. I help Mom plan to catch a cross-Canada train out of Montreal back to Vancouver, a spectacular cross-continental journey I hope will make up for her mixed stay with us.

THIRTY-THREE

Every morning, I enjoy walking our white mongrel, Tui. I stroll around the neighborhood, giving Tui space to sniff and do his business. One morning, as Tui and I walk through the nearby cemetery, I meet a fellow dog owner, a neighbor. Our dogs sniff each other, approve, and proceed to play. The dog's owner, a bespectacled senior citizen, eyes me curiously.

"You're new here," he says. "My name's Roy Heath." Thus begins a morning ritual of walking our dogs together.

It turns out that Roy is a former Princeton University psychology professor. We become friends. I tell him a bit about my life, and he regales me with stories about his research at Princeton years before. He wrote a book called *The Reasonable Adventurer – A study of the development of thirty-six undergraduates at Princeton*.

"It's all about the personality attributes for enjoying a deeply satisfying life in college," Roy explains.

I'm interested in learning more about reasonable adventuring, but I blurt out, "Well, I didn't get through college. I got turned onto acid and dropped out after two years. After my psychedelic experiences, school seemed barren." I anticipate an insurmountable generational gulf, but Roy doesn't skip a beat.

"What did you do instead of school?" he asks.

"Well . . . I cofounded a yoga community in Vancouver, but we left there. Now it's a new chapter. I've written a few books . . . and more are coming out soon." I stumble around for a tangible way to articulate in a few sentences what I've done since dropping out of SFU.

The next morning, I bring a copy of *The Marriage and Family Book* to show Roy. I'd put my heart into the book. It's something I can point to with pride.

"May I borrow your book for a few days?" Roy asks.

"I'm sure it's not up to academic standards, Roy, but if you'd like to look at it, that would be fine." I'm honored that this learned professor wants to read my book. I'm also curious about his reaction to the New Age spiritual vibe that permeates its pages.

A few mornings later, I meet up with Roy again. Right away, he hands back my book.

"Very impressive!" Then, he adds, "Have you thought about going back to school?" I appreciate that a former Ivy League professor and clinical psychologist has made positive noises about my book. But his question catches me completely off guard.

"I'm thirty-four, with a seven-year-old and a newborn," I say. "I'm too old to go back to school. I'd be with twenty-year-old kids. I blew that possibility years ago."

Roy quickly cut me off. "No, I'm talking about graduate school. You've contributed to knowledge and have demonstrated independent scholarship. There's a master's degree program at UMass, right here in Amherst, that recognizes contributions like yours. The dean of the School of Education runs it. Her name's Norma-Jean Anderson. Go see her. I'll give her a call."

The possibility of getting into a master's degree program intrigues me. I've never considered shortcuts on the academic ladder a possibility. I'm thrilled that an insider has pointed the way. I don't know what questions to ask or what the possible career tracks might be. But I have an intuition that jump-starting my academic career will somehow translate into good results.

Ten days later, I walk into Dean Anderson's office carrying the books Nina and I have published, including the German translation of *Yoga for Pregnancy and Birth*—an impressive pile of books. Dean Anderson's eyes light up as she ogles our books.

"Did you write all these books?" she asks with obvious satisfaction.

"Yes, Dean Anderson," I respond. "My wife and I are a writing team."

I place the books on the coffee table, and Dean Anderson flips through them. She looks up for a moment and says, "Please call me Norma-Jean. Professor Heath told me about you. We would be delighted for you to join us here as a full-time master's student. You could continue studying marriage and family dynamics in our family therapy program. You'd have access to the counseling courses in the School of Education, as well as the Psychology Department. We can offer you a teaching assistantship and waive tuition fees."

I'm over the moon. After my checkered past, academia represents a real way forward. In the fall, I join the program in counseling psychology.

The School of Education—or the *School of Ed*, as it's known—provides the freedom to explore education in the widest sense of the word. There are the obvious education-related career tracks—like teaching—but there's also guidance counseling, school psychology, and individual, couple, and family counseling. I'm thrilled to be in an academic setting where I can study counseling and psychology. The family therapy program captures my interest from the outset. It opens my eyes to a new way of seeing and understanding human relations.

In contrast to the focus of the other counseling programs—which emphasize the intrapersonal, what happens inside a person's psyche—family therapy focuses on the interactions *between* individual family members. The central idea is that a person always operates in a systemic context—their families, workgroups, etc. In that sense, there's no such thing as an individual in isolation. The premise of the human systems school boils down to a *no blame* approach, a focus on patterns of interaction between people. I learn to map family dynamics, the underlying structures that set the stage for individual interactions. This is a powerful tool, a lens through which to understand all human systems, couples, families, as well as teams. A skilled therapist can help a dysfunctional family develop new and positive patterns of interaction.

I'm fortunate to get into Dr. Evan Coppersmith's class, family therapy training that takes place over a year. Evan's a popular and dynamic professor; her classes are always filled.

Family therapy classes are like a clinical lab where budding therapists learn techniques and interventions from the inside out. In other words, under Evan's watchful eye, we're our own guinea pigs. In class, we perform simulations, playing roles in one another's families, while others play therapists. Sometimes it's a lot of fun, hilarious, and sometimes more poignant. We interview real families and become skilled diagnosticians of family dynamics—too tight or too loose boundaries, inappropriate parent-child alliances, dysfunctional family triangles, etc. It's exciting to learn systems thinking and how to apply our insights to real family dynamics, including our own families of origin.

I view my family history through a systemic lens—my parents:

an emotionally unskilled and temperamentally ill-suited couple, each with their unhealed trauma from World War II and the Holocaust. I begin to understand the role played by external stressors—the circumstances of post-WWII apartheid society, economic pressures, South Africa's history of racism and bigotry, and the overwhelming systemic oppression. The violence of the society. I feel compassion for everyone in our family, including myself.

Gaining this systemic family perspective softens my heart. Some families are close-knit, and others, like ours, scatter their members to far-flung places. I feel the blessing of the force that pushed me out of my family at thirteen, how boarding school taught me self-reliance and saved me from my family's daily tensions and dysfunctions. I gain far more than mere academic knowledge. I've been initiated into a process of understanding my family history and healing from it.

One day, Evan gives us a new exercise about differentiation in our families of origin. Essentially, differentiation refers to the degree to which, as children, we've been programmed to relate to our parents as a unit rather than nurturing a unique relationship with each parent. Evan instructs us to write letters to each of our parents, inviting them to a date independent of the other parent. Each student is free to do the exercise in their own style. This simple instruction causes quite a stir because some students have never considered having a relationship with their mother or father independent of the other parent. I'm not sure how this exercise applies to me. Unlike the other students whose parents are all somewhere in the US, and many in Massachusetts, my parents are far away. By this time, Evan is familiar with my family situation, having heard much of the story in class during simulations.

"Michael," she says. "Please see me after class. I want to discuss the exercise with you."

When we're alone, she says, "Sorry, I don't expect you to do this exercise. Your relationship with your parents is too fraught—especially with your father. I don't have faith that any good would come from you contacting him."

I take this in and agree it's probably not a good idea to contact Dad out of the blue, at least not for the purposes of this exercise. I think of my parents as separate people, so that aspect of the exercise doesn't hold that much for me. But privately, I think Evan's wrong about there being no hope for my relationship with my father. Surely, hope should always be kept alive?

As I approach the completion of my master's degree, I realize that my training has merely skimmed the surface. I will soon have a master's, and that's great, especially after my previous checkered education. But I'm not prepared to head into a new career yet.

I'm at yet another crossroad. What should I do now? Should I continue to the doctoral level? I'm still stunned to be in graduate school. In my wildest dreams, I've never considered that I would have the opportunity to become a "doctor." I apply to the most sought-after next step for graduating master's students—the doctoral program in counseling psychology. To my surprise, I'm one of five applicants accepted. Though I've gained access to further study, I'm confused and anxious about exactly how to make the best of the academic opportunity.

In the meantime, Jeff and Dee offer me a side gig editing their quarterly journal—*Many Hands*—a magazine that focuses on spirituality and restorative arts. It advertises the valley's various healers and therapists. I've taken on the job to make a bit of extra money and learn about digital layout, just emerging in 1981.

One morning, a tall, fair-haired woman comes by our house to drop off a listing for *Many Hands*. Her name's Corinne. She and her husband, Jack, are placing an ad about a couples' workshop they periodically offer. Corinne is outgoing, and we strike up a conversation. She's one of the many compatible new people who've shown up in our lives. I share that I'm a doctoral candidate and confused about what specific direction I want to take in my studies.

"You should talk to my husband," Corinne says. "He has a doctorate from the School of Ed too. He juiced the program for all it's worth. I'll tell him about you. I'm sure he'd help you think this through."

Pleased to hear of someone who might be able to guide my direction, I call Jack. Corinne has given him a few details. His voice is warm, but I detect a certain impatience. Jack, it seems, doesn't suffer fools gladly.

"Look, Michael, I might be able to help you. Corinne mentioned that I know UMass well. Can I interview you over the phone? It'll help me to understand your background."

Jack's interviewing style is incisive but appropriate. I appreciate how he frames his questions. Some people might be intimidated by his brusqueness, but I resonate with his no-bullshit, brass-tacks attitude. After a half-hour of pointed questions, Jack invites me to his home office. He and Corinne live in South Deerfield, a neighboring town.

A few days later, I drive down a meandering road following the Deerfield River to Jack and Corinne's house at the top of a hill with an expansive westerly view of Mt. Greylock. It's obvious from the outset that Jack and Corinne are people of some means. Their house is large and sprawling. Jack is nine years older than me, a balding guy with penetrating blue eyes, dark, bushy eyebrows, and an intense, task-focused demeanor. He earned his undergraduate degree at Brown University, then graduated from Yale Law, before attending the doctoral program at the School of Ed. There, he studied groups and organizational psychology.

Jack wastes no time. "Michael, I enjoyed talking to you the other day. I'm impressed with what you've done. You started your work career working in your father's business and on the shop floor in a factory in Joburg. You've been a salesman, Ram Dass's road manager. Arica trainer, event organizer, yoga teacher, meditator. Workshop leader. Author. Researcher. Lumber mill worker. Janitor. Community builder. Last but not least, an incompetent bartender." He chuckles. I laugh. "You've done many things. Quite a background for a guy of your age."

I'm grateful that Jack sees value in my spotty past work experiences.

"Look, Michael, everything you've done should be considered manure for feeding your tree. Your history points strongly toward a possible career. Let me unpack what I'm thinking so you can understand where I'm coming from."

Jack reframes my work background and my interests in psychology and spirituality. He informs me my experiences are compatible with an emerging career path called *organization development.* The approach applies principles of humanistic psychology, systems thinking, synergistic teamwork, win-win ethics, and visionary leadership to business. This new discipline is all about helping managers and executives collaborate to achieve a desired collective future. It involves coaching leaders to be better leaders and teaching groups and teams to optimally function. My career path, failures and all, is useful in a way I've not previously considered. I have a sense of what Jack's talking about. Suddenly, the opportunities at the School of Ed take on a whole new potential. Jack has pointed toward a career path that I've never imagined. But much of what he explains resonates. At last, a direction has been revealed. I'll take a page from Jack's book and follow his example.

As I take my leave, he gives me one last bit of information. "Organization development pays a whole lot better than counseling or therapy."

This news doesn't fall on deaf ears. I've struggled so much with *filthy lucre* for as far back as I can remember. But the most important thing the meeting with Jack has given me is fresh optimism. I'm a good teacher and trainer, and those skills can be applied in business. Jack has opened up a world I had no idea existed, a career path that will give me a sense of purpose and pay well. I'm psyched!

THIRTY-FOUR

The fall of 1983 arrives. I'm on a high, about to graduate with a doctorate. Thanks to Jack, I've found a direction for my studies, a path that satisfies a number of my intellectual, emotional, and psychological proclivities. I've now spent years immersed in individual psychotherapy, healing and counseling, family therapy, leadership training, group dynamics, and courses in the business school, sociology, and psychology departments—a learning process that's launched me on a journey of intellectual discovery, personal growth, and maturation.

I'm finally making something of myself. My parents would be proud of me. I certainly hadn't shown any academic inclinations as a kid. There was that 19 percent in Latin. Mom is surprised that her wayward hippie son has become an organization development consultant. It isn't quite "my son, the doctor," but it's close enough. Academic labels like "master's" and "doctorate" would no doubt astonish Dad. If he knew, he might have a tough time believing I wasn't fabricating these grandiose titles. I last saw Dad in Cape Town a few days before I left for Israel. I was twenty. Sixteen years have passed. Much water under the bridge, as they say.

Once I began psychological training, my relationship with Dad showed up repeatedly—a glaring piece of unfinished psychological business. I've successfully defended my dissertation; an epiphany comes: *Break the pattern between you and Dad. Why wait for him? Call him and tell him directly that his son has become a doctor in the world of business and organizations.* If Dad gets wind of my academic success, he might be proud. But *if* is a small word with a big meaning, like Jack's fond saying, "If my granny had balls, she'd be my grandfather."

Maybe I'm deluded, filled with unreasonable hope, but I cast caution to the wind and call Dad's office in Cape Town.

Ms. Rose, Dad's secretary all these years, answers the phone. Her voice sounds exactly the way I remember it—prim, proper, helpful. I can picture her there, sitting at her desk outside Dad's office with the blue tortoiseshell glasses. She's kind of pretty, though she hides it very well. Ms. Rose remembers me. She's surprised to hear my voice.

"I'm calling from the United States," I tell her. "I'm wondering if my dad's there? I've got some exciting news to share with him."

"Your father is on a business trip in the United States," she replies.

Stunning news. How can Dad be in the States? What a weird coincidence.

"If you call me back in fifteen minutes, I'll have a number where you can reach him in Los Angeles." Dad's in the States and hasn't contacted me. There's a pang of ancient hurt. Is this further confirmation that he wants nothing to do with me?

Fifteen minutes later, I call Ms. Rose back. She gives me a phone number. I call the number and ask to speak to Dad. An unfamiliar female voice tells me to hold on. There's a brief delay. Then Dad's voice comes on the line. "Hello?"

"Hello, Dad. It's Gary."

Seconds pass. Then Dad says, "I've been thinking about you. I was going to call you myself. Eve and I are here in LA, and then we're heading to New York for a trade show in a few days. Can we meet there?" The words are ordinary, like any father might say to his son. But to me, this is a bigger opening than I imagined.

"But how did you know I was in Los Angeles?" Dad asks, his voice irritated, suspicious.

"Well, that's why I'm calling, Dad. I've got some very exciting news I want to share with you. I called your office. Ms. Rose gave me this number."

"But someone in Cape Town must have told you I was in the States. Who was it?" Dad's convinced that someone has tipped me off.

"Really, Dad. I just called Ms. Rose. She gave me this number. I don't have much contact with anyone in South Africa anymore."

"Well, someone must have told you. Otherwise, how did you know I was in the States?"

Dad barely conceals his impatience.

I leave it at that. In a way, it's the same old story. Father discounts son's reality. Oh well.

"Dad, I'd love to meet you in New York. I'll come down with my wife, Nina, and our daughters Manju and Sara. Manju's ten and Sara's three. I have a master's degree, and I just completed my doctorate at the University of Massachusetts!"

It's evident that Dad can't quite compute the information: the inexplicable call, two grandchildren, his wayward son reemerging as a doctor. His circuits are blown. "Hold on for a minute," he says. Poor man has to take a few deep breaths.

He comes back on the line with a different attitude.

"Well, that's wonderful news! Let's all meet in New York. And may I offer my congratulations? You can tell me about it when we meet."

A week later, the four of us pile into the huge gray Chrysler—a boat of a car Carl and Mabel gifted us—and head to Manhattan. I've been on a professional track. I've shaved my beard and wear my curly black hair at a respectable length. Nina's fashionable, with her hair lightened and flipped away from her face. She's begun wearing a bit of makeup, which brings out her dazzling eyes.

We meet up with Dad and Eve, his younger, glamorous wife. I have to rearrange my head a little. Here's my dad. Older, a little thicker, and slower than when I left South Africa. Still a handsome man, with gray hair and a movie-star face.

And Eve is only about ten years older than me—a big girl when I was a little boy. I remember her mother, Traute. She was Mom's perfumed friend who suffocated me in her enormous bosom as she pinched my cheek and called me *Liebchen*. Here's her daughter, Eve, the girl for whose teenage beauty Mom claimed proud responsibility. She evolved into the blond bombshell I last saw at bioscope in Oudtshoorn when I was at boarding school. Eve—my stepmother? Really? Together, she and Dad make an attractive couple. Like middle-aged versions of Gregory Peck and Farrah Fawcett.

Dad—moved by seeing me and meeting Nina, Manju, and Sara—hugs us, his eyes welling with tears. He takes quiet joy in the kids. He keeps pronouncing Manju's name as "Manyu"—the Afrikaans way of pronouncing a 'j' as 'y.' I understand.

We take photos together. We're all happy, acknowledging the momentousness of the occasion. Nina and Eve hit it off. The two of them could pass as sisters, both beautiful blonds.

We eat in a Jewish deli and hang out for hours. Dad's softer and more engaged. Interested in us, not the brooding, unhappy camper I grew up with. Eve has had a positive influence on him. I'm warming to her.

"I was in love with your dad since I was a teenager," she tells me. "I used to hide in the field across the road from your Buchan Road house just to get a glimpse of him when the two of you played cricket in the driveway. I married a guy from England and had two boys. Then I got divorced, and so did your dad. We met by chance at a New Year's Eve party. We were both free. We've been together ever since. Your dad helped to raise my sons. Together, we have Candice, who's now almost thirteen."

Eve and Dad are happy together. Their relationship is a more natural fit than my parents' volatile chemistry. Dad tells us he had a serious heart attack some years before. In the process, his doctors discovered an aneurysm in his aorta. His heart's too weak for an operation. He's matter-of-fact about dying of a burst aneurysm. He doesn't know how long he has. He's been told to stop smoking and take it easy. I sense an impatient edge just below the surface.

For her part, Eve's keen that Dad and I reconcile. Her support is appreciated. When we have a private moment, she shares, "You know, I was cleaning your dad's desk some years ago, and I found a drawer filled with the letters you wrote him over the years. I asked him, 'How could you not reply to all these letters?' but he didn't say anything."

Eve's confirmation that my letters arrived and that Dad kept them means something to me. One tends to keep things that one values.

Eve, Nina, and the girls take off to explore Manhattan. Dad and I are on our own. This is the first time we've been face-to-face since I was twenty. After small talk, I change the subject.

"You know, Dad, I still carry around baggage about what happened in our family. I'd like to talk to you about it."

That's as far as I get.

"I've thought about the past, and I don't have any regrets," Dad replies. "If you want to have a relationship with me, it will have to be from this day forward. I'm not interested in discussing the past."

Dad is clear. I have a choice to make. Part of me wants to shout, *You stubborn old asshole! You were a lousy father and still won't take responsibility.* I feel the righteous indignation rising. But where will it lead if I react in the same old way? Not to the result I want. A therapeutic approach—understanding empathically how it was for each of us—perhaps will bring us to mutual forgiveness, but Dad doesn't want to talk, at least not about what happened.

Sorting through the mess together is out of the question.

I face that if I want a relationship with my father, I will have to accept him as he is. Nothing prevents me from working on my own emotional process, not even Dad's refusal to discuss the past or acknowledge any responsibility. I'm in charge of my own healing.

All this comes to me in a flash. "Okay, Dad," I say. "Let's go forward from here."

The meeting with Dad and Eve in New York signals a new

beginning. Not quite the one I hoped for, but a fresh start. I'm relieved and awed. Relieved that Dad and I have connected after all this time and awed at how Providence brought us together again. I'm sure some kind of telepathy has been at work. Somehow, through the ethers, our mind-streams have connected.

I've been given another chance, or we've been granted a fresh opportunity to develop a meaningful father-son relationship. It will be adult to adult. Maybe I'm getting ahead of myself, but that's my vision.

Having the support of Nina and the kids helps enormously. Something bigger is being rekindled. At its core, a relationship between Dad and me, but also with Nina, Manju, and Sara on my side. And on Dad's side, his new family with Eve and Candice, their daughter, the half sister I have yet to meet. It's all different now. We're all different people. I'm optimistic.

THIRTY-FIVE

A few months after the dramatic meeting with Dad and Eve in New York, we invite Mom to visit us in Amherst. We haven't seen her since her visit after Sara's birth, three summers ago. We've learned from that rather disastrous visit. We do our best to be gracious hosts. Her visit should be carefully choreographed. Unlike Nina's parents, who demand little attention, Mom requires our full focus. She loves art and culture. Nina concludes that providing a daily special excursion will keep Mom entertained and happy.

We take turns. One day, Nina takes her on a small adventure. The next day, I take her. We alternate. So begins a series of interesting, successful outings. It's a pleasure being around Mom when she's happy and entertained. Her charming wit and natural enthusiasm are contagious.

Mom hits it off with our friends, who take her in as one of their own. Mom's great when she's relaxed. Corinne invites her for dinner, and Mom's quite taken with Jack's storytelling and crisp punchlines. She feels a natural simpatico with our friend Ervin, himself a Holocaust child survivor and social psychology professor who's dedicated his life to educating people about prosocial behavior.

From Mom's side, she loves to give small gifts to us all. She takes great pride in her refined taste and loves to find beautiful things to share with her granddaughters. She brings parcels containing small gifts, like an old-fashioned music box or a silk scarf. Sometimes, she misses the mark, like when she gifts a fancy perfume to Nina, who hates perfume. We all understand the loving intention. Having physical keepsakes from their grandma, who lives a continent away, nurtures a connection with Manju and Sara.

One afternoon, after Mom has been with us for a week, we're sitting around the kitchen table having tea. The subject of my reconciliation with Dad comes up in conversation. I mention that we met Dad in New York. But I don't say a word about Eve for fear of putting salt in the wound.

"What did you think of his father?" Mom asks, turning to Nina. I know from the tone in her voice that this innocent inquiry is laced with cyanide. Nina doesn't hesitate. She says, "I quite liked him."

This is not the answer Mom wants. Smoke pours out of her ears. She's smoldering, ready to explode.

"How can you say that after the way he treated your husband?" It's not really a question. It's filled with contempt. She turns to me, expecting wholehearted agreement, but that's not where I'm at. I'm grateful that Nina supports my efforts to reunite with Dad. I'm in no mood to have Mom interfere with what I consider sacred work.

"Mom, you shouldn't have asked if you didn't want the truth."

Mom doesn't say anything, but it's obvious she has her own

opinion. In her mind, my loyalty to Dad means I'm disloyal to her. How can I possibly be loyal to both? I have to choose, and apparently, I've chosen Dad. But her assumption is wrong. I want a relationship with both my parents. I can make appropriate boundaries.

THIRTY-SIX

Still in the flush of success from completing my doctorate, I invite Babaji for a visit to Amherst. Five years have passed since we left Vancouver. I've continued an occasional correspondence with him, although it's not as intimate as our earlier relationship. In the mode of continuing to take care of unfinished business, I propose Babaji stop in Amherst after his retreat near Toronto in September. He'll be in Eastern Canada and fairly close by. I expect a polite demurral, but Babaji writes back, "It can be possible for me to come to Amherst." Then, in late August, he writes again, informing us he'll visit after the Toronto retreat in mid-September.

Babaji arrives with an entourage of seven or eight of his California devotees, including Ma Renu, the older retired art professor, who has sponsored his stay in the States from the beginning. Although we're unprepared for so many people, we find neighborhood homes for them to stay. Babaji and Ma stay with us. The next morning, Ma takes me aside.

"R.D.," she says, looking me right in the eye, "Babaji came to Amherst to see you." I take this in, not entirely sure what she's communicating.

I'm still confused about my relationship with Babaji. His visit has coincided with a terrible allergic reaction to the Valley's late summer pollen. My face is swollen, my eyes bloodshot and itchy. My nose is running. I'm miserable. Babaji's not my guru anymore, but he's been an important spiritual teacher. I respect him, but I'm thankful I've outgrown the spiritual dependency of my Vancouver days. I take Ma's words in with some satisfaction. I appreciate her integrity and kindness and the unassuming but vital role she plays behind the scenes. She softens Babaji's outspoken and sometimes insensitive comments. His visit is a recognition of our service, a kind of amends.

The next day, we host a Satsang for about forty of our Amherst friends and acquaintances. Most of them have heard about Babaji from Ram Dass's book, *Be Here Now*, which has become a bestseller, the so-called *counterculture bible*. They're curious about meeting this silent Himalayan yogi. It's a pleasant day. People gather under the blue sky on the big lawn outside our old farmhouse, in the shade of a massive pine in which I've built a treehouse for Manju.

Babaji joins people outside. He makes no pretense at social niceties and sits down cross-legged on the cushion of a simple wicker couch. The group is quiet, somewhat surprising in this very verbal, academic community. Gradually, people ask questions. A lively interchange ensues.

Later, Babaji comments, "Very good and intelligent people." I wonder if he thinks Amherst might be good soil for a Satsang, but he indicates no interest. Initially, I'm disappointed, but reflecting further, I'm relieved. We're all moving forward.

As we get on with our lives in Amherst, the Vancouver Satsang has dwindled. The Salt Spring Center of Yoga, devoted to Babaji's teachings, is slowly coming into being on this beautiful British Columbia Gulf island. A core group of yogis from the old days have moved there. A.D. and his new wife, Kalpana, have relocated to Santa Cruz to be closer to Babaji.

In 1986, A.D. calls and tells us he has Parkinson's disease. He has a strong tremor that makes his life intolerable. He's decided to seek a radical new solution—an electrode implant in his brain. A few months later, he undergoes the operation.

Babaji writes to the Satsang communities in Santa Cruz and Vancouver, "A.D. was slow, but he was very dedicated to yoga. He was very friendly and compassionate, with a heart full of love. His sadhana developed, but his physical body deteriorated. He never stopped his sadhana, even though he was unable to walk or control his body from trembling. But he controlled his mind. He left his body in the operating room. His last words were, 'I know that I am *Brahman–the supreme cosmic spirit*—but these doctors don't know that I'm *Brahman*.' He never regained consciousness."

The news of A.D.'s death deeply saddens me. He's one of my oldest and dearest friends. We lived communally in hippie houses, took our first acid trips together, simultaneously became spiritual aspirants, discovered Ram Dass and Babaji, and cofounded the Vancouver Satsang. We truly came of age together. He was a good friend, a real brother. Now he's left his body while still a young man, barely forty. I honor his presence and the love we've shared. A.D. was a sweet soul.

THIRTY-SEVEN

After our dramatic New York meeting, Dad begins demonstrating the softer side of his nature. Parcels arrive in the mail every few months. They're filled with the chocolates of my youth—Crunchie Bars, Peppermint Crisps, and Whole Nut Chocolate bars. Dad's chocolate parcels are a connection to the sweeter parts of my South African sojourn. Of course, they're a big hit with Manju and Sara, who rarely get sweet treats at home.

Before our troubles, Dad was always a letter writer, and now I begin receiving regular letters by fax, the prevailing technology. I'll arrive in my office early in the morning, and there'll be an overnight fax waiting for me. Like Babaji, Dad handwrites his letters in neat print:

MY DEAR SON,

Thank you for your last letter. Candice is doing well. She's a beautiful girl and makes us very proud. My new business, importing paper goods from the Far East and distributing them to tourist shops, is developing very nicely.

What has happened to your writing career? Please tell me about your books. I would love to have copies of them. I'm so proud of all you've accomplished. You've managed to get a stellar education without help from anyone. It should make you puff out your chest and exclaim, 'I am somebody despite hardships which I've had to endure. My achievements are my own, and I owe no one anything.'

With lots of love to all,
YOUR DAD

Of course, what Dad has written isn't entirely true. I've received help from lots of people. I've been blessed with good fortune along the way. But I know that what Dad means is that *he* hadn't helped me. I appreciate the acknowledgment. I fax back my news.

DEAR DAD,

Thank you for your last letter. It's great to hear the news about your family. So interesting to hear about your new business too. Very exciting.

Manju is doing well in school. Nina has decided to become a child psychologist and is enrolled in a doctoral program at UMass. She's opened a small day care at our house to bring in some more money. The house is filled with two-year-old kids from Monday to Friday. Sara is surrounded by friends all day. The day care means that Nina doesn't have to be separated from her for substantial periods. Nina's a dynamo and somehow balances her graduate work and the day care, and she still manages to cook up great meals for us too. We've figured things out so that when she has to go to class, I look after the day care.

We've published seven books but haven't been writing while both of us have been in graduate school. I'll send copies for you. We always seem to have a lot on our plates!

Love to Eve and Candice,
MICHAEL

From the outset, I always sign my letters "Michael." Dad reciprocates by addressing his letters to "Gary Fuchs c/o Dr. Michael Shandler" and begins his letters with—"My Dear Son."

Dad values what's emerging in our relationship more than his feelings about my stubborn insistence on being called Michael. He doesn't make an issue of the name thing, but he finds a way to both retain the old and accept the new. The faxing of letters back and forth reignites the coals of a relationship that had all but died. These letters become our way of bridging the 7,500-mile distance between us.

THIRTY-EIGHT

It's early 1984. South Africa is still in the grip of apartheid. The country has become what Nelson Mandela will call "the skunk of the world's nations." The surrounding African nations and the developed world condemn the racist regime's policies. International sanctions are exerting pressure on the country's economy. Bishop Desmond Tutu has been awarded the Nobel Peace Prize for his activism, giving an internationally recognized face to the struggle for equality while Nelson Mandela is still imprisoned.

Within the nation, the townships have begun to erupt in violence. *Swartgevaar*, the Black rage that's haunted South Africa, periodically boils over. The police run amuck in the townships, and Black factions wage war. Hundreds are dying. Many Whites are leaving, creating a wealth and brain drain. While South Africa has maintained physical and social isolation at the bottom of Africa, in 1976, the government finally allowed television broadcasts in the country, but even this is still limited. They're trying to hold on. It's a country in transition, with violence and racial war looming as a distinct possibility.

As Nina, Manju (now almost eleven), Sara (almost four), and I step onto the tarmac at the Cape Town airport, dozens of Black soldiers armed with assault weapons encircle the plane. It seems that a few things have changed. But who are these Black soldiers, and why are they working for the racist government?

This is the first return trip to my country of origin. I boarded a plane to Israel, eighteen years ago. I'm curious. What's changed? What's stayed the same? How will it feel to be back? So much has happened to me. I'm a different person than the one who left in 1967. Now, as a thirty-eight-year-old with a whole set of life experiences behind me, I'm returning with my own young family and an emerging professional career.

During my time in North America, I've become a student of South African culture and history. Studying various aspects of apartheid is central to my self-education. I've gained a far better understanding of the system in which I grew up. I remember the feeling of apartheid, its dark rigidities and the racist assumptions at its core. The cold legal apparatus and the brutal police state oppress millions and provide privilege to others by virtue of their White skin.

I've seen it for what it is: a pigmentocracy.

But while I maintain no illusions about the pariah nation of my youth, it's still the land that I came from. I miss South Africa's unique beauty and culture. I've longed to share it with Nina and the kids. We'll spend most of our South African trip in Cape Town with Penny and Benny and visit Dad and Eve.

What will it be like for Nina and the girls to be in the heart of affluent White South Africa with all its inequity and oppression? Even for me—a native—flying into the apartheid nation is shocking. At the same time, Table Mountain's dominant presence and its swirling white tablecloth of clouds, the warmth of the sun, and the familiar Mediterranean fauna and flora provide the same soothing ambiance I remember from my youth.

Penny and Benny's house is a generous Mediterranean-style home with a swimming pool and manicured garden. Their beautiful home is surrounded by high walls topped with razor wire and sharp glass embedded in the cement, the same as all the other homes in the neighborhood.

Penny introduces us to her son—my nephew—a handsome twelve-year-old named Paul who lets me know right away that he's into the Springboks, South Africa's national team. "We're the best rugby players in the world!" he tells me with the same enthusiasm I remember at his age.

Penny's daughter, my fourteen-year-old niece, Loren, and Candice, my half sister about the same age, are both away for their summer holiday at a Jewish Camp near Hermanus, an Indian Ocean coastal town near the southerly tip of Africa, eighty miles from Cape Town. I've loved Hermanus since boyhood. In a few weeks, we'll make an excursion to pick them up. I find it remarkable that my father's granddaughter from his first marriage and his daughter from his second marriage are the same age, only three years older than my older daughter, Manju.

Penny introduces us to Rosie, her long-standing maid. Rosie's a dignified Xhosa woman from the Eastern Cape.

"Welcome, master," Rosie says, shaking my hand. Understanding the apartheid way and embarrassed to be called "master," I protest.

"Please don't call me master, Rosie. Call me Michael."

Rosie seems pleased at my gesture of equality, or maybe she's just amazed at my naïveté.

"Okay, Michael," she says with a small smile.

At that juncture, Penny chimes in. "Rosie's a part of our family.

She's been with me for years. She'll feed you all while you're here. Just ask Rosie for anything you want."

Later, we're relaxing around the pool. I mention Penny's comments about Rosie to Nina.

"Well, if Rosie's a member of the family, why doesn't she swim in the pool with everyone else?" Nina demands.

She has a point. I'm not about to argue. Nina was a civil rights activist when she was barely seventeen, marching on Washington with Dr. King and again at nineteen marching in Selma, Alabama. She can't ignore the injustice of the South African system.

Soon after we arrive, we head down to the nearby Indian Ocean coast. I'm keen to show my family the amazing beaches and warm waters of False Bay, to explore the shore I swam and fished in as a boy. We stop in St. James, a seaside village, and collect shells on the beach.

Above us, the railroad wends its way along the coast, stopping at all the beaches. Just then, a train thunders by. We admire it steaming along, but then the "WHITES ONLY" signs on the carriages remind us where we are.

That's it in a nutshell—unbelievable nature, but always apartheid's presence, its ubiquitous reminders of the racist way of life that governs the people of this paradise. We make our way along the coast, eventually stopping at Seaforth, a protected bay, perfect for swimming. All this seaside along Cape Town's coast is dedicated to so-called *White* beaches. It's a hot summer day, and the blue-green Indian Ocean waters beckon invitingly. As we head for the water's edge, a small group of young Black kids sits on a rock about thirty yards away. They're looking enviously at the White kids frolicking in the water. Nina approaches them. "Come. I'll take you in."

The kids look at her with curiosity but don't move. Suddenly, a nanny to a few White kids nearby jumps to her feet and rushes over.

"*Aikhona!*—Cannot do it!" *Aikhona*, means "no" or "definitely not" in isiZulu. The Zulu adds a certain emphasis. Then, sensing Nina's not a White South African, the woman asks, "Where do you come from?"

"From the USA," Nina answers.

"Oh, that explains it!" the woman says, shooing the children further from the water's edge. The kids are quiet, a look of resignation on their faces, early training about their place in this society.

A couple of weeks later, Penny and Benny take us on a road trip to Oudtshoorn, the dusty town where I went to boarding school. We all pile into Benny's big BMW for the long drive to the barren desert town. It's been twenty-two years since my days in Oudtshoorn. The boarding house grounds are the same, except the bamboo bushes where the boys used to smoke their pipes are bushier and taller. The housefather, in the same role as Wan in my day, greets us. I tell him I lived in the boarding house for three years in the early sixties. He offers to give us a tour.

I ask Nina her impressions. She doesn't hold back.

"I've worked in mental institutions that are better than this place."

It's a bit shocking to hear Nina's blunt assessment. I allow myself to feel what it took to survive in this reformatory run by bullies like Dolos and Loftus and their cronies. I stand on the power spot where I knocked Fanie out. I walk by the red-tiled quad where Loftus beat me with the rubber hose. I hear his voice yelling, "*Fokken Jood.*"

I remember my roommates: Moerbei, Renoster, Spook, Katderm, and Mike. I silently thank the boys who made a positive difference—Boompie, Kuiken, Zirk, and Hoepel, the boy who cut my hair for ten cents. I wonder where fate has taken each of them. We drive by Mrs. Kushner's old house, and I silently express my gratitude for her kindness and generosity. I'm not sure what's become of her, but we don't stop. By God's grace, and with the kindness of strangers, I survived this place. Now I can say I'm richer for my experiences here.

On our way out of Oudtshoorn, we stop at Safari Ostrich Farm, the ranch where I celebrated the Passover Seder all those years ago. The kids will get a kick out of being up close to ostriches. Besides, it'll be interesting to visit there for old times' sake.

At Safari, we're taken to a kraal where a huge ostrich is herded in preparation to be ridden bareback. The jockey, a wiry Cape Colored, wears large white trunks and an oversized green and yellow shirt that billows in the wind. A ridiculous white top hat, with multicolored tassels streaming behind him, adds a festive touch to his outfit. A black sock is placed over the ostrich's head, and the jockey climbs up a ladder held by a few attendants. He climbs onto the ostrich's back. Her massive wings—an almost seven feet span—clamp the jockey in place. He holds the ostrich's neck with both hands. The bird doesn't like it, but the jockey just laughs. He yanks her neck back and forth to guide her movement. The huge creature takes off, quickly reaching thirty-five miles an hour. After a few minutes, the jockey pulls her long neck back toward him like a brake. The creature comes to a halt. The jockey climbs down, bowing. Everyone claps. When tourists are invited to ride the ostrich, I volunteer. Something about being back in Oudtshoorn has caused temporary insanity.

A large black-and-white male ostrich is tethered between two posts. A ladder for climbing onto the ostrich's back is held in place by a pair of attendants. A black sock is stretched over the giant bird's head. I climb up to the height of the creature's back. Its enormous wings are lifted. I place my legs around its sinuous back, sit, and grab its leathery neck. Without warning, the giant raptor bolts.

My ostrich ride lasts all of three, maybe four seconds before I'm thrown off by an effortless flick of his powerful body. I tumble through the air and land on my ass. The ostrich stands over me, its bloodshot eyes signaling rage. I instinctively raise my arm to protect my face. His huge claws rip the flesh from my forearm. The attendants quickly control the beast, but my arm is badly lacerated.

I'm taken to the main house, a so-called "feather palace," a sandstone mansion built around the turn of the twentieth century when ostrich feathers were South Africa's fourth-largest export, after gold, diamonds, and wool. I remember the Seder so many years ago. The big room where we kids got *shikker*.

My wound is cleaned and dressed. Then a familiar woman comes into the room to check on me, the idiot tourist who has no business riding ostriches. Something clicks.

"Mrs. Lipschitz, I was at boarding school here in Oudtshoorn over twenty years ago, and I came to a Seder here. I remember it well. It was a wonderful event." Mrs. Lipschitz looks at me carefully.

"Oh, I remember you. Once a *wilde chaya*, always a *wilde chaya*—you're still a wild animal!"

I guess I haven't changed that much after all. I've come full circle with Oudtshoorn. I hope my ostrich karma has finally been appeased.

Penny suggests a convoy with Dad to pick up Loren and Candice from summer camp. Nina begs off, saying she needs some space from the family intensity.

Dad and I are in the front, and Manju and Sara are in the back of Dad's Mercedes. Benny and Penny are in their BMW behind us. We stop at the summer camp to pick up the teenagers. It's great to meet Candice, my half sister, who has the best of her parents' genes, and my niece, Loren, who's blessed with the same shocking blue eyes and sense of humor as Benny.

The two-car convoy arrives in the center of the town of Hermanus. We're stopped at a traffic light, what they called a "robot" in South Africa. Candice, Manju, and Sara—the newly acquainted young auntie and her two little nieces—sit in the back.

When the light turns green, Dad floors the Mercedes. Penny and Benny are left in the dust. Dad turns down side streets to avoid being followed. Penny, Benny, Loren, and Paul are lost in the traffic.

"What about Penny and Benny?" I exclaim. I can't help myself.

"They know their way around," Dad growls.

Despite my intention to keep my cool, my blood's boiling.

"Can't you wait for them, Dad? I thought we were all traveling together."

Dad waves his hand in dismissal.

I'm seething, ashamed to show this side of myself to my half sister, whom I've met minutes before for the first time. She's probably heard stories about Dad and me, and now she's witnessing our strife firsthand. There's a major difference between having an intention for reconciliation and maintaining it when the going gets tough.

I'm transported back into childhood, into feelings of helplessness, my world out of control. I've been in this place with Dad many times. But what have I learned since I was a boy? How can I work through my triggered state? I don't want to blow it with Dad. We've had a breakthrough. Even though he's being a stubborn jerk. Then the inner work I've been doing for years—my sadhana—kicks in.

First, stop.
Exhale.
Don't do anything.
Inhale.
Don't say anything.
Exhale.
Don't escalate.
Inhale.
Don't try to change anything.
Exhale.

Now is not the time to trust your thoughts.
Or your feelings.

Dad inadvertently cuts off a car in the neighboring lane. The car brakes violently to avoid colliding with us. The driver honks furiously and accelerates until his car is level with ours. Dad gives him the finger. The driver rolls down his window and yells, "That's not very nice for an old fart!" Dad laughs. We all laugh. The atmosphere is suddenly lighthearted. I regain my composure. Dad has changed. He's smiling. He's not as uptight as the unhappy camper of my youth. We've all changed.

THIRTY-NINE

Two days after our return to Massachusetts, still jetlagged, I'm sitting in an upscale event room surrounded by executives of major and minor industries, all of us paying rapped attention to the charismatic presenters in front of the room. The course is called Leadership and Mastery.

Jack has sent me here with his usual understated encouragement. "Okay, babe. Doctorate done. Next step, Leadership and Mastery. I'm telling you it will change your life. These guys at Innovation Associates, they're genius. They're into something big, a major paradigm shift in organizational understanding, and it complements our studies at UMass. They've figured out practical language and sophisticated lenses for leaders to create and sustain high-performing teams and organizations. They've hit on a method to present radical ideas to businesses otherwise resistant to psychobabble. Straight corporate types are eating it up. You'll see. Your psychospiritual training will be a profound asset."

Jack's right on the money. I greet every session with genuine appreciation and delight.

New worlds of understanding and practical application are opening. By the end, I'm a convert to IA's approach. My commitment shows. IA offers me a job as a consultant. I'm thrilled. The newly anointed Dr. Shandler has landed a job in one of the most innovative consultancies in the world. Talk about impostor syndrome.

The first months at IA are intense. It's something like a paid postdoctoral fellowship on steroids. IA's embrace of intuition, humanistic psychology, and systems thinking combine to create a powerful human technology for managing change and creating desired results. Clients are prepared to pay handsomely for the privilege of learning from these innovative wizards.

After a few months, I begin working directly with clients. The learning curve is steep, but IA's founder, Charlie Kiefer, takes me under his wing. We work side by side. I've become increasingly adept at helping teams to plan their futures around a common vision. Charlie models playful chutzpah that routinely blows the stubborn mindsets of the toughest senior executives.

Two years on, I'm sufficiently confident to start my own consulting firm. We move back to Amherst.

I call my consultancy *Vision Action Associates*. Shortly after I've opened the doors, I receive an invitation to give a talk at a business conference in Atlanta.

After the question and answer period, an elderly, balding guy in a dull gray suit shuffles up to me. He introduces himself. "Good afternoon, Dr. Shandler. I'm Jack Chin from Madison Paper Industries. We're a small outfit up in Maine. I liked your talk. Here's my card. When you get back to your office, please call me."

He hands me the card, shakes my hand, and slowly walks away. The card reads:

Jack Chin
Chairman & CEO
Madison Paper Industries
A Division of the *New York Times*

The following day, I call Mr. Chin.

"Can you visit us up here in Maine?" he asks. "I want you to meet some of my people." I agree. We make an appointment. I'm excited to have a real client interested in my services. I drive the 280 miles north, speeding most of the way. Four hours later, I pull into the parking lot of Madison Paper Industries, a huge mill covering several acres. In my suit and tie, I look the part of a yuppie consultant.

After welcoming me, Mr. Chin introduces his staff. He leaves me with them to sort things out. This group of executives is responsible for planning the firm's annual management retreat in Fort Lauderdale in a few months. They take me on a tour of the plant—a series of gigantic machines spread-eagled through several interconnected buildings. This complex maze of equipment ultimately produces the paper for the *New York Times*. I can't follow all the technical details of the process, but it doesn't matter. I'm not there as a technical expert. The tour has given me a glimpse of the territory.

After some conversation, they invite me to facilitate an afternoon leadership workshop at the firm's retreat. I'm okay with the gig, but I have a nagging sense that Jack Chin might be open to something more.

I saw the look in his eyes when I met him after my talk in Atlanta, and again this morning in his office. He's excited about me being here. There are bigger fish to fry.

I head over to Chin's office. His secretary recognizes me from my earlier visit.

"Dr. Shandler, I'm sorry, but Mr. Chin's off playing golf. He plays on Wednesday afternoons."

"Oh, that's too bad," I persist. "I would love to finish my conversation with him before I leave town."

"Well, let's see. What time is it? 2:10. You can probably catch him somewhere around the ninth hole if you go over there right now. Let me write down the directions. It's only about seven miles from here."

I gather all my latent chutzpah, head over to the course, and walk down toward the ninth hole. Everyone on the links is dressed in golfing attire, pastel pants with white polo shirts and golf caps. In my dark suit, tie, and shiny dress shoes, I look rather conspicuous. I see all of Mr. Chin's friends' caps turn in unison to observe me walking toward them. Mr. Chin meets me halfway. A good sign.

"Sorry to disturb you on the links, Mr. Chin. But I wanted to catch you before I leave. The folks in charge of organizing the Fort Lauderdale meeting have invited me to do a leadership workshop. But to be completely candid, it's not what you need."

Mr. Chin's eyes widen. "What do we need?" he asks.

"MPI's management team needs a vision of the future and a plan for how to implement that vision. Fort Lauderdale is an opportunity to begin a meaningful change process." I blurt out my proposal with the confidence of a business mogul.

Mr. Chin looks at me over his glasses, leans on his golf club, and says, "Dr. Shandler, go back to your office and write up a proposal for what you think we need. Mail it to me. I'll speak to my people and explain. Thank you."

He turns and meanders back to the ninth hole.

I don't completely get what's driving me. It's like fishing. You feel the nibble on the line.

You strike at the right moment, or you lose the fish. I'm angling for something big here. I brainstorm a strategic intervention for Madison Paper Industries, essentially a blueprint for creating a new culture aligned around a commonly held vision of a desired future with a collective commitment to becoming a learning organization. The total package comes to seven figures over a four-and-a-half-year period. It's outrageous. On a wave of confidence, I send it off to Mr. Chin.

Two weeks go by. I've heard nothing. I'm nervous that Mr. Chin has dismissed my wildly optimistic proposal. After all, in one fell swoop, I've gone from a very nice weekend gig in Fort Lauderdale to a sweeping cultural change project. Am I manic? Grandiose? Arrogant? Or just plain stupid?

I call Mr. Chin.

"Oh, Dr. Shandler. Forgive me. I've been up to my eyeballs. But I like your proposal. Let's get started. We'll use the Fort Lauderdale meeting as a kickoff. Okay with you? I'll cut a check for the first phase."

I've hooked a huge fish on ten-pound line. I have to get my act together. And pronto. I can't do this project alone. I hire a few high-quality people to take some of the load.

My economic karma has taken a decidedly positive turn. I've endured many lean years, but now a period begins where money flows in. From the Madison Paper project, other opportunities arise, both in the for-profit sector and then, increasingly, by word of mouth, in large public nonprofits. Madison Paper leads to projects with the clothing giant, Phillips Van Heusen, the senior leadership of the MacArthur Foundation, The Global Alliance for Vaccine and Immunization (GAVI) in its merger into the UN, and Campbell Hausfeld, a compressor manufacturer in Ohio.

I've gone from being an erratic provider to success, from being a poor immigrant to living the American dream. We pay off our mortgage and stash away our daughters' outlandish future college fees.

FORTY

I visit Mom in Vancouver once or twice a year. Usually, I stay for about ten days. She meets me at the airport in her beat-up old Subaru, all tears and smiles. I always insist on driving. She's a terrible driver. She vaguely gets it and usually tells me to keep the car while I'm in town. Mom's settled into a plumper body in her older age, but she's as vivacious as ever. She still dyes her hair a vivid auburn.

She often regales me with stories of her new sewing pupils, primarily Chinese immigrants who'll get jobs tailoring after receiving a certificate. This is a new world version of the same career she had in South Africa.

The Austrian government has begun sending her a monthly stipend as reparations for her Nazi-interrupted education in Graz. This small amount of extra income is helpful. Ernst and Walter have helped her buy a modest apartment. She's not rich by any means, but she's independent and has many new friends.

But two things are the same. She's charming, and she's volatile, flying off the handle when I least expect. Sometimes, it takes tremendous energy on my part to maintain peaceful visits.

Over time, I've learned to pace myself, to give Mom my undivided attention for at most three hours at a time. I try to keep her busy doing things I know she likes. I take her for drives through Stanley Park or to Horseshoe Bay, to her favorite art galleries, or for outdoor luncheons. Occasionally, I take her to Seasons in the Park, a fine restaurant with magnificent views of the city and the surrounding snow-topped mountains. Mom loves nature. It's where she's usually most relaxed.

But there are no guarantees.

I protect my sanity on these trips to Vancouver through the amazing generosity of my old friends, Andrew and Wendy. Their home provides a haven where I can relax and lick my wounds if necessary before visiting Mom again. Andrew, Wendy, and I go back to the days with Babaji and the Vancouver Satsang. My twice-yearly ten-day incursions into their home have strengthened our friendship and made me an uncle of sorts to their kids.

I see Sammy and his wife, Anne, too. It's good to spend a pleasant evening with old friends when you're far from home in a now strange city. They've made friends with Mom too. They visit her, get her out, make a fuss of her, celebrate her birthday with Anne's homemade chocolate cake and the like. Mom can be a charming friend. I don't think Sammy or Anne quite get why I'm sometimes so exasperated with her. Mom can be vivacious, attentive, curious, emotionally vulnerable, *"a feeling person with a soul!"* as she puts it, but she's not their mother.

My relationship with Ernst has been strained since my hippie-spiritual phase. Things haven't been the same since the night Jerry dunked his head in Barbara's white cake, a sure sign of how far Jerry and

I had fallen from rationality. One day, out of the blue, Mom announces that Ernst is pissed off with me. I call him to see what it's about.

"My mother tells me you're annoyed with me. Why don't you speak directly to me?"

"I'll tell you what it's about," he says. He's loaded for bear. "You took down the pictures in my room. You didn't ask me."

It's true. In the early days when I first arrived in Vancouver, I spent endless nights listening to Ernst's incessant ramblings. When he moved in with Barbara, I tried to make that dungeon into a home for myself. I took down his pictures and put up my own. He rarely stopped by the old hovel. At the time, it seemed reasonable. Getting permission hadn't entered my brain.

"This is what you're pissed with me about?" The tone of my voice betrays my lack of empathy. My exasperation is like spilling blood to lure a shark. Ernst goes on a tirade for a good ten minutes. The gist of it is that I was an ungrateful asshole. Which I was. I should have expressed my gratitude to him for supporting me when I first came to Canada. I'm grateful he arranged for my immigration, set me up with a job at the mill, and gave me a way to make money and a place to live. He's played an important role in my life. He's cantankerous, but I've always been fond of his flamboyant personality, his jokes, and his outlandish stories.

One day, Mom calls and tells me that Ernst has suffered a heart attack. He called her from the hospital, late at night, desperate to chat his way through his insomnia. She told him he needed to rest, but shortly after, he suffered a second fatal heart attack. Though Mom is often at war with Ernst, the suddenness of his death has left her shocked. She will miss having her confidant and sparring partner.

For Walter, Ernst's death is a great loss. He and Ernst were partners, joined at the hip, really, and life will simply not be the same without his brother. He begins reaching out to me more. He calls every month or so, and we schmooze about unimportant things. We get to know each other in a new way, man to man. It's an enjoyable relationship. Even though Walter's a brash stickler—conservative and slow to change with the times—I also respect him. He's well-read—especially about history. I enjoy learning from him.

On my trips to Vancouver, Walter and I sometimes meet for lunch at a Middle Eastern restaurant near his house in Kerrisdale. Walter is friendly with the Egyptian owners of the restaurant, and the first few minutes of our lunches are always consumed with pleasantries and jokes, a kind of unspoken celebration of mutual liberation from the days before the wars between Egypt and Israel, before they all came to Canada. This is a new country, and a Jew and an Arab can greet one another in peace. That's the best appetizer. Walter loves eating there, and so do I.

On one of my trips to Vancouver, I've gotten caught up in a stupid blowup with Mom. I meet Walter at the Egyptian restaurant. I'm still sputtering, and Walter knows right away what's going on.

"No doubt you've been at your mother's. The look on your face tells everything!" he says with a smile of half-pity and half-compassion. "You're so stupid. It's just unbelievable! Don't you know your own mother by now? Don't get so caught up. She's complicated. Crazy. She's always been like that. But I tell you, that mother of yours has another side.

"I fought against the Egyptians in Sinai in '56, and I saw the deep character of people under the stress of battle. Some people couldn't handle it, but for some, it brought out tremendous bravery. Let me tell you a little story about your mother.

"After Kristallnacht, the Nazis arrested Papa and sent him to Dachau. A few weeks later, they arrested Mama too and took her to the Graz police station. We kids were left to fend for ourselves. I was six, and Ernst was ten, but I remember it like it happened yesterday. Your mother was fifteen, a spoiled Jewish princess. But it fell to her to take care of us. She didn't know how to cook. The food ran out. Your mother marched the three of us off to the police station. She burst through the door, holding us by the hand, and demanded to see the chief of police."

"She scolded him. 'You've arrested my mother, and my father has been sent to Dachau. We three children are alone, without help. I can't take care of these two boys by myself! How will I get food for them? I have no money. I don't know how to cook! Do you want us to starve? Let my mother go! She's done nothing!'"

"The police chief took pity. Perhaps it was because he was Papa's customer before the Nazis came to Graz, but he released Mama, and she came home with us that same day. It never would have happened if it were not for your mother's guts.

"Okay, she gets meshuga sometimes. Paranoid. She convinces herself that people are against her. Don't get caught. It always passes."

This story is a reminder of our family's suffering under Naziism and Mom's courage. She's tough to take when she's meshuga—so angry, convinced everyone's against her. That she's right. Those who don't see it her way are shallow fools, including Walter, not to mention me.

One day, driving through Vancouver, Mom proudly announces, "I finally told Walter the truth. I told him, 'You're nothing but a fat, scared little Jew.'"

I imagine Walter reacting to this assessment of his character with a knowing smirk. He is right. Mom has always been courageous, put herself out there. Taken a risk—left Austria for Israel, Israel for South Africa, and Cape Town for Vancouver. She's made her way in the world against terrible odds. And she's sometimes a loose cannon.

I have work to do. A lot of work. I must become a master matador, learn to brandish an invisible red cape, and get the fuck out of her way.

Meanwhile, in South Africa, 1990 marks the beginning of apartheid's wind down. The process of change is fraught with violence and keeps the country in a state of deep insecurity. Frederik Willem de Klerk, an Afrikaner politician who supported apartheid, takes power as the new president of the country. He promises change. De Klerk's government is ahead of many of its White supporters and light-years ahead of the racist police who attempt to maintain the political status quo by force and deception. Black fury mounts. The long-feared *swartgevaar*—the pent-up rage of the Black majority—explodes in violence.

There are numerous police massacres: hundreds are killed, and thousands are shot, often in the back as they run away. Behind the scenes, the police aid and abet violence between the rival factions of the African National Congress (ANC) and the Inkatha Freedom Party (IFP).

To maintain peace, the de Klerk government suspends some aspects of apartheid. Segregation in government schools is relaxed, and public amenities are open to all. But demonstrations in the townships regularly boil over in violent paroxysms. The country is unstable, and no one knows what will happen.

Many fear the worst. Civil war. In my safe perch in America, I believe a racial bloodbath is imminent in the country of my childhood.

It's a miracle. On February 11, 1990, Nelson Mandela takes his first steps to freedom after twenty-seven years of incarceration. I watch on television as the tall, unfamiliar figure of Mandela walks through the gates of Victor Verster Prison near Cape Town. I see his dignity and sense of purpose. Tears roll down my cheeks. I pray he'll be successful.

Penny, Benny, Loren, and Paul emigrate to Canada, leaving South Africa, now teetering on the edge of civil war. They settle in Toronto, determined to make a go of things in their new country. Loren is a first-year college student, and Paul is a high school senior. Benny finds an executive position in the textile industry, and Penny gets a job assisting an optometrist. They settle into a modest apartment and begin their new lives as immigrants. My sister, my childhood companion, my fierce protector, now lives on the same continent.

FORTY-ONE
MARCH 1998

Dad's visited us in the States a few times. I've visited him in South Africa. Years have come and gone since our last meeting. I've hardly noticed the passage of time. I've been consumed with trying to keep my consulting practice afloat.

Then Dad calls. A rare event. International calls out of South Africa are expensive, and Dad is frugal.

"I want to see you. I'm not well enough to travel. Please come. I'll pay for your ticket." There's an urgency and vulnerability in his words. So unlike him to admit frailty. I hop on a plane. Dad picks me up at the airport. It's mid-March, the tail end of the summer. Dad's dressed in shorts. He's all smiles. His joy at the sight of me is irrepressible. Outside the terminal, a jobless young man appears in the parking lot and tries to help with my suitcase. "Just to make a rand or two, please, *baas*!"

Dad stands more upright and shoos the guy away, insisting on pushing the heavy bag to his Mercedes and lifting it into the trunk himself. I've barely landed in Cape Town. I'm reminded that Dad will insist on being strong and in charge till the day he dies. Touching, really. How he wants to be the father serving his son, even as age takes its toll.

We spend the first few days catching up, sitting on the balcony of Dad and Eve's new apartment high on the slopes of Table Mountain, overlooking the city bowl and the harbor. The view's magnificent. Dad and Eve point out various sights, the city twinkling below and ships moored in Table Bay.

Robben Island, where Nelson Mandela was incarcerated for so many years, is visible offshore. I remember how I used to play on Clifton's beaches with the mysterious island in the distance. At the time, I didn't know that political prisoners were incarcerated there, but even if I had known, I wonder what my childhood self would have thought. It's a great gift to be back in Cape Town with the thirty-year perspective of my education and experience in other countries and cultures and as a witness to the massive changes in South Africa. Mandela's president of South Africa. Wow. What a change from the White pigmentocracy in which I grew up.

After all my travels, Cape Town remains the most beautiful city. Dad loans me his old Mercedes to drive around. I visit my old haunts. On the fourth day, Dad invites me to lunch. He tells me to pick him up at his office downtown at 1 p.m.

I'm a bit late, and Dad's irritable. He says, "Take me home. I want to get my little Honda. I love that car, and I want to drive it."

So, I drive three or four miles out of our way to switch cars. The Honda is only a few months old, glossy white, and still has that new car smell. It's smooth and responsive.

"I like it better than my old Mercedes," Dad remarks. I offer to drive, but Dad dismisses my offer and squeezes into the driver's seat.

Dad always drives.

"I want us to have lunch at Groot Constantia," Dad says as we drive down Table Mountain toward De Waal Drive. "You may have forgotten that Groot Constantia is one of the original wine farms in the Cape. Their wines have received worldwide acclaim."

I look forward to sitting on Groot Constantia's patio, under the ancient oak trees in front of the gracious old Cape Dutch mansion. Like Dad, I relish the food, scenery, and a glass or two.

We enter De Waal Drive, Cape Town's main highway. It's packed with cars zooming into and out of the city center. In the distance, the mountains that separate the Cape from the interior glisten in the sunlight.

Dad's on one of his political rants, talking a mile a minute. "Mandela has been a fantastic spokesman for South Africa, but he hasn't governed half as well. I suppose one can't blame these ANC chaps. After all, it's only been a few years since they were all sitting in cells on Robben Island. But there's too much incompetency. They just don't have the experience we need to keep the economy going. At the moment, the conversion rate is just under two rands to the dollar, but I'm telling you, in the years to come, we'll see the rand slide tremendously. I wouldn't be surprised if we see fifteen or eighteen rands to the dollar. We have to make this country fit for investment and not scare financiers off."

I'm surprised at Dad's respect for Mandela's international stature on the one hand and his contempt for his governing ability on the other. I'd like to ask questions about the situation, but it's clear that this is a lecture and the question and answer period has not yet begun.

"I'm a longtime student of politics in this country. I'm telling you that these ANC chaps better get their act together, Mandela or no Mandela. If they don't, we're headed for very tough times. Already, the brain drain is enormous."

We're speeding around Hospital Bend, a stretch of De Waal Drive that goes directly past Groote Schuur Hospital, Cape Town's largest hospital, where Christiaan Barnard performed the first heart transplant. On the right, on the slopes of Table Mountain, antelopes and zebras graze in large fenced-in fields. Dad inhales and gasps. "I've got a bad pain!"

"Where?" I ask, alarmed by his tone.

"Here in my stomach. I've got to stop the car."

But as Dad says these words, his body goes limp. He collapses over the steering wheel.

His eyes roll back into his forehead.

The car speeds on at sixty miles an hour. The highway traffic whizzes around us.

I act without thinking.

I lean to the right toward Dad, place my right arm underneath his crumpled body, and push him away from the steering wheel. With my right hand, I grab the wheel and steer, his weight pressing on my arm. With my free left hand, I pull up the handbrake. I hope to God it won't send the car into a skid. Somehow, we avoid other cars by inches; their drivers speed by, unaware of the drama unfolding in the Honda.

The handbrake works. The Honda comes to a safe halt near the median dividing the highway.

Dad is still.

He's not breathing.

I can't find a pulse.

I put my arms around his lifeless body. I hug him. How can this be? He was in the middle of his lecture about Mandela! Maybe he's still alive? Groote Schuur Hospital is just 300 yards from where I've stopped the car, but Dad is solidly wedged behind the wheel. The hospital may as well be 300 light-years away. I don't have a phone to call for help, but a part of me knows that no one can help Dad.

I'm in shock. My mind struggles to comprehend the suddenness and finality of death. He told me when we met in New York that he had an aneurysm in his aorta. That he'd probably die from it one day. Probably, it burst. That's why he complained of the pain in his abdomen before he collapsed over the wheel.

Dad's dead. Gone. Just like that. I know what the Hindus and Buddhists mean when they describe dying as the "spirit leaving the body."

Just a few minutes ago, Dad's spirit animated his body. He was completely himself—grumpy, articulate, totally into his favorite subject, South African politics. It's all happened so fast. Someone wise once noted that *character is destiny*. Dad was always impatient. He left his body in a hurry.

In the Honda, with my arms around Dad's body, I remember the holiest of Jewish prayers—the *Shema*.

> "*Shema Yisrael, Adonai Elohainu, Adonai Ehud.*
> *Hear o Israel, the Lord our God, the Lord is One.*"

By now, the traffic is crawling along, everyone rubbernecking, trying to figure out what's going on. Not a single car stops. This is South Africa. People are afraid of the unusual. It might be some bizarre gangster car hijacking. They could get robbed. The traffic's backed up, way back. I don't know what to do.

I get out of the car and stand there, pathetically waving my arms. Then a car pulls over, and through a crack in his window, a man asks me what's up. I tell him I think my father has just died in the car. Realizing I'm sincere, the good Samaritan gets out of his car to help.

He goes to the white Honda and checks Dad's pulse.

After a few seconds, he mutters, "I think you're right. This doesn't look good. Here, use my mobile phone. You can call the police and your loved ones."

He hands me the phone. I call the police emergency number, explaining the situation. They're aware something is happening on De Waal Drive. The traffic's backed up for miles, all the way into the center city.

Then I call Eve. I'm apprehensive.

"Eve, a terrible thing has happened. Dad just died on De Waal Drive right on Hospital Bend, opposite Groote Schuur."

The silence on the other end of the phone is deafening.

"Ach, Michael, don't say things like that. Don't ever say things like that."

With that, the phone goes dead.

The police arrive in ten minutes. I'm blown away by how young they are. One of them still has bumfluff on his chin. He opens the driver's door and feels Dad's pulse at his neck.

Then he shakes his head and turns to me.

"*Hy's weg*. He's gone," he says. He speaks to the other police in rapid Afrikaans. They order an ambulance to take Dad's body to the morgue.

Then, a car speeds toward us along the shoulder of the highway. It halts nearby. Candice and my stepbrother, Greg, get out of the car. Eve sits in the passenger seat, frozen in place, her face a mask of pain and disbelief. Silently, the three of us walk over to the ambulance and pay our respects to Dad.

Dad's dramatic final exit stuns everyone who knows him.

The funeral is a blur. I make a short speech eulogizing Dad. In the beginning, it had been a rocky road, but Dad and I came through things okay. We met each other halfway. We had bad years and good years. Now I can honestly say, "I'm grateful for it all."

After the funeral, Eve tells me, "You know, Michael, your dad died a happy man because he was with you."

Dad and I could have easily remained estranged, but our karma together has ended differently. We've both gone through the door in the wall, each in our way, and come back better people. I've received the greatest honor—to be present at my father's death in love, without regret, resentment, or recrimination.

EPILOGUE

Twenty-one years after Dad's death, March 2019, I'm back in South Africa. I'm seventy-two and an avid cyclist. I'm riding in the Cape Town Cycle Tour, a seventy-mile course around the Cape Peninsula, my boyhood playground. It's the biggest timed cycling event in the world. The route goes through my old haunts—around Table Mountain, past Newlands Ave, through Wynberg, onto the Indian Ocean coastline, crossing the tip of the peninsula near Simonstown, toward Hout Bay and the mountainous Atlantic Seaboard—a wonderful opportunity to take in the magic of the Cape Peninsula from the seat of a bike.

The race begins in the shadow of the Castle of Good Hope, where I was inducted into the army. The winds are gusting up to forty-five miles an hour, and cyclists discuss conditions, hoping the wind will die down. Along the Atlantic coast, a strong gust can blow a cyclist off the cliffs. Thirty-six thousand riders line up waiting. Waves of two or three hundred are released every few minutes. My start time is 7:50—early morning sunshine and cool cycling conditions. The starter's gun goes off. In seconds, I'm on Nelson Mandela Boulevard, formerly De Waal Drive. We climb for a few miles and then reach the top of Hospital Bend. Groote Schuur Hospital lies to my left, a half-mile away. I remember the unforgettable scene in Dad's white Honda.

In no time, I'm where Dad left his body.

I want to say a prayer from the seat of my bike, riding at 40 mph. "Dad, may you be in peace." I sense him smiling and cheering me on.

May his memory be for a blessing.

Much has changed. Jean, Walter's wife, died tragically in 2003 from Creutzfeldt-Jakob disease. Jean was my main ally when I first came to Canada in early 1968. She later got into yoga and meditation, and we always shared a connection. She accepted me from the very beginning and quietly helped me. I'm still smiling with her—our secret smile of understanding about our family's neuroses.

May her memory be a blessing.

In 2004, Carl and I spent a week together in Amherst while Nina and Mabel were away. Carl and I were good friends and enjoyed hanging out. He was ninety-three and feeble, but one morning during his stay, he was strong enough to take a gentle walk. I took special care to choose an easy route. Carl was delighted that he was able to successfully complete the half-mile circuit. This turned out to be his final walk.

After his funeral, the family gathered at our house in Amherst. I took my first grandchild, Mayrav, Manju's fourteen-month-old daughter, for a walk in her carriage along the same route Carl and I had taken. As we came around a turn, I looked down, and there lay two 500 Swedish krona bills. I picked them up. I knew that this was a communication from Carl—my Swede Finn father-in-law and friend. I cannot explain finding those Swedish krona in this place in any other way. I mounted and framed the bills, and they still hang in our dining room.

After Carl's death, Mabel lived independently in the stone house in Sturbridge for five years. When it became impossible for her to live alone, she came to stay with us. In her last years, she suffered from Lewy body dementia. We took care of her in our home until she died in 2013. Even in her steep decline, Mabel remained a sweet soul.

I remember Carl and Mabel with great fondness. They unfailingly modeled tolerance, acceptance, steadiness, loyalty, generosity, and service. They came into my life at exactly the right moment and became my family.

May their memories be a blessing.

Mom died in 2014. She faced her last five years as a paraplegic with courage and rarely complained. My twice-yearly visits to see her in Vancouver ended after thirty years. I miss Mom's presence, her childlike delight in nature and all things beautiful. Mom comes to me in the bathroom every morning when I wash my face. I hear her unmistakable voice admonishing me, "Look after your skin, or it will turn to leather. Use moisturizer!"

Okay, Mom. Thank you. I finally get your loving intention. Indeed, Mom had the most wonderful skin even into her nineties.

May her memory be a blessing.

Walter died in 2016. In the years before he died, he reached out to me regularly, and we enjoyed many conversations about the twists and turns of life. Despite his gruff exterior, Walter was an intelligent and sensitive man. I'm grateful our paths crossed.

May his memory be a blessing.

Ram Dass died in 2019. I remain grateful to him for making the connection between psychedelics and the spiritual path and for leading me to Baba Hari Dass. I met up with Ram Dass again around 2005 when we both attended a celebration of Maharaji's birthday at a mutual friend's farm. Ram Dass had with him a wooden box filled with dozens of Sandalwood *malas* or rosaries. He gazed at me with his infectious enthusiasm and dazzling smile. "I'm still doing the same old thing. Giving away *malas* so people will remember God."

May his memory be a blessing.

Babaji died in 2018. He was a mentor from whom I learned a great deal, painful as it sometimes was. His teachings are my companions. "Be equal! Never above or below." "Cultivate contentment." Namaste, Babaji. Deepest gratitude.

May his memory be a blessing.

Our dear friends, Jack and Corinne, died in 2020 and 2021, within a year of one another.

We miss them.

May their memories be blessings.

Life goes on. The story continues—though I am mindful that one day, it stops for each of us and is carried into the future by our children and grandchildren and their children's children.

I am one of the lucky ones—one of those who escapes the confines of his karma and finds healing, love, reconciliation, purpose, and belonging. I am filled with gratitude for my good fortune and for the kindness of so many; without help, this journey would not have been possible.

I am eternally grateful to Nina—my wife and partner of over fifty years, whose kindness, companionship, and love have blessed my journey at every turn. And to my dearest daughters—Manju and Sara—who have brought such joy, love, and gratitude. And for my amazing grandchildren—Mayrav, Tatiana, Hazel, Rowan, and Arlo—you will continue the story and make your own contributions. From what I've seen, there's no doubt you will make the world a better place.

I am aware that for many people, escaping their karmic lot is impossible, that many suffer under a heavy load of challenging outer circumstances and painful suffering. How was I able to overcome the life that was handed to me? Karma and kismet? Action and fate. God's grace and human will.

Finally, I'm filled with gratitude that I am no longer a link in the chain of abuse. The journey has been long and sometimes strange. At times, I lost faith, but, at crucial points, people—often strangers—showered me with kindness and all kinds of help along the way. I have found love and belonging. I pray that my children and grandchildren have been spared the Holocaust's evil tentacles and will grow up in freedom, love, and curiosity. This is my vision and prayer.

May it be so.

ACKNOWLEDGMENTS

My loving wife, the author and psychologist Nina Shandler, took in my story from the outset of our journey more than fifty years ago. The grace of her deep listening has played no small part in my healing. Her deft editing clarified and brightened every page of the manuscript.

My talented and loving artist daughter, Manju Shandler Estrin, has known this family history almost as long as Nina. She believed in the book and spent months with the manuscript, poring over every line and paragraph, cajoling and suffering me with enormous grace, and in the process, she made me a better writer.

My loving and talented daughter, Sara Shandler Banks—whose creativity transforms everything she touches—read and imparted invaluable insights about the book's structure from her well of experience seeing many books to fruition.

I'm grateful to my family. Without their individual and collective contributions, *Karma and Kismet* would not be the book you have just read.

Numerous other people helped as well. James Steinberg's early enthusiasm sparked the "serious" phase of writing. Andrew Jordan read every draft thoroughly and maintained a steadfast belief in what he called my emerging "Torah." Joel Agee read an early draft aloud to his wife, Susan Agee, and they provided helpful feedback and support. My sister, Penny Bravo, shared her eye-witness corroborations of our family-of-origin dynamics. Our long conversations were healing and delightful. About sixty friends—too many to mention by name—read drafts of the manuscript. My gratitude to all of you.

Koehler Books has played an important role in making *Karma and Kismet* a reality. John Koehler guided me through the publishing process and did it with realism and humor. My gratitude to Greg Fields, Koehler's senior acquisitions editor, for his belief and encouragement, and to my editor, Miranda Dillon, for her meticulous fine-tuning of the manuscript. I'm also grateful to Suzanne Bradshaw who brought her wonderful artistic talents to the internal book and cover design of *Karma and Kismet*.

www.ingramcontent.com/pod-product-compliance
Lightning Source LLC
LaVergne TN
LVHW091711070526
838199LV00050B/2349